Chaos Engineering
System Resiliency in Practice

Casey Rosenthal and Nora Jones

Beijing · Boston · Farnham · Sebastopol · Tokyo

Chaos Engineering

by Casey Rosenthal and Nora Jones

Copyright © 2020 Casey Rosenthal and Nora Jones. All rights reserved.

Published by O'Reilly Media, Inc., 1005 Gravenstein Highway North, Sebastopol, CA 95472.

O'Reilly books may be purchased for educational, business, or sales promotional use. Online editions are also available for most titles (*http://oreilly.com*). For more information, contact our corporate/institutional sales department: 800-998-9938 or *corporate@oreilly.com*.

Acquisitions Editor: John Devins
Development Editor: Amelia Blevins
Production Editor: Deborah Baker
Copyeditor: Jasmine Kwityn
Proofreader: Charles Roumeliotis

Indexer: Judith McConville
Interior Designer: David Futato
Cover Designer: Karen Montgomery
Illustrator: Rebecca Demarest

April 2020:   First Edition

Revision History for the First Edition
2020-04-03:   First Release

See *http://oreilly.com/catalog/errata.csp?isbn=9781492043867* for release details.

978-1-492-04386-7

[LSI]

This book is dedicated to David "The Dude" Hussman. Dave was the spark that turned Chaos Engineering into a community.

Table of Contents

Part II.   Principles in Action

Part IV.   Business Factors

Part V. Evolution

Preface

Chaos Engineering has taken off. Thousands of companies of all shapes and sizes, in all verticals, have adopted Chaos Engineering as a core practice to make their products and services safer and more reliable. Many resources exist on the topic, particularly conference talks, but none of these paint an entire picture.

Nora and Casey set out to write the most complete book on Chaos Engineering. This was no small task, given the breadth of implementations across the industry and the evolving nature of the discipline. In this book we attempt to capture the history behind Chaos Engineering, the fundamental theories that ground it, the definitions and principles, implementations across the software industry, examples from beyond traditional software, and the future of where we see practices like this going.

Conventions Used in This Book

The following typographical conventions are used in this book:

Italic
: Indicates new terms, URLs, email addresses, filenames, and file extensions.

`Constant width`
: Used for program listings, as well as within paragraphs to refer to program elements such as variable or function names, databases, data types, environment variables, statements, and keywords.

O'Reilly Online Learning

O'REILLY® For more than 40 years, *O'Reilly* has provided technology and business training, knowledge, and insight to help companies succeed.

Our unique network of experts and innovators share their knowledge and expertise through books, articles, and our online learning platform. O'Reilly's online learning platform gives you on-demand access to live training courses, in-depth learning paths, interactive coding environments, and a vast collection of text and video from O'Reilly and 200+ other publishers. For more information, visit *http://oreilly.com*.

How to Contact Us

Please address comments and questions concerning this book to the publisher:

O'Reilly Media, Inc.
1005 Gravenstein Highway North
Sebastopol, CA 95472
800-998-9938 (in the United States or Canada)
707-829-0515 (international or local)
707-829-0104 (fax)

We have a web page for this book, where we list errata and any additional information. You can access this page at *https://oreil.ly/Chaos_Engineering*.

Email us at *bookquestions@oreilly.com* to comment or ask technical questions about this book.

For more information about our books, courses, and news, see our website at *http://www.oreilly.com*.

Find us on Facebook: *http://facebook.com/oreilly*

Follow us on Twitter: *http://twitter.com/oreillymedia*

Watch us on YouTube: *http://www.youtube.com/oreillymedia*

Acknowledgments

As with any large book, there are countless people who contributed time, energy, and emotional support to the authors, editors, and contributors. As a compendium including sixteen authors total (Nora and Casey plus fourteen contributing authors), the span of the support to make this book happen is difficult to grasp. We appreciate all of the effort from the contributing authors, their patience with us as we refined ideas and scope, and pushing through the editing process.

We were blessed to work with great editors and staff at O'Reilly. Amelia Blevins, Virginia Wilson, John Devins, and Nikki McDonald were all instrumental in making this book happen. In many ways this book is a work of creation willed into existence by Amelia and Virginia as much as by the authors. Thank you for your patience with us, and the many, many negotiated deadlines.

We appreciate the enthusiastic contributions of our reviewers: Will Gallego, Ryan Frantz, Eric Dobbs, Lane Desborough, Randal Hansen, Michael Kehoe, Mathias Lafeldt, Barry O'Reilly, Cindy Sridharan, and Benjamin Wilms. Your comments, suggestions, and corrections dramatically improved the quality of this work. Beyond that, it provided ample opportunities for us to expand our own understanding of this complex field and led to additional research that we incorporated back into the work. This book is truly a collaborative work enhanced by your review.

We are indebted in so many ways to the contributing authors: John Allspaw, Peter Alvaro, Nathan Aschbacher, Jason Cahoon, Raji Chockaiyan, Richard Crowley, Bob Edwards, Andy Fleener, Russ Miles, Aaron Rinehart, Logan Rosen, Oleg Surmachev, Lu Tang, and Hao Weng. Obviously this book would not have happened without you. Each one of you made a necessary and fundamental contribution to the content as a whole. We appreciate you as peers and as friends.

We want to thank David Hussman, Kent Beck, and John Allspaw. David, to whom this book is dedicated, encouraged us to evangelize Chaos Engineering outside our limited scope in Silicon Valley. It is in large part because of his support and encouragement that Chaos Engineering became an actual "thing"—a standalone discipline within the broader software engineering community. Likewise, Kent Beck encouraged us to view Chaos Engineering as a construct bigger than us that has the power to transform the way people think about building, deploying, and operating software. John Allspaw gave us the language to explain the fundamentals of Chaos Engineering, by encouraging us to study Human Factors and Safety Systems at Lund University in Sweden. He introduced us to the field of Resilience Engineering, which has proved to be foundational for Chaos Engineering, and is the lens through which we see issues of safety (including availability and security) when we look at sociotechnical systems such as software deployed at scale. All instructors and peers in the program at Lund have also shaped our thinking, especially Johan Bergstrom and Anthony "Smokes" Smoker.

We thank you all for the impact you have had on us, giving us the courage to push Chaos Engineering forward, and the indelible impact you have had on our thinking.

Introduction: Birth of Chaos

Chaos Engineering is still a relatively new discipline within software development. This introduction lays out the history, from the humble beginnings of the practice through to the current epoch of all major industries adopting the practice in some form. Over the past three years, the question has changed from "Should we do Chaos Engineering?" to "What's the best way to get started doing Chaos Engineering?"

The history of our nascent discipline explains how we transitioned from the first to the second question just posed. We don't want to merely tell a story of dates and motions to get the facts straight. We want to tell the story of how this emerged, so that you understand why it emerged the way that it did, and how you can learn from that path in order to get the most out of the practice.

The story begins at Netflix, where the authors of this book, Casey Rosenthal (*https://oreil.ly/FE9EE*) and Nora Jones (*https://oreil.ly/Rx9-1*), both worked when the Chaos Team defined and evangelized Chaos Engineering.[1] Netflix found real business value in the practice, and when others saw that, a community grew up around the discipline to spread it throughout tech.

Management Principles as Code

Beginning in 2008, Netflix made a very public display[2] of moving from the datacenter to the cloud. In August of that year, a major database corruption event in the datacenter left Netflix unable to ship DVDs for three days. This was before streaming video was ubiquitous; DVD delivery was the bulk of their business.

---

1 Casey Rosenthal built and managed the Chaos Engineering Team for three years at Netflix. Nora Jones joined the Chaos Engineering Team early on as an engineer and technical leader. She was responsible for significant architectural decisions about the tools built as well as implementation.

2 Yury Izrailevsky, Stevan Vlaovic, and Ruslan Meshenberg, "Completing the Netflix Cloud Migration," Netflix Media Center, Feb. 11, 2016, *https://oreil.ly/c4YTI*.

The thinking at the time was that the datacenter locked them into an architecture of single points of failure, like large databases, and vertically scaled components. Moving to the cloud would necessitate horizontally scaled components, which would decrease the single points of failure.

Things didn't go exactly as planned. For one thing, it took eight years to fully extract themselves from the datacenter. More relevant to our interests, the move to horizontally scaled cloud deployment practices did not coincide with the boost to uptime of the streaming service that they expected.[3]

To explain this, we have to recall that in 2008, Amazon Web Services (AWS) was considerably less mature than it is now. Cloud computing was not yet a commodity, and not nearly the no-brainer, default deployment option that we have today. Cloud service back then did hold a lot of promise, and one of those promises was that instances[4] would occasionally blink out of existence with no warning. This particular form of failure event was rare in a datacenter, where big powerful machines were well tended and often the idiosyncrasies of specific machines were well understood. In a cloud environment, where that same amount of power was provided by many smaller machines running on commodity hardware, it was an unfortunately common occurrence.

Methods of building systems that are resilient to this form of failure event were well known. Perhaps half a dozen common practices could have been listed that help a system automatically survive one of its constituent components failing unexpectedly: redundant nodes in a cluster, limiting the fault domain by increasing the number of nodes and reducing the relative power of each, deploying redundancies in different geographies, autoscaling and automating service discovery, and so on. The specific means for making a system robust enough to handle instances disappearing was not important. It might even be different depending on the context of the system. The important thing was that it had to be done, because the streaming service was facing availability deficits due to the high frequency of instance instability events. In a way, Netflix had simply multiplied the single-point-of-failure effect.

Netflix wasn't like other software companies. It proactively promoted cultural principles that are derived from a unique management philosophy outlined in a culture deck. This manifested in several practices that had a strong bearing on how Netflix solved the availability deficit. For example:

---

3 Throughout this book, we'll generally refer to the availability of the system as the perceived "uptime."

4 In a cloud-based deployment, an "instance" is analogous to a virtual machine or a server in prior industry lingo.

- Netflix only hired senior engineers who had prior experience in the role for which they were hired.

- They gave all engineers full freedom to do anything necessary to satisfy the job, concomitant with the responsibility of any consequences associated with those decisions.

- Crucially, Netflix trusted the people doing the work to decide how the work got done.

- Management didn't tell individual contributors (ICs) what to do; instead, they made sure that ICs understood the problems that needed to be solved. ICs then told management how they planned to solve those problems, and then they worked to solve them.

- High performance teams are highly aligned and loosely coupled. This means that less effort needs to be put into process, formal communication, or task management if everyone shares the same goal across teams.

This interesting dynamic is part of what contributed to Netflix's high-performance culture, and it had an interesting consequence in the development of Chaos Engineering. Because management's job wasn't to tell ICs what to do, there was essentially no mechanism at Netflix for any one person or team or group to tell the rest of the engineers how to write their code. Even though a half dozen common patterns for writing services robust enough to handle vanishing instances could have been written down, there was no way to send an edict to the entire engineering organization demanding that everyone follow those instructions.

Netflix had to find another way.

Chaos Monkey Is Born

Many things were tried, but one thing worked and stuck around: Chaos Monkey. This very simple app would go through a list of clusters, pick one instance at random from each cluster, and at some point during business hours, turn it off without warning. It would do this every workday.

It sounds cruel, but the purpose wasn't to upset anyone. Operators knew that this type of failure—vanishing instances—was going to happen to every cluster at some point anyway. Chaos Monkey gave them a way to proactively test everyone's resilience to the failure, and do it during business hours so that people could respond to any potential fallout when they had the resources to do so, rather than at 3 a.m. when pagers typically go off. Increasing the frequency to once per day then acts somewhat like a regression test, making sure they would not experience drift into this failure mode down the line.

Netflix lore says that this was not instantly popular. There was a short period of time when ICs grumbled about Chaos Monkey. But it seemed to work, so more and more teams eventually adopted it.

One way that we can think of this application is that it took the pain of the problem at hand—vanishing instances affected service availability—and brought that pain to the forefront for every engineer. Once that problem was right in front of them, engineers did what they did best: they solved the problem.

In fact, if Chaos Monkey was bringing their service down every day, then they couldn't get any work done until they solved *this* problem. It didn't matter how they solved it. Maybe they added redundancy, maybe scaling automation, maybe architectural design patterns. That didn't matter. What did matter is that the problem got solved somehow, quickly, and with immediately appreciable results.

This reinforces the "highly aligned, loosely coupled" tenet of Netflix's culture. Chaos Monkey forced everyone to be highly aligned toward the goal of being robust enough to handle vanishing instances, but loosely coupled as to how to solve this particular problem since it doesn't suggest the solution.

Chaos Monkey is a management principle instantiated in running code. The concept behind it seemed unique and a bit wonky, so Netflix blogged about it. Chaos Monkey became a popular open source project, and even a recruiting tool that introduced Netflix to potential candidates as a creative software engineering culture, not just an entertainment company. In short, Chaos Monkey was designated a success. This set a precedent and helped establish this form of risk-taking/creative solutioning as a part of Netflix's cultural identity.

Fast-forward to December 24, 2012, Christmas Eve.[5] AWS suffered a rolling outage of elastic load balancers (ELBs). These components connect requests and route traffic to the compute instances where services are deployed. As the ELBs went down, additional requests couldn't be served. Since Netflix's control plane ran on AWS, customers were not able to choose videos and start streaming them.

The timing was terrible. On Christmas Eve, Netflix should have been taking center stage, as early adopters showed their extended family how easy it was to stream actual movies over the internet. Instead, families and relatives were forced to speak to each other without the comforting distraction of Netflix's content library.

Inside Netflix, this hurt. Not only was it a hit to the public image of the company and to engineering pride, but no one enjoyed being dragged out of the Christmas Eve

---

5 Adrian Cockcroft, "A Closer Look at the Christmas Eve Outage," The Netflix Tech Blog, Dec. 31, 2012, *https:// oreil.ly/wCftX*.

holiday by a paging alert in order to watch AWS stumble through the remediation process.

Chaos Monkey had been successfully deployed to solve the problem of vanishing instances. That worked on a small scale. Could something similar be built to solve the problem of vanishing regions? Would it work on a very, very large scale?

Going Big

Every interaction that a customer's device has with the Netflix streaming service is conducted through the control plane. This is the functionality deployed on AWS. Once a video starts streaming, the data for the video itself is served from Netflix's private network, which is by far the largest content delivery network (CDN) in the world.

The Christmas Eve outage put renewed attention internally on building an active–active solution to serving traffic for the control plane. In theory, the traffic for customers in the Western hemisphere would be split between two AWS regions, one on each coast. If either region failed, infrastructure would be built to scale up the other region and move all of the requests over there.

This capability touched every aspect of the streaming service. There is a propagation delay between coasts. Some services would have to modify things to allow for eventual consistency between coasts, come up with new state-sharing strategies, and so on. Certainly no easy technical task.

And again, because of Netflix's structure, there is no mechanism to mandate that all engineers conform to some centralized, verified solution that would certifiably handle a regional failure. Instead, a team backed by support from upper management coordinated the effort among the various affected teams.

To ensure that all of these teams had their services up to the task, an activity was created to take a region offline. Well, AWS wouldn't allow Netflix to take a region offline (something about having other customers in the region) so instead this was simulated. The activity was labeled "Chaos Kong."

The first several times Chaos Kong was initiated, it was a white-knuckle affair with a "war room" assembled to monitor all aspects of the streaming service, and it lasted hours. For months, Chaos Kong was aborted before moving all of the traffic out of one region, because issues were identified and handed back to service owners to fix. Eventually the activity was stabilized and formalized as a responsibility of the Traffic Engineering Team. Chaos Kongs were routinely conducted to verify that Netflix had a plan of action in case a single region went down.

On many occasions, either due to issues on Netflix's side of things or otherwise to issues with AWS, a single region did in fact suffer significant downtime. The regional failover mechanism used in Chaos Kong was put into effect in these cases. The benefits of the investment were clear.[6]

The downside of the regional failover process was that it took about 50 minutes to complete in the best-case scenario because of the complexity of the manual interpretation and intervention involved. In part by increasing the frequency of Chaos Kong, which in turn had an impact on the internal expectations regarding regional failover within the engineering organization, the Traffic Engineering Team was able to launch a new project that ultimately brought the failover process down to just six minutes.[7]

This brings us to about 2015. Netflix had Chaos Monkey and Chaos Kong, working on the small scale of vanishing instances and the large scale of vanishing regions, respectively. Both were supported by the engineering culture and made demonstrable contributions to the availability of the service at this point.

Formalizing the Discipline

Bruce Wong (*https://oreil.ly/jh7hr*) created a Chaos Engineering Team at Netflix in early 2015 and left the task of developing a charter and roadmap to Casey Rosenthal. Not quite sure what he had gotten himself into (he was originally hired to manage the Traffic Engineering Team, which he continued to do simultaneously with the Chaos Engineering Team), Casey went around Netflix asking what people thought Chaos Engineering was.

The answer was usually something along the lines of, "Chaos Engineering is when we break things in production on purpose." Now this sounded cool, and it might make a great addition to a LinkedIn profile summary, but it wasn't very helpful. Anyone at Netflix with access to a terminal had the means to break things in production, and chances are good that it wouldn't return any value to the company.

Casey sat down with his teams to formally define Chaos Engineering. They specifically wanted clarity on:

- What is the definition of Chaos Engineering?
- What is the point of it?
- How do I know when I'm doing it?
- How can I improve my practice of it?

---

6 Ali Basiri, Lorin Hochstein, Abhijit Thosar, and Casey Rosenthal, "Chaos Engineering Upgraded," The Netflix Technology Blog, Sept. 25, 2015, *https://oreil.ly/UJ5yM*.

7 Luke Kosewski et al., "Project Nimble: Region Evacuation Reimagined," The Netflix Technology Blog, March 12, 2018, *https://oreil.ly/7bafg*.

After about a month of working on a manifesto of sorts, they produced the Principles of Chaos Engineering (*https://principlesofchaos.org*). The discipline was officially formalized.

The super-formal definition settled upon was: "Chaos Engineering is the discipline of experimenting on a distributed system in order to build confidence in the system's capability to withstand turbulent conditions in production." This established that it is a form of *experimentation*, which sits apart from *testing*.

The point of doing Chaos Engineering in the first place is to build confidence. This is good to know, so that if you don't need confidence, then this isn't for you. If you have other ways of building confidence then you can weigh which method is most effective.

The definition also mentions "turbulent conditions in production" to highlight that this isn't about creating chaos. Chaos Engineering is about making the chaos inherent in the system visible.

The Principles goes on to describe a basic template for experimentation, which borrows heavily from Karl Popper's principle of falsifiability. In this regard, Chaos Engineering is modeled very much as a science rather than a techne.

Finally, the Principles lists five advanced practices that set the gold standard for a Chaos Engineering practice:

- Build a hypothesis around steady-state behavior
- Vary real-world events
- Run experiments in production
- Automate experiments to run continuously
- Minimize blast radius

Each of these is discussed in turn in the following chapters.

The team at Netflix planted a flag. They now knew what Chaos Engineering was, how to do it, and what value it provided to the larger organization.

Community Is Born

As mentioned, Netflix only hired senior engineers. This meant that if you want to hire Chaos Engineers, you needed a pool of experienced people in that field from which to hire. Of course, since they had just invented the discipline, this was difficult to do. There were no senior Chaos Engineers to hire, because there were no junior ones, because outside of Netflix they didn't exist.

In order to solve this problem, Casey Rosenthal decided to evangelize the field and create a community of practice. He started by putting together an invitation-only conference called "Chaos Community Day" in Autumn 2015. It was held in Uber's office in San Francisco, and about 40 people attended. The following companies were represented: Netflix, Google, Amazon, Microsoft, Facebook, DropBox, WalmartLabs, Yahoo!, LinkedIn, Uber, UCSC, Visa, AT&T, NewRelic, HashiCorp, PagerDuty, and Basho.

Presentations were not recorded, so that people could speak freely about issues they had convincing management to adopt the practice, as well as discuss "failures" and outages in an off-the-record manner. Presenters were chosen in advance to speak about how they approached issues of resilience, failure injection, fault testing, disaster recovery testing, and other topics associated with Chaos Engineering.

One of Netflix's explicit goals in launching Chaos Community Day was to inspire other companies to specifically hire for the role "Chaos Engineer." It worked. The next year, Chaos Community Day was held in Seattle in Amazon's Blackfoot office tower. A manager from Amazon announced that after the first Chaos Community Day, they had gone back and convinced management to build a team of Chaos Engineers at Amazon. Other companies were now embracing the title "Chaos Engineer" as well.

That year, 2016, attendance went up to 60 people. Companies represented at the conference included Netflix, Amazon, Google, Microsoft, Visa, Uber, Dropbox, Pivotal, GitHub, UCSC, NCSU, Sandia National Labs, Thoughtworks, DevJam, ScyllaDB, C2, HERE, SendGrid, Cake Solutions, Cars.com, New Relic, Jet.com, and O'Reilly.

At the encouragement of O'Reilly, the following year the team at Netflix published a report on the subject, *Chaos Engineering*, which coincided with several presentations and a workshop at the Velocity conference in San Jose.

Also in 2017, Casey Rosenthal and Nora Jones organized Chaos Community Day in San Francisco at Autodesk's office at 1 Market Street. Casey had met Nora at the previous Chaos Community Day when she worked at Jet.com. She had since moved over to Netflix and joined the Chaos Engineering Team there. More than 150 people attended, from the usual suspects of large Silicon Valley companies operating at scale as well as various startups, universities, and everything in between. That was in September.

A couple of months later, Nora gave a keynote on Chaos Engineering at the AWS re:Invent conference in Las Vegas to 40,000 attendees in person and an additional 20,000 streaming. Chaos Engineering had hit the big time.

Fast Evolution

As you will see throughout this book, the concepts threaded throughout Chaos Engineering are evolving rapidly. That means much of the work done in this area has diverged from the original intent. Some of it might even seem to be contradictory. It's important to remember that Chaos Engineering is a pragmatic approach pioneered in a high-performance environment facing unique problems at scale. This pragmatism continues to drive the field, even as some of its strength draws from science and academia.

Setting the Stage

Throughout history, competitive advantages have presented themselves as complex systems. Military science, construction, maritime innovations—to the humans who had to interact with those systems at the time, there were so many moving parts interacting in unforeseeable ways that it was impossible to predict the result with confidence. Software systems are today's complex systems.

Chaos Engineering was deliberately created as a proactive discipline to understand and navigate complex systems. Part I of this book introduces examples of complex systems and grounds the principles of Chaos Engineering within that context. The content of Chapter 1 and Chapter 2 is laid out in the natural order that experienced engineers and architects learn to manage complexity: contemplate, encounter, confront, embrace, and finally navigate it.

Chapter 1 explores the properties of complex systems, illustrating those properties with three examples taken from software systems: "In complex systems, we acknowledge that one person can't hold all of the pieces in their head." In Chapter 2 we turn our attention to navigating complexity as a systemic approach: "The holistic, systemic perspective of Chaos Engineering is one of the things that sets it apart from other practices." Two models, the Dynamic Safety Model and the Economic Pillars of Complexity Model, are presented as ways to think about working with the complexity.

Chapter 3 builds on that exploration of complex systems presented in the previous chapters to frame the principles and definition of Chaos Engineering: "The facilitation of experiments to uncover systemic weaknesses." This chapter encapsulates the theoretical evolution of the discipline so far, and provides the touchstones for subsequent chapters as they address implementations and permutations of Chaos Engineering. "The Principles defines the discipline so that we know when we are doing Chaos Engineering, how to do it, and how to do it well."

CHAPTER 1

Encountering Complex Systems

In the first part of this chapter we explore the problems that arise when dealing with complex systems. Chaos Engineering was born of necessity in a complex distributed software system. It specifically addresses the needs of operating a complex system, namely that these systems are nonlinear (*https://oreil.ly/PiC5D*), which makes them unpredictable, and in turn leads to undesirable outcomes. This is often uncomfortable for us as engineers, because we like to think that we can plan our way around uncertainty. We are often tempted to blame these undesirable behaviors on the people who build and operate the systems, but in fact surprises are a natural property of complex systems. Later in this chapter we then ask whether we can extricate the complexity out of the system, and in doing so extricate the undesirable behaviors with it. (Spoiler: no, we cannot.)

Contemplating Complexity

Before you can decide whether Chaos Engineering makes sense for your system, you need to understand where to draw the line between simple and complex. One way to characterize a system is in the way changes to input to the system correspond to changes in output. Simple systems are often described as linear. A change to input of a linear system produces a corresponding change to the output of the system. Many natural phenomena constitute familiar linear systems. The harder you throw a ball, the further it goes.

Nonlinear systems have output that varies wildly based on changes to the constituent parts. The bullwhip effect is an example from systems thinking[1] that visually captures this interaction: a flick of the wrist (small change in system input) results in the far

---

[1] See Peter Senge, *The Fifth Discipline* (New York, NY: Doubleday, 2006).

end of the whip covering enough distance in an instance to break the speed of sound and create the cracking sound that whips are known for (big change in system output).

Nonlinear effects can take various forms: changes to system parts can cause exponential changes in output, like social networks that grow faster when they are big versus when they are small; or they can cause quantum changes in output, like applying increasing force to a dry stick, which doesn't move until it suddenly breaks; or they can cause seemingly random output, like an upbeat song that might inspire someone during their workout one day but bore them the next.

Linear systems are obviously easier to predict than nonlinear ones. It is often relatively easy to intuit the output of a linear system, particularly after interacting with one of the parts and experiencing the linear output. For this reason, we can say that linear systems are simple systems. In contrast, nonlinear systems exhibit unpredictable behavior, particularly when several nonlinear parts coexist. Overlapping nonlinear parts can cause system output to increase up to a point, and then suddenly reverse course, and then just as suddenly stop altogether. We say these nonlinear systems are complex.

Another way we can characterize systems is less technical and more subjective, but probably more intuitive. A simple system is one in which a person can comprehend all of the parts, how they work, and how they contribute to the output. A complex system, by contrast, has so many moving parts, or the parts change so quickly that no person is capable of holding a mental model of it in their head. See Table 1-1.

Table 1-1. Simple and complex systems

Simple systems	Complex systems
Linear	Nonlinear
Predictable output	Unpredictable behavior
Comprehensible	Impossible to build a complete mental model

Looking at the accumulated characteristics of complex systems, it's easy to see why traditional methods of exploring system safety are inadequate. Nonlinear output is difficult to simulate or accurately model. The output is unpredictable. People can't mentally model them.

In the world of software, it's not unusual to work with complex systems that exhibit these characteristics. In fact, a consequence of the Law of Requisite Variety[2] is that

---

2 See commentary on W. Ross Ashby's "Law of Requisite Variety," in W. Ross Ashby, "Requisite Variety and Its Implications for the Control of Complex Systems," *Cybernetica* 1:2 (1958), pp. 83-99. To oversimplify, a system A that fully controls system B has to be at least as complex as system B.

any control system must have at least as much complexity as the system that it controls. Since most software involves writing control systems, the great bulk of building software increases complexity over time. If you work in software and don't work with complex systems today, it's increasingly likely that you will at some point.

One consequence of the increase in complex systems is that the traditional role of software architect becomes less relevant over time. In simple systems, one person, usually an experienced engineer, can orchestrate the work of several engineers. The role of the architect evolved because that person can mentally model the entire system and knows how all the parts fit together. They can act as a guide and planner for how the functionality is written and how the technology unfolds in a software project over time.

In complex systems, we acknowledge that one person can't hold all of the pieces in their head. This means that software engineers need to have greater involvement in the design of the system. Historically, engineering is a bureaucratic profession: some people have the role of deciding what work needs to be done, others decide how and when it will be done, and others do the actual work. In complex systems, that division of labor is counterproductive because the people who have the most context are the ones doing the actual work. The role of architects and associated bureaucracy becomes less efficient. Complex systems encourage nonbureaucratic organizational structures to effectively build, interact with, and respond to them.

Encountering Complexity

The unpredictable, incomprehensible nature of complex systems presents new challenges. The following sections provide three examples of outages caused by complex interactions. In each of these cases, we would not expect a reasonable engineering team to anticipate the undesirable interaction in advance.

Example 1: Mismatch Between Business Logic and Application Logic

Consider the microservice architecture described here and illustrated in Figure 1-1. In this system, we have four components:

Service P
> Stores personalized information. An ID represents a person and some metadata associated with that person. For simplicity, the metadata stored is never very large, and people are never removed from the system. P passes data to Q to be persisted.

Service Q
> A generic storage service used by several upstream services. It stores data in a persistent database for fault tolerance and recovery, and in a memory-based cache database for speed.

Service S

A persistent storage database, perhaps a columnar storage system like Cassandra or DynamoDB.

Service T

An in-memory cache, perhaps something like Redis or Memcached.

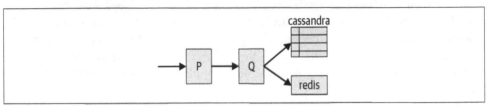

Figure 1-1. Diagram of microservice components showing flow of requests coming in to P and proceeding through storage

To add some rational fallbacks to this system, the teams responsible for each component anticipate failures. Service Q will write data to both services: S and T. When retrieving data, it will read from Service T first, since that is quicker. If the cache fails for some reason, it will read from Service S. If both Service T and Service S fail, then it can send a default response for the database back upstream.

Likewise, Service P has rational fallbacks. If Q times out, or returns an error, then P can degrade gracefully by returning a default response. For example, P could return un-personalized metadata for a given person if Q is failing.

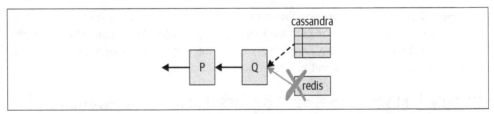

Figure 1-2. The in-memory cache T fails, causing the fallback in Q to rely on responses from the persistent storage database S

One day, T fails (Figure 1-2). Lookups to P start to slow down, because Q notices that T is no longer responding, and so it switches to reading from S. Unfortunately for this setup, it's common for systems with large caches to have read-heavy workloads. In this case, T was handling the read load quite well because reading directly from memory is fast, but S is not provisioned to handle this sudden workload increase. S slows down and eventually fails. Those requests time out.

Fortunately, Q was prepared for this as well, and so it returns a default response. The default response for a particular version of Cassandra when looking up a data object when all three replicas are unavailable is a 404 [Not Found] response code, so Q emits a 404 to P.

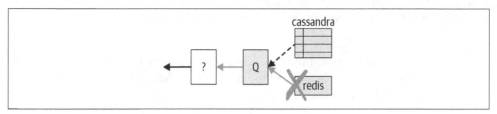

Figure 1-3. With T unresponsive, and S unable to handle the load of the read-heavy workload, Q returns a default response to P

P knows that the person it is looking up exists because it has an ID. People are never removed from the service. The 404 [Not Found] response that P receives from Q is therefore an impossible condition by virtue of the business logic (Figure 1-3). P could have handled an error from Q, or even a lack of response, but it has no condition to catch this impossible response. P crashes, taking down the entire system with it (Figure 1-4).

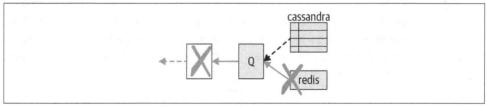

Figure 1-4. The default 404 [Not Found] response from Q seems logically impossible to P, causing it to fail catastrophically

What is at fault in this scenario? The entire system going down is obviously undesirable system behavior. This is a complex system, where we allow that no person can hold all of the moving parts in mind. Each of the respective teams that own P, Q, S, and T made reasonable design decisions. They even went an extra step to anticipate failures, catch those cases, and degrade gracefully. So what is to blame?

No one is at fault and no service is at fault. There is nothing to blame. This is a well-built system. It would be unreasonable to expect that the engineers should have anticipated this failure, since the interaction of the components exceeds the capability of any human to hold all of the pieces in their head, and inevitably leads to gaps in assumptions of what other humans on the team may know. The undesirable output from this complex system is an outlier, produced by nonlinear contributing factors.

Let's look at another example.

Example 2: Customer-Induced Retry Storm

Consider the following snippet of a distributed system from a movie streaming service (Figure 1-5). In this system, we have two main subsystems:

System R

> Stores a personalized user interface. Given an ID that represents a person, it will return a user interface customized to the movie preferences of that individual. R calls S for additional information about each person.

System S

> Stores a variety of information about users, such as whether they have a valid account and what they are allowed to watch. This is too much data to fit on one instance or virtual machine, so S separates access and reading and writing into two subcomponents:

S-L

> Load balancer that uses a consistent hash algorithm to distribute the read-heavy load to the S-D components.

S-D

> Storage unit that has a small sample of the full dataset. For example, one instance of S-D might have information about all of the users whose names start with the letter "m" whereas another might store those whose names start with the letter "p."[3]

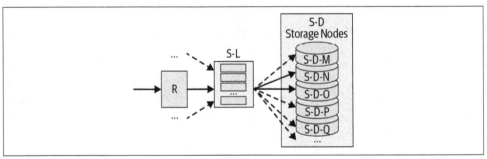

Figure 1-5. request path from R to S-L to S-D-N for user Louis's data

The team that maintains this has experience in distributed systems and industry norms in cloud deployment. This includes measures like having rational fallbacks. If R can't retrieve information about a person from S, then it has a default user interface. Both systems are also conscientious about cost, and so they have scaling policies that

---

3 It doesn't work exactly this way, because the consistent hash algorithm distributes data objects pseudo-randomly across all S-D instances.

keep the clusters appropriately sized. If disk I/O drops below a certain threshold on S-D, for example, S-D will hand off data from the least busy node and shut that node down, and S-L will redistribute that workload to the remaining nodes. S-D data is held in a redundant on-node cache, so if the disk is slow for some reason, a slightly stale result can be returned from the cache. Alerts are set to trigger on increased error ratios, outlier detection will restart instances behaving oddly, etc.

One day, a customer who we will call Louis is watching streaming video from this service under nonoptimal conditions. Specifically, Louis is accessing the system from a web browser on his laptop on a train. At some point a strange thing happens in the video and surprises Louis. He drops his laptop, on the ground, some keys are pressed, and when he situates the laptop again to continue watching, the video is frozen.

Louis does what any sensible customer would do in this situation and hits the refresh button 100 times. The calls are queued in the web browser, but at that moment the train is between cell towers, so a network partition prevents the requests from being delivered. When the WiFi signal reconnects, all 100 requests are delivered at once.

Back on the server side, R receives all 100 requests and initiates 100 equal requests to S-L, which uses the consistent hash of Louis's ID to forward all of those requests to a specific node in S-D that we will call S-D-N. Receiving 100 requests all at once is a significant increase since S-D-N is used to getting a baseline of 50 requests per second. This is a threefold increase over baseline, but fortunately we have rational fallbacks and degradations in place.

S-D-N can't serve 150 requests (baseline plus Louis) in one second from disk, so it starts serving requests from the cache. This is significantly faster. As a result, both disk I/O and CPU utilization drop dramatically. At this point, the scaling policies kick in to keep the system right-sized to cost concerns. Since disk I/O and CPU utilization are so low, S-D decides to shut down S-D-N and hand off its workload to a peer node. Or maybe anomaly detection shut off this node; sometimes it's difficult to say in complex systems (Figure 1-6).

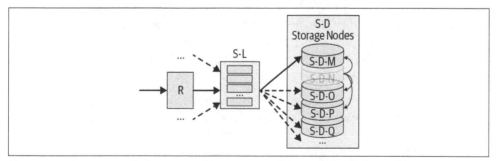

Figure 1-6. Request path from R to S-L to S-D-M for user Louis's data after S-D-N shuts down and hands off data

S-L returns responses to 99 of Louis's requests, all served from S-D-N's cache, but the 100th response is lost due to the configuration of the cluster being changed as S-D-N shuts down and data handoff takes place. For this last response, since R gets a timeout error from S-L, it returns a default user interface rather than the personalized user interface for Louis.

Back on his laptop, Louis's web browser ignores the 99 proper responses and renders the 100th response, which is the default user interface. To Louis, this appears to be another error, since it is not the personalized user interface to which he is accustomed.

Louis does what any sensible customer would do in this situation and hits the refresh button another 100 times. This time, the process repeats but S-L forwards the requests to S-D-M, which took over from S-D-N. Unfortunately, data handoff has not completed, so the disk on S-D-M is quickly overwhelmed.

S-D-M switches to serving requests from cache. Repeating the procedure that S-D-N followed, this significantly speeds up requests. Disk I/O and CPU utilization drop dramatically. Scaling policies kick in and S-D decides to shut down S-D-M and hand off its workload to a peer node (Figure 1-7).

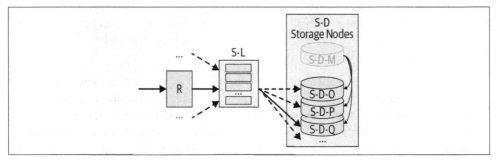

Figure 1-7. Request path from R to S-L to S-D for user Louis's data after S-D-M and S-D-N both shut down and hand off data

S-D now has a data handoff situation in flight for two nodes. These nodes are responsible not just for the Louis user, but for a percentage of all users. R receives more timeout errors from S-L for this percentage of users, so R returns a default user interface rather than the personalized user interface for these users.

Back on their client devices, these users now have a similar experience to Louis. To many of them this appears to be another error, since it is not the personalized user interface to which they are accustomed. They too do what any sensible customer would do in this situation and hit the refresh button 100 times.

We now have a user-induced retry storm.

The cycle accelerates. S-D shrinks and latency spikes as more nodes are overwhelmed by handoff. S-L struggles to satisfy requests as the request rate increases dramatically from client devices while timing out simultaneously keeps requests sent to S-D open longer. Eventually R, keeping all of these requests to S-L open even though they will eventually time out, has an overwhelmed thread pool that crashes the virtual machine. The entire service falls over (Figure 1-8).

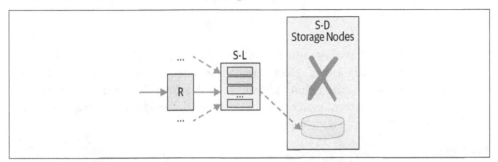

Figure 1-8. Request path as S-D is scaled down and R is pummeled by user-induced retry storms

To make matters worse, the outage causes more client-induced retries, which makes it even more difficult to remediate the issue and bring the service back online to a stable state.

Again we can ask: what is at fault in this scenario? Which component was built incorrectly? In a complex system no person can hold all of the moving parts in their mind. Each of the respective teams that built R, S-L, and S-D made reasonable design decisions. They even went an extra step to anticipate failures, catch those cases, and degrade gracefully. So what is to blame?

As with the prior example, no one is at fault here. There is nothing to blame. Of course, with the bias of hindsight, we can improve this system to prevent the scenario just described from happening again. Nevertheless, it would be unreasonable to expect that the engineers should have anticipated this failure. Once again nonlinear contributing factors conspired to emit an undesirable result from this complex system.

Let's look at one more example.

Example 3: Holiday Code Freeze

Consider the following infrastructure setup (Figure 1-9) for a large online retail company:

Component E

a load balancer that simply forwards requests, similar to an elastic load balancer (ELB) on the AWS cloud service.

Component F

An API Gateway. It parses some information from the headers, cookies, and path. It uses that information to pattern-match an enrichment policy; for example, adding additional headers that indicate which features that user is authorized to access. It then pattern matches a backend and forwards the request to the backend.

Component G

A sprawling mess of backend applications running with various levels of criticality, on various platforms, serving countless functions, to an unspecified set of users.

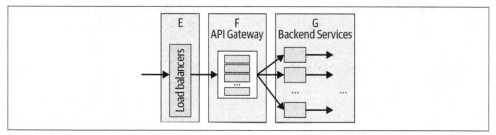

Figure 1-9. Request path for large online retail company

The team maintaining F has some interesting obstacles to manage. They have no control over the stack or other operational properties of G. Their interface has to be flexible to handle many different shapes of patterns to match request headers, cookies, and paths and deliver the requests to the correct place. The performance profile of G runs the full spectrum, from low-latency responses with small payloads to keep-alive connections that stream large files. None of these factors can be planned for because the components in G and beyond are themselves complex systems with dynamically changing properties.

F is highly flexible, handling a diverse set of workloads. New features are added to F roughly once per day and deployed to satisfy new use cases for G. To provision such a functional component, the team vertically scales the solution over time to match the increase in use cases for G. Larger and larger boxes allow them to allocate more memory, which takes time to initiate. More and more pattern matching for both enrichment and routing results in a hefty ruleset, which is preparsed into a state machine and loaded into memory for faster access. This too takes time. When all is said and done, these large virtual machines running F each take about 40 minutes to provision from the time that the provisioning pipeline is kicked off to the time that all of the caches are warm and the instance is running at or near baseline performance.

Because F is in the critical path of all access to G, the team operating it understands that it is a potential single point of failure. They don't just deploy one instance; they deploy a cluster. The number of instances at any given time is determined so that the entire cluster has an additional 50% capacity. At any given time, a third of the instances could suddenly disappear and everything should still keep working.

Vertically scaled, horizontally scaled, and overprovisioned: F is an expensive component.

To go above and beyond with regard to availability, the team takes several additional precautions. The CI pipeline runs a thorough set of unit and integration tests before baking an image for the virtual machine. Automated canaries test any new code change on a small amount of traffic before proceeding to a blue/green deployment model that runs a good chunk of the cluster in parallel before completely cutting over to a new version. All pull requests to change the code to F undergo a two-reviewer policy and the reviewer can't be someone working on the feature being changed, requiring the entire team to be well informed about all aspects of development in motion.

Finally, the entire organization goes into a code freeze at the beginning of November until January. No changes are allowed during this time unless it is absolutely critical to the safety of the system, since the holidays between Black Friday and New Year's Day are the peak traffic seasons for the company. The potential of introducing a bug for the sake of a noncritical feature could be catastrophic in this timeframe, so the best way to avoid that possibility is to not change the system at all. Since many people take vacation around this time of year, it works out to have restricted code deployments from an oversight perspective as well.

Then one year an interesting phenomenon occurs. During the end of the second week in November, two weeks into the code freeze, the team is paged for a sudden increase in errors from one instance. No problem: that instance is shut down and another is booted up. Over the course of the next 40 minutes, before the new instance becomes fully operational, several other machines also experience a similar increase in errors. As new instances are booted to replace those, the rest of the cluster experiences the same phenomenon.

Over the course of several hours, the entire cluster is replaced with new instances running the same exact code. Even with the 50% overhead, a significant number of requests go unserved during the period while the entire cluster is rebooted over such a short interval. This partial outage fluctuates in severity for hours before the entire provisioning process is over and the new cluster stabilizes.

The team faces a dilemma: in order to troubleshoot the issue, they would need to deploy a new version with observability measures focused in a new area of code. But the code freeze is in full swing, and the new cluster appears by all metrics to be stable. The next week they decide to deploy a small number of new instances with the new observability measures.

Two weeks go by without incident when suddenly the same phenomenon occurs again. First a few then eventually all of the instances see a sudden increase in error rates. All instances that is, *except* those that were instrumented with the new observability measures.

As with the prior incident, the entire cluster is rebooted over several hours and seemingly stabilizes. The outage is more severe this time since the company is now within its busiest season.

A few days later, the instances that were instrumented with new observability measures begin to see the same spike in errors. Due to the metrics gathered, it is discovered that an imported library causes a predictable memory leak that scales linearly with the number of requests served. Because the instances are so massive, it takes approximately two weeks for the leak to eat up enough memory to cause enough resource deprivation to affect other libraries.

This bug had been introduced into the codebase almost nine months earlier. The phenomenon was never seen before because no instance in the cluster had ever run for more than four days. New features caused new code deployment, which cycled in new instances. Ironically, it was a procedure meant to increase safety—the holiday code freeze—that caused the bug to manifest in an outage.

Again we ask: what is at fault in this scenario? We can identify the bug in the dependent library, but we learn nothing if we point the blame to an external coder who does not even have knowledge of this project. Each of the team members working on F made reasonable design decisions. They even went an extra step to anticipate failures, stage deployment of new features, overprovision, and "be careful" as much as they could think to do. So who is to blame?

As with both prior examples, no one is at fault here. There is nothing to blame. It would be unreasonable to expect that the engineers should have anticipated this failure. Nonlinear contributing factors produced an undesirable and expensive output in this complex system.

Confronting Complexity

The three preceding examples illustrate cases where none of the humans in the loop could reasonably be expected to anticipate the interactions that ultimately led to the undesirable outcome. Humans will still be writing software for the foreseeable future, so taking them out of the loop is not an option. What then can be done to reduce systemic failures like these?

One popular idea is to reduce or eliminate the complexity. Take the complexity out of a complex system, and we will not have the problems of complex systems anymore.

Perhaps if we could reduce these systems to simpler, linear ones then we would even be able to identify who is to blame when something goes wrong. In this hypothetical simpler world, we can imagine a hyper-efficient, impersonal manager could remove all errors simply by getting rid of the bad apples who create those errors.

To examine this possible solution, it is helpful to understand a few additional characteristics of complexity. Roughly speaking, complexity can be sorted into two buckets: accidental and essential, a distinction made by Frederick Brooks in the 1980s.[4]

Accidental Complexity

Accidental complexity is a consequence of writing software within a resource-limited setting, namely this universe. In everyday work there are always competing priorities. For software engineers the explicit priorities might be feature velocity, test coverage, and idiomaticity. The implicit priorities might be economy, workload, and safety. No one has infinite time and resources, so navigating these priorities inevitably results in a compromise.

The code we write is imbued with our intentions, assumptions, and priorities at one particular point in time. It cannot be correct because the world will change, and what we expect from our software will change with it.

A compromise in software can manifest as a slightly suboptimal snippet of code, a vague intention behind a contract, an equivocating variable name, an emphasis on a later-abandoned code path, and so on. Like dirt on a floor, these snippets accumulate. No one brings dirt into a house and puts it on the floor on purpose; it just happens as a byproduct of living. Likewise, suboptimal code just happens as a byproduct of engineering. At some point these accumulated suboptimals exceed the ability of a person to intuitively understand them and at that point we have complexity—specifically, accidental complexity.

---

4 Frederick Brooks, "No Silver Bullet—Essence and Accident in Software Engineering," from *Proceedings of the IFIP Tenth World Computing Conference*, H.-J. Kugler ed., Elsevier Science BV, Amsterdam (1986).

The interesting thing about accidental complexity is that there is no known, *sustainable* method to reduce it. You can reduce accidental complexity at one point in time by stopping work on new features to reduce the complexity in previously written software. This can work, but there are caveats.

For example, there is no reason to assume that the compromises that were made at the time the code was written were any less informed than the ones that will be made in a refactoring. The world changes, as does our expectation of how software should behave. It is often the case that writing new software to reduce accidental complexity simply creates new forms of accidental complexity. These new forms may be more acceptable than the prior, but that acceptability will expire at roughly the same rate.

Large refactors often suffer from what is known as the second-system effect, a term also introduced by Frederick Brooks, in which the subsequent project is supposed to be better than the original because of the insight gained during development of the first. Instead, these second systems end up bigger and more complex due to unintentional trade-offs inspired by the success of writing the first version.

Regardless of the approach taken to reduce accidental complexity, none of these methods are sustainable. They all require a diversion of limited resources like time and attention away from developing new features. In any organization where the intention is to make progress, these diversions conflict with other priorities. Hence, they are not sustainable.

So as a byproduct of writing code, accidental complexity is always accruing.

Essential Complexity

If we cannot sustainably reduce accidental complexity, then perhaps we can reduce the other kind of complexity. Essential complexity in software is the code that we write that purposefully adds more overhead because that is the job. As software engineers we write new features, and new features make things more complex.

Consider the following example: you have the simplest database that you can imagine. It is a key/value datastore, as seen in Figure 1-10: give it a key and a value, and it will store the value. Give it a key, and it will return the value. To make it absurdly simple, imagine that it runs in-memory on your laptop.

Now imagine that you are given the task of making it more available. We can put it into the cloud. That way when we shut the laptop lid the data persists. We can add multiple nodes for redundancy. We can put the keyspace behind a consistent hash and distribute the data to multiple nodes. We can persist the data on those nodes to disk so we can bring them on- and offline for repair or data handoff. We can replicate a cluster to another in different regions so that if one region or datacenter becomes unavailable we can still access the other cluster.

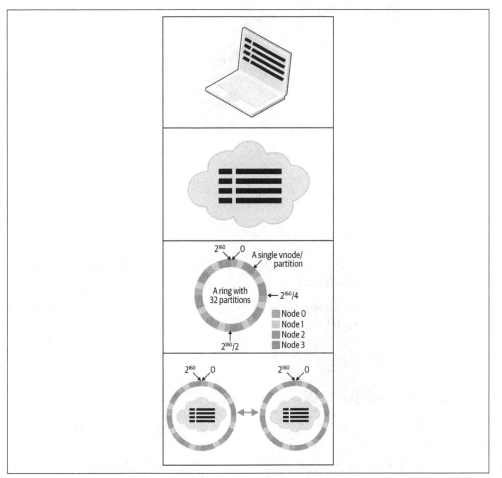

Figure 1-10. Progression of a simple key/value database to a highly available setup

In one paragraph we very quickly can describe a slew of well-known design principles to make a database more available.

Now let's go back to our simple key/value datastore running in-memory on our laptop (Figure 1-11). Imagine that you are given the task of making it more available, and simpler, simultaneously. Do not spend too much time trying to solve this riddle: it cannot be done in any meaningful way.

Figure 1-11. Rewind to the simple key/value database

Adding new features to software (or safety properties like availability and security) requires the addition of complexity.

Taken together, the prospect of trading in our complex systems for simple systems is not encouraging. Accidental complexity will always accrue as a byproduct of work, and essential complexity will be driven by new features. In order to make any progress in software, complexity will increase.

Embracing Complexity

If complexity is causing bad outcomes, and we cannot remove the complexity, then what are we to do? The solution is a two-step process.

The first step is to embrace complexity rather than avoid it. Most of the properties that we desire and optimize for in our software require adding complexity. Trying to optimize for simplicity sets the wrong priority and generally leads to frustration. In the face of inevitable complexity we sometimes hear, "Don't add any unnecessary complexity." Sure, but the same could be said of anything: "Don't add any unnecessary _____." Accept that complexity is going to increase, even as software improves, and that is not a bad thing.

The second step, which is the subject of Chapter 2, is to learn to navigate complexity. Find tools to move quickly with confidence. Learn practices to add new features without exposing your system to increased risks of unwanted behavior. Rather than sink into complexity and drown in frustration, surf it like a wave. As an engineer, Chaos Engineering may be the most approachable, efficient way to begin to navigate the complexity of your system.

CHAPTER 2

Navigating Complex Systems

The previous chapter described complex systems in much the same way one would describe the water to someone who is drowning. This chapter focuses on how to stop drowning and surf the waves instead. To learn how to navigate complex systems, we present two methods:

- Dynamic Safety Model
- Economic Pillars of Complexity Model

Both of these models are foundational to the construction of Chaos Engineering as a discipline within software engineering.

Dynamic Safety Model

This model is an adaptation of Jens Rasmussen's Dynamic Safety Model,[1] which is well known and highly regarded within the field of Resilience Engineering. The adaptation presented here simply reframes the model in a context relevant to software engineers.

The Dynamic Safety Model has three properties: Economics, Workload, and Safety (Figure 2-1). You can imagine an engineer in the middle of these three properties, attached to each by a rubber band. Throughout their workday, the engineer can move about, stretching the rubber band; however, if the engineer strays too far from a property, then the rubber band snaps and it is game over for that engineer.

---

1 Jens Rasmussen, "Risk Management in a Dynamic Society," Jens Rasmussen, "Risk Management in a Dynamic Society," *Safety Science* 27(2-3), 1997.

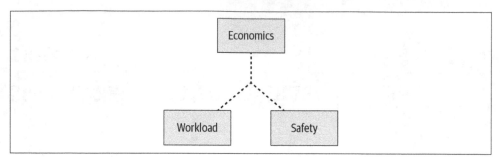

Figure 2-1. The Dynamic Safety Model

The fascinating thing about this model is that engineers implicitly optimize their work in order to prevent any of the rubber bands from snapping. We will touch on each of the three properties in turn.

Economics

You probably do not have a rule for software engineers that they are not allowed to spin up a million instances on the cloud on their first day of work. Why don't you have such a rule? Because it isn't necessary. Engineers implicitly understand that they have a cost, their team has a cost, and their resources have a cost. It's common sense. Without anyone having to tell them so, engineers know that spinning up a million instances on the cloud would be prohibitively expensive, and could bankrupt the organization. There are countless other expenses that could in theory be incurred by an engineer but aren't, because this is a form of complexity that we are already comfortable navigating. We can say that engineers have an intuition for the Economics margin, and they don't cross that boundary to where that rubber band would snap.

Workload

Likewise, engineers understand that they cannot work 170 hours or anywhere close to that in a given week. They have a limit to the workload that they can handle. Their team has a limit to the features they can deliver in a sprint. Their tools and resources have limits to how much load they can handle. No engineer would expect to deploy a system at scale on a laptop, because they implicitly know that all of that traffic would exceed the workload capabilities of a laptop and it would crash. There are countless other forms of workload constraints that engineers understand, but again we don't often consider these explicitly because this is also a form of complexity that we are already comfortable navigating. We can say that engineers have an intuition for the Workload margin, and they don't cross that boundary to where that rubber band would snap.

Safety

The third property in the model is Safety. In the context of software systems this can refer to either the availability of the system or to security in the cybersecurity sense of the word.[2] Here is where we have a departure from the first two properties. Whereas with Economics and Workload we can say that engineers have an intuition for the margin, the same cannot be said for Safety. In general, software engineers do not have an intuition for how close they are to the boundary beyond which that rubber band would snap, resulting in an incident, be it an outage or a security breach.

We are comfortable making that broad generalization over software engineers because incidents are ubiquitous in software. If an engineer knew that they were within the Safety margin, approaching the boundary, then they would change their behavior in order to avert the incident. This rarely happens because in almost all cases the incident is a surprise. Engineers simply do not have enough information to assess the Safety of the system and so they stumble across that line.

To make matters worse, engineers tend to optimize for what they can see. Since they have an intuition for the Economics and Workload properties, they see those properties in their day-to-day work, and so they move toward those poles in the diagram (see Figure 2-2). This inadvertently leads them further away from Safety. This effect sets up conditions for a silent, unseen drift toward failure as the success of their endeavor provides opportunities to optimize toward Economics and Workload, but away from Safety.

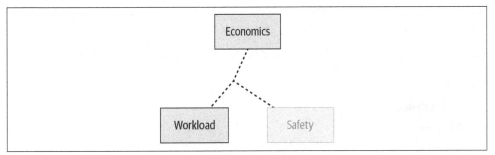

Figure 2-2. In the Dynamic Safety Model, when the Safety property is unseen, engineers tend to drift away from it, and toward the Economic and Workload properties, which are more visible

One way to interpret the benefit of Chaos Engineering on an organization is that it helps engineers develop an intuition for Safety where it is otherwise lacking. The empirical evidence provided by the experiments inform the engineer's intuition. A

---

2 See Chapter 20, *The Case for Security Chaos Engineering*, by Aaron Rinehart, for an explicit exploration of security in Chaos Engineering.

specific result may teach an engineer about a specific vulnerability and they can patch that. There is some value there, but by far the greater value is in teaching the engineer things they did not anticipate about how safety mechanisms interplay in the complexity of the entire system.

Even better, the Dynamic Safety Model tells us that once an engineer has an intuition for that boundary, they will implicitly change their behavior to optimize away from it. They will give themselves a margin to prevent that rubber band from snapping. No one has to tell them that an incident is to be avoided, or remind them to be careful, or encourage them to adopt best practices. They will implicitly modify their behavior in a way that leads to a more resilient system. In this way, the Dynamic Safety Model is foundational for the efficacy of Chaos Engineering.

Economic Pillars of Complexity

This model is an adaptation of a model presented by Kent Beck,[3] which was informed by a presentation by Professor Enrico Zaninotto, Dean of Economics at the University of Trento. The adaptations presented in this version specifically address concerns of software engineers.

As described in the previous chapter, complexity can make designing, delivering, operating, and maintaining software a difficult job. The gut instinct most engineers have when faced with complexity is to avoid or reduce it. Unfortunately, simplification removes utility and ultimately limits business value. The potential for success rises with complexity. This model provides a method of understanding one of the ways software engineers navigate that complexity.

There are four pillars in the Economic Pillars of Complexity model (Figure 2-3):

- Statess
- Relationships
- Environment
- Reversibility

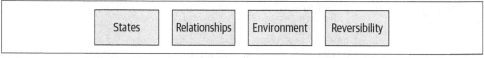

Figure 2-3. Economic Pillars of Complexity

---

3 Kent Beck, "Taming Complexity with Reversibility," Facebook post, July 7, 2015, *https://oreil.ly/jPqZ3*.

The model states that the degree to which an organization can control one of these pillars corresponds to the success with which that organization can navigate the complexity of a competitive production process. Each of the pillars is best illustrated with an example, and the car manufacturing company Ford in the mid-1910s is commonly invoked as the quintessential example.

State

> Therefore in 1909 I announced one morning, without any previous warning, that in the future we were going to build only one model, that the model was going to be "Model T," and that the chassis would be exactly the same for all cars, and I remarked: "Any customer can have a car painted any colour that he wants so long as it is black."
>
> —Henry Ford[4]

As illustrated in Henry Ford's famous quote, Ford drastically limited the number of States in his production, sales, and maintenance process—by design. Parts were standardized. Variance was removed. This contributed to their success in navigating the complex and competitive automobile business.

Relationships

Ford did not stop with just the product. Implementing their own flavor of scientific management, the company also limited the number of Relationships in the manufacturing process. Other automobile companies had teams that would build an entire car. This required high communication and coordination of effort throughout the production process. At Ford, tasks were broken down into small, prescribed movements that incorporated the intelligence of assembly into process and predetermined, mechanical motions. Relationships were no longer required to communicate, coordinate, and improvise the assembly. This also contributed to their success in navigating the complexity of the automobile business at the time. Henry Ford knew this and fluctuated between jealously guarding and flaunting this advantage.

Environment

Most organizations do not have the resources to control or affect their Environment. Ford was able to do so by countersuing the Association of Licensed Automobile Manufacturers (ALAM), which ultimately led to the breakup of that monopoly. ALAM had stifled innovation in the automobile industry through patent licensing and litigation for decades, and after that victory Ford had the freedom to produce more innovative engine designs and sell them without paying prohibitive license fees to ALAM. After some years Ford itself had enough power to influence legislation, literally

---

4 Henry Ford, *My Life and Work* (New York: Doubleday, 1922), p. 45.

paving the Environment to enable more predictable operation of their product across the United States. This obviously enabled the company to navigate the complexity of automobile production with more confidence.

Reversibility

That brings us to the fourth pillar, Reversibility. Unfortunately for Ford, undoing the manufacturing process is not as simple as putting a car in reverse. A car cannot easily be un-built. The efficiency of the factory designs proposed by scientific management also made it very difficult to improvise a design decision. Ford could not do much to control or affect this pillar.

Economic Pillars of Complexity Applied to Software

In the example we just looked at, Ford was able to streamline the first three pillars but not the fourth. How does this relate to software?

Most business goals encourage the proliferation of State. This is true in the sense of creating and saving more data over time (application state) but also the increase in functionality and different possible states of the product. People usually want more features, not less. So software cannot usually streamline State.

Software is also largely an undertaking of adding in layers of abstraction. These new layers require new Relationships. Even compared to a few years ago, the number of components in the average software stack has increased significantly. Taking a typical system at scale deployment as an example, several layers of virtualization have become the norm from cloud instances to containers to functions as a service. With a general migration toward microservice architectures, the industry seems to have acted against its best interest in terms of managing complexity by purposefully increasing the Relationships between parts within a system. Many software companies are migrating to remote organizational structures, relaxing control over even the human Relationships involved in the process.

Most software engineers don't have the means to reign in Relationships in order to better navigate complexity; in fact, the opposite seems to be the case. Very few software companies have the size or scale to affect the Environment in a meaningful way. This puts this pillar out of reach for nearly all software engineers as well.

This brings us to the final pillar in the model: Reversibility. This is where software shines. The word "software" itself refers to the ability to manipulate the execution of a program easier than if it were implemented in hardware. The great improvements in software Reversibility started in the extreme programming (XP) and Agile movements. The prior general method of building software, known as Waterfall, involved up-front planning, design, and lengthy delivery. The product would finally be put in front of the customer, perhaps after a year of development, and if the customer didn't like it then there was not much that could be done. Software back then did not have much Reversibility. Short iterations in XP changed that formula. Something unfinished could be put in front of a customer in a couple of weeks. If they didn't like it, then throwing that out (reversing the design decisions) was not a prohibitive action. The next iteration would be closer to what the customer wanted, and then the third even closer, until hopefully by the fourth iteration they are tracking really closely to what the customer wants and needs. This was a process-based method of improving Reversibility.

The great advantage of software is that you can make explicit design decisions that improve Reversibility as well. Development of applications on the web, where a browser reload is all that is required to deploy a new codebase, drastically improved the Reversibility of applications. Version control, blue–green deployment methods, automated canaries, feature flags, continuous integration/continuous delivery (CI/CD)—these are all examples of technical solutions and architectural decisions that explicitly improve Reversibility. Any technique that improves the ability of a software engineer to get code into production, change their mind, and roll back or roll forward that decision, improves their Reversibility. That in turn improves their ability to navigate the complex systems of modern software development.

Seen through this lens, optimizing for Reversibility is a virtue in contemporary software engineering. Optimizing for Reversibility pays dividends down the road when working with complex systems. This is also a foundational model for Chaos Engineering. The experiments in Chaos Engineering expose properties of a system that are counterproductive to Reversibility. In many cases these might be efficiencies that are purposefully built by engineers.

Efficiency can be a business goal, but efficiency is also brittle. Chaos experiments can surface brittleness, and then that can be un-optimized for efficiency, or it can be optimized for Reversibility, so that the rest of the system can improvise and make different decisions if that brittle piece breaks. Chaos Engineering acts like a floodlight, highlighting in broad strokes the places that software engineers can optimize for Reversibility.

The Systemic Perspective

The holistic, systemic perspective of Chaos Engineering is one of the things that sets it apart from other practices. Helping engineers build an intuition of the Safety boundary implicitly changes their behavior toward better safety outcomes. Helping engineers explicitly identify targets for Reversibility helps them optimize for the improvisation characteristic of resilient systems. Both of these models can be understood in terms of grounding Chaos Engineering as a practice that helps engineers move with complexity instead of fight it, swim with the current, and navigate it. In the following chapters you will read several examples of Chaos Engineering as practiced at many different organizations. For each of them, think back to how Chaos Engineering improves their intuition of the Safety boundary, and identifies targets for improving Reversibility. These are the keys to navigating complex systems safely.

CHAPTER 3

Overview of Principles

In the early days of Chaos Engineering at Netflix, it was not obvious what the discipline actually was. There were some catchphrases about pulling out wires or breaking things or testing in production, many misconceptions about how to make services reliable, and very few examples of actual tools. The Chaos Team was formed to create a meaningful discipline, one that proactively improved reliability through tooling. We spent months researching Resilience Engineering and other disciplines in order to come up with a definition and a blueprint for how others could also participate in Chaos Engineering. That definition was put online (*https://principlesofchaos.org*) as a sort of manifesto, referred to as "The Principles." (See the Introduction: Birth of Chaos for the story of how Chaos Engineering came about.)

As is the case with any new concept, Chaos Engineering is sometimes misunderstood. The following sections explore what the discipline *is*, and what it *is not*. The gold standard for the practice is captured in the section "Advanced Principles" on page 29. Finally, we take a look at what factors could change the principles going forward.

What Chaos Engineering Is

"The Principles" defines the discipline so that we know when we are doing Chaos Engineering, how to do it, and how to do it well. The common definition today for *Chaos Engineering* is "The facilitation of experiments to uncover systemic weaknesses." "The Principles" website outlines the steps of the experimentation as follows:

1. Start by defining "steady state" as some measurable output of a system that indicates normal behavior.

2. Hypothesize that this steady state will continue in both the control group and the experimental group.

3. Introduce variables that reflect real-world events like servers that crash, hard drives that malfunction, network connections that are severed, etc.

4. Try to disprove the hypothesis by looking for a difference in steady state between the control group and the experimental group.

This experimentation constitutes the basic principles of Chaos Engineering. By design, there is great latitude in how to implement these experiments.

Experimentation Versus Testing

One of the first distinctions we found necessary to make at Netflix is that Chaos Engineering is a form of experimentation, not testing. Arguably both fall under the umbrella of "quality assurance," but that phrase often has negative connotations in the software industry.

Other teams at Netflix would initially ask the Chaos Team something along the lines of, "Can't you just write a bunch of integration tests that look for the same thing?" This sentiment was pragmatic in theory, but in practice it was impossible to get the desired result from integration tests.

Testing, strictly speaking, does not create new knowledge. Testing requires that the engineer writing the test knows specific properties about the system that they are looking for. As illustrated in the previous chapter, complex systems are opaque to that type of analysis. Humans are simply not capable of understanding all of the potential side effects from all of the potential interactions of parts in a complex system. This leads us to one of the key properties of a test.

Tests make an assertion, based on existing knowledge, and then running the test collapses the valence of that assertion, usually into either true or false. Tests are statements about known properties of the system.

Experimentation, on the other hand, creates new knowledge. Experiments propose a hypothesis, and as long as the hypothesis is not disproven, confidence grows in that hypothesis. If it is disproven, then we learn something new. This kicks off an inquiry to figure out why our hypothesis is wrong. In a complex system, the reason why something happens is often not obvious. Experimentation either builds confidence, or it teaches us new properties about our own system. It is an exploration of the unknown.

No amount of testing in practice can equal the insight gained from experimentation, because testing requires a human to come up with the assertions ahead of time. Experimentation formally introduces a way to discover new properties. It is entirely possible to translate newly discovered properties of a system into tests *after* they are discovered. It also helps to encode new assumptions about a system into new hypotheses, which creates something like a "regression experiment" that explores system changes over time.

Because Chaos Engineering was born from complex system problems, it is essential that the discipline embody experimentation over testing. The four steps of experimentation distilled in "The Principles" roughly adheres to commonly accepted definitions, from the point of view of exploring availability vulnerabilities in systems at scale.

A combination of real-world experience applying the previously outlined steps to systems at scale as well as thoughtful introspection led the Chaos Team to push the practice further than just experimentation. These insights became the "Advanced Principles," which guide teams through the maturity of their Chaos Engineering programs and help set a gold standard toward which we can aspire.

Verification Versus Validation

Using definitions of verification and validation inspired by operations management and logistical planning, we can say that Chaos Engineering is strongly biased toward the former over the latter.

Verification
> Verification of a complex system is a process of analyzing output at a system boundary. A homeowner can *verify* the quality of the water (output) coming from a sink (system boundary) by testing it for contaminants without knowing anything about how plumbing or municipal water service (system parts) functions.

Validation
> Validation of a complex system is a process of analyzing the parts of the system and building mental models that reflect the interaction of those parts. A homeowner can *validate* the quality of water by inspecting all of the pipes and infrastructure (system parts) involved in capturing, cleaning, and delivering water (mental model of functional parts) to a residential area and eventually to the house in question.

Both of these practices are potentially useful, and both build confidence in the output of the system. As software engineers we often feel a compulsion to dive into code and validate that it reflects our mental model of how it should be working. Contrary to this predilection, Chaos Engineering strongly prefers verification over validation. Chaos Engineering cares *whether* something works, not *how*.

Note that in the plumbing metaphor we could validate all of the components that go into supplying clean drinking water, and yet still end up with contaminated water for some reason we did not expect. In a complex system, there are always unpredictable interactions. But if we verify that the water is clean at the tap, then we do not necessarily have to care about how it got there. In most business cases, the output of the system is much more important than whether or not the implementation matches our mental model. Chaos Engineering cares more about the business case and output than about the implementation or mental model of interacting parts.

What Chaos Engineering Is Not

There are two concepts that are often confused with Chaos Engineering, namely breaking stuff in production and Antifragility.

Breaking Stuff

Occasionally in blog posts or conference presentations we hear Chaos Engineering described as "breaking stuff in production." While this might sound cool, it doesn't appeal to enterprises running at scale and other complex system operators who can most benefit from the practice. A better characterization of Chaos Engineering would be: fixing stuff in production. "Breaking stuff" is easy; the difficult parts are around mitigating blast radius, thinking critically about safety, determining if something is worth fixing, deciding whether you should invest in experimenting on it, the list goes on. "Breaking stuff" could be done in countless ways, with little time invested. The larger question here is, how do we reason about things that are already broken, when we don't even know they are broken?

"Fixing stuff in production" does a much better job of capturing the value of Chaos Engineering since the point of the whole practice is to proactively improve availability and security of a complex system. Plenty of disciplines and tools already exist to reactively respond to an incident: alerting tools, incident response management, observability tools, disaster recovery planning, and so on. These aim to reduce time-to-detect and time-to-resolve after the inevitable incident. An argument could be made that Site Reliability Engineering (SRE) straddles both reactive and proactive disciplines by generating knowledge from past incidents and socializing that to prevent future ones. Chaos Engineering is the only major discipline in software that focuses solely on *proactively* improving safety in complex systems.

Antifragility

People familiar with the concept of Antifragility, introduced by Nassim Taleb,[1] often assume that Chaos Engineering is essentially the software version of the same thing. Taleb argues that words like "hormesis" are insufficient to capture the ability of complex systems to adapt, and so he invented the word "antifragile" as a way to refer to systems that get stronger when exposed to random stress. An important, critical

---

1 Nassim Taleb, *Antifragile: Things That Gain from Disorder* (New York, NY: Penguin, 2012).

distinction between Chaos Engineering and Antifragility is that Chaos Engineering educates human operators about the chaos already inherent in the system, so that they can be a more resilient team. Antifragility, by contrast, adds chaos to a system in hopes that it will grow stronger in response rather than succumbing to it.

As a framework, Antifragility puts forth guidance at odds with the scholarship of Resilience Engineering, Human Factors, and Safety Systems research. For example, Antifragility proposes that the first step in improving a system's robustness is to hunt for weaknesses and remove them. This proposal seems intuitive but Resilience Engineering tells us that hunting for what goes *right* in safety is much more informative than what goes *wrong*. The next step in Antifragility is to add redundancy. This also seems intuitive, but adding redundancy can cause failure just as easily as it can mitigate against it, and the literature in Resilience Engineering is rife with examples where redundancy actually contributes to safety failures.[2]

There are numerous other examples of divergence between these two schools of thought. Resilience Engineering is an ongoing area of research with decades of support, whereas Antifragile is a theory that exists largely outside of academia and peer review. It is easy to imagine how the two concepts become conflated, since both deal with chaos and complex systems, but the spirit of Antifragile does not share the empiricism and fundamental grounding of Chaos Engineering. For these reasons we should consider them to be fundamentally different pursuits.[3]

Advanced Principles

Chaos Engineering is grounded in empiricism, experimentation over testing, and verification over validation. But not all experimentation is equally valuable. The gold standard for the practice was first captured in the "Advanced Principles" section of "The Principles." The advanced principles are:

- Build a hypothesis around steady-state behavior
- Vary real-world events
- Run experiments in production
- Automate experiments to run continuously
- Minimize blast radius

---

2 Perhaps the most famous example is the 1986 *Challenger* disaster. The redundancy of O-rings was one of three reasons that NASA approved the continuation of the launches, even though damage to the primary O-ring was well known internally for over fifty of the prior launch missions over the span of five years. See Diane Vaughan, *The Challenger Launch Decision* (Chicago: University of Chicago Press, 1997).

3 Casey Rosenthal, "Antifragility Is a Fragile Concept," LinkedIn post, Aug. 28, 2018, *https://oreil.ly/LbuIt*.

Build a Hypothesis Around Steady-State Behavior

Every experiment begins with a hypothesis. For availability experiments, the form of the experiment is usually:

Under _____ circumstances, customers still have a good time.

For security experiments by contrast, the form of the experiment is usually:

Under _____ circumstances, the security team is notified.

In both cases, the blank space is filled in by the variables mentioned in the next section.

The advanced principles emphasize building the hypothesis around a steady-state definition. This means focusing on the way the system is expected to behave, and capturing that in a measurement. In the preceding examples, customers presumably have a good time by default, and security usually gets notified when something violates a security control.

This focus on steady state forces engineers to step back from the code and focus on the holistic output. It captures Chaos Engineering's bias toward verification over validation. We often have an urge to dive into a problem, find the "root cause" of a behavior, and try to understand a system via reductionism. Doing a deep dive can help with exploration, but it is a distraction from the best learning that Chaos Engineering can offer. At its best, Chaos Engineering is focused on key performance indicators (KPIs) or other metrics that track with clear business priorities, and those make for the best steady-state definitions.

Vary Real-World Events

This advanced principle states that the variables in experiments should reflect real-world events. While this might seem obvious in hindsight, there are two good reasons for explicitly calling this out:

- Variables are often chosen for what is easy to do rather than what provides the most learning value.

- Engineers have a tendency to focus on variables that reflect their experience rather than the users' experience.

Avoid Choosing the Easy Route

Chaos Monkey[4] is actually pretty trivial for such a powerful program. It's an open source product that randomly turns off instances (virtual machines, containers, or servers) about once a day for each service. You can use it as is, but the same functionality can be provided by a bash script at most organizations. This is basically the low-hanging fruit of Chaos Engineering. Cloud deployment and now container deployment ensure that systems at scale will have instances (virtual machines or containers) spontaneously disappear on a somewhat regular basis. Chaos Monkey replicates that variable and simply accelerates the frequency of the event.

This is useful and fairly easy to do if you have root-level privileges to the infrastructure so that you can make those instances disappear. Once you have root-level privileges, the temptation exists to do other things that are easy to do as root. Consider the following variables introduced on an instance:

- Terminate an instance
- Peg the CPU of an instance
- Utilize all available memory on an instance
- Fill up the disk of an instance
- Turn off networking on the instance

These experiments have one thing in common: they predictably cause the instance to stop responding. From a system perspective, this looks the same as if you terminated the instance. You learn nothing from the last four experiments that you didn't learn from the first. These experiments are essentially a waste of time.

From the distributed system perspective, almost all interesting availability experiments can be driven by affecting latency or response type. Terminating an instance is a special case of infinite latency. In most online systems today response type is often synonymous with status code, like changing HTTP 200s to 500s. It follows that most availability experiments can be constructed with a mechanism to vary latency and change status codes.

Varying latency is much more difficult to do than simply pegging a CPU or filling up the RAM on an instance. It requires coordinated involvement with all relevant inter-process communication (IPC) layers. That might mean modifying sidecars, software-defined networking rules, client-side library wrappers, service meshes, or even lightweight load balancers. Any of these solutions requires a nontrivial engineering investment.

---

4 Chaos Monkey was the germinal Chaos Engineering tool. See the Introduction: Birth of Chaos for the history of how Chaos Engineering came about.

Run Experiments in Production

Experimentation teaches you about the system you are studying. If you are experimenting on a Staging environment, then you are building confidence in *that* environment. To the extent that the Staging and Production environments differ, often in ways that a human cannot predict, you are not building confidence in the environment that you really care about. For this reason, the most advanced Chaos Engineering takes place in Production.

This principle is not without controversy. Certainly in some fields there are regulatory requirements that preclude the possibility of affecting the Production systems. In some situations there are insurmountable technical barriers to running experiments in Production. It is important to remember that the point of Chaos Engineering is to uncover the chaos inherent in complex systems, not to cause it. If we know that an experiment is going to generate an undesirable outcome, then we should not run that experiment. This is especially important guidance in a Production environment where the repercussions of a disproved hypothesis can be high.

As an advanced principle, there is no all-or-nothing value proposition to running experiments in Production. In most situations, it makes sense to start experimenting on a Staging system, and gradually move over to Production once the kinks of the tooling are worked out. In many cases, critical insights into Production are discovered first by Chaos Engineering on Staging.

Automate Experiments to Run Continuously

This principle recognizes a practical implication of working on complex systems. Automation has to be brought in for two reasons:

- To cover a larger set of experiments than humans can cover manually. In complex systems, the conditions that could possibly contribute to an incident are so numerous that they can't be planned for. In fact, they can't even be counted because they are unknowable in advance. This means that humans can't reliably search the solution space of possible contributing factors in a reasonable amount of time. Automation provides a means to scale out the search for vulnerabilities that could contribute to undesirable systemic outcomes.

- To empirically verify our assumptions over time, as unknown parts of the system are changed. Imagine a system where the functionality of a given component relies on other components outside of the scope of the primary operators. This is the case in almost all complex systems. Without tight coupling between the given functionality and all the dependencies, it is entirely possible that one of the dependencies will change in such a way that it creates a vulnerability. Continuous experimentation provided by automation can catch these issues and teach the primary operators about how the operation of their own system is changing over time. This could be a change in performance (e.g., the network is becoming saturated by noisy neighbors) or a change in functionality (e.g., the response bodies of downstream services are including extra information that could impact how they are parsed) or a change in human expectations (e.g., the original engineers leave the team, and the new operators are not as familiar with the code).

Automation itself can have unintended consequences. In Part III, Chapter 11 and Chapter 12 explore some of the pros and cons of automation. The advanced principles maintain that automation is an advanced mechanism to explore the solution space of potential vulnerabilities, and to reify institutional knowledge about vulnerabilities by verifying a hypothesis over time knowing that complex systems will change.

Minimize Blast Radius

This final advanced principle was added to "The Principles" after the Chaos Team at Netflix found that they could significantly reduce the risk to Production traffic by engineering safer ways to run experiments. By using a tightly orchestrated control group to compare with a variable group, experiments can be constructed in such a way that the impact of a disproved hypothesis on customer traffic in Production is minimal.

How a team goes about achieving this is highly context-sensitive to the complex system at hand. In some systems it may mean using shadow traffic; or excluding requests that have high business impact like transactions over $100; or implementing automated retry logic for requests in the experiment that fail. In the case of the Chaos Team's work at Netflix, sampling of requests, sticky sessions, and similar functions were added into the Chaos Automation Platform (ChAP),[5] which is discussed more in Chapter 16. These techniques not only limited the blast radius; they had the added benefit of strengthening signal detection, since the metrics of a small variable group can often stand out starkly in contrast to a small control group. However it is achieved, this advanced principal emphasizes that in truly sophisticated implementations of Chaos Engineering, the potential impact of an experiment can be limited by design.

All of these advanced principles are presented to guide and inspire, not to dictate. They are born of pragmatism and should be adopted (or not) with that aim in mind.

---

5 Ali Basiri et al., "ChAP: Chaos Automation Platform," The Netflix Technology Blog, July 26, 2017, *https://oreil.ly/U7aaj*.

Focus on the Users' Experience

There is a lot to be said for improving the experience for developers. DevUX is an underappreciated discipline. Concerted effort to improve the experience of software engineers as they write, maintain, and deliver code to production, and revert those decisions, has huge long-term payoff. That said, most business value from Chaos Engineering is going to come from finding vulnerabilities in the production system, not in the development process. Therefore, it makes sense to instead focus on variables that might impact the user experience.

Since software engineers (not users) are usually choosing the variables in chaos experiments, this focus is sometimes lacking. An example of this misguided focus is the enthusiasm on the part of Chaos Engineers for introducing data corruption experiments. There are many places where data corruption experiments are warranted and highly valuable. Verifying the guarantees of databases is a clear example of this. Corruption of response payload in transit to the client is probably *not* a good example.

Consider the increasingly common experiments whereby response payload is corrupted to return mis-formed HTML or broken JSON. This variable isn't likely to happen in the real world, and if it does, it's likely to happen on a per-request basis that is easily accommodated by user behavior (a retry event), by fallbacks (a different kind of retry event), or be graceful clients (like web browsers).

As engineers, we may run into contract mismatches frequently. We see that libraries interacting with our code behave in ways that we don't want. We spend a lot of time adjusting our interaction to get the behavior we want from those libraries. Since we've seen a lot of behavior we didn't want, we then assume that it's worthwhile to build experiments that expose those cases. This assumption is false; chaos experimentation isn't necessary in these cases. Negotiating contract mismatches is part of the development process. It is discovery for the engineer. Once the code is working, once the contract is figured out, it's extremely unlikely that a cosmic ray or fried transistor is going to garble the library output and corrupt the data in transit. Even if that is something we want to address, because of library drift or something to that effect, it is a known property of the system. Known properties are best addressed with testing.

Chaos Engineering hasn't been around long enough to formalize the methods used to generate variables. Some methods are obvious, like introducing latency. Some require analysis, like adding the right amount of latency to induce queuing effects without actually surpassing alert limits or an SLO. Some are highly context-sensitive, like degrading the performance of a second-tier service in such a way that it causes a different second-tier service to temporarily become a first-tier service.

As the discipline evolves, we expect these methods to either deliver formal models for generating variables, or at least have default models that capture generalized experience across the industry. In the meantime, avoid choosing the easy route, focus on the users' experience, and vary real-world events.

The Future of "The Principles"

In the five years since "The Principles" was published, we have seen Chaos Engineering evolve to meet new challenges in new industries. The principles and foundation of the practice are sure to continue to evolve as adoption expands through the software industry and into new verticals.

When Netflix first started evangelizing Chaos Engineering at Chaos Community Day in earnest in 2015, they received a lot of pushback from financial institutions in particular (see the Introduction: Birth of Chaos for more about Chaos Community Day and early evangelism). The common concern was, "Sure, maybe this works for an entertainment service or online advertising, but we have real money on the line." To which the Chaos Team responded, "Do you have outages?"

Of course, the answer is "yes"; even the best engineering teams suffer outages at high-stakes financial institutions. This left two options, according to the Chaos Team: either (a) continue having outages at some unpredictable rate and severity, or (b) adopt a proactive strategy like Chaos Engineering to understand risks in order to prevent large, uncontrolled outcomes. Financial institutions agreed, and many of the world's largest banks now have dedicated Chaos Engineering programs.

The next industry to voice concerns with the concept was healthcare. The concern was expressed as, "Sure, maybe this works for online entertainment or financial services, but we have human lives on the line." Again, the Chaos Team responded, "Do you have outages?"

But in this case, even more direct appeal can be made to the basis of healthcare as a system. When empirical experimentation was chosen as the basis of Chaos Engineering, it was a direct appeal to Karl Popper's concept of falsifiability (*https://oreil.ly/6M5zW*), which provides the foundation for Western notions of science and the scientific method. The pinnacle of Popperian notions in practice is the clinical trial.

In this sense, the phenomenal success of the Western healthcare system is built on Chaos Engineering. Modern medicine depends on double-blind experiments with human lives on the line. They just call it by a different name: the clinical trial.

Forms of Chaos Engineering have implicitly existed in many other industries for a long time. Bringing experimentation to the forefront, particularly in the software practices within other industries, gives power to the practice. Calling these out and explicitly naming it Chaos Engineering allows us to strategize about its purpose and application, and take lessons learned from other fields and apply them to our own.

In that spirit, we can explore Chaos Engineering in industries and companies that look very different from the prototypical microservice-at-scale examples commonly associated with the practice. FinTech, Autonomous Vehicles (AV), and Adversarial Machine Learning can teach us about the potential and the limitations of Chaos Engineering. Mechanical Engineering and Aviation expand our understanding even further, taking us outside the realm of software into hardware and physical prototyping. Chaos Engineering has even expanded beyond availability into security, which is the other side of the coin from a system safety perspective. All of these new industries, use cases, and environments will continue to evolve the foundation and principles of Chaos Engineering.

PART II

Principles in Action

We felt it was important to showcase different voices from different organizations throughout this book. There is no one-size-fits-all Chaos Engineering program. Some of the opinions and guidance presented herein are not entirely consistent, and that's okay. We did not shy away from disagreement and opposing viewpoints. You will find common themes like building a "big red button" into chaos programs, as well as conflicting opinions like whether Chaos Engineering is a form of testing or experimentation.[1]

We specifically chose perspectives from Slack, Google, Microsoft, LinkedIn, and Capital One. We bring forth the most compelling examples and narratives and we leave it to the reader to pick and choose which are most relevant to their own circumstances. In complex systems, context is king.

We begin with Chapter 4, "Slack's Disasterpiece Theater" with Richard Crowley describing the particular approach to Chaos Engineering at Slack. With a combination of legacy and modern systems, Slack provides a target-rich environment for exploring different methods of Chaos Engineering. Richard chose to develop a unique approach to Game Days with particular flair: "Through more than twenty exercises it has discovered vulnerabilities, proven the safety of systems new and old, and affected the roadmaps of many engineering teams."

---

1 The authors of the book hold that Chaos Engineering is a form of experimentation. Some of the contributing authors disagree, and use the term "testing." See the section "Experimentation Versus Testing" on page 26 in Chapter 3.

Jason Cahoon takes us inside Google's analog to Chaos Engineering, called "DiRT," in Chapter 5, "Google DiRT: Disaster Recovery Testing." This is one of the most experienced explorations of Chaos Engineering, since Google has been operating the DiRT program for quite some time. This chapter explores the philosophy behind Google's approach: "Merely hoping a system behaves reliably in extreme circumstances is not a good strategy. You have to expect things to fail, design them with failure in mind, and constantly prove that those designs are still valid." It also describes the focus and value of the long-running program, reinforcing themes we see in complex system analysis: "DiRT is not about breaking things only for the sake of breaking them; its value comes from uncovering failures modes you don't already know about."

"Unfortunately, nothing went as planned," could summarize many of the surprises we have experienced operating systems at scale. In Chapter 6, "Microsoft Variation and Prioritization of Experiments," Oleg Surmachev provides a very structured perspective on how to prioritize experiments. The potential impact of incidents are front and center to the multitude of considerations presented in this chapter. Vigorously pursuing the conceivable weaknesses can build a more robust system and save unnecessary experimentation, prior to searching for the "unknown events/unexpected consequences."

In Chapter 7, "LinkedIn Being Mindful of Members," Logan Rosen emphasizes the importance of the customer experience. Fortunately there are many strategies to minimize the blast radius and potential impact to customers during chaos experimentation. Logan takes us on a journey through LinkedIn's projects to implement a few such strategies. "While some minor impact may be inevitable, it's very important that you minimize how much harm a chaos experiment can cause to your end users and have a simple recovery plan that can get everything back to normal."

Rounding out this part of the book, we have Chapter 8, "Capital One Adoption and Evolution of Chaos Engineering in Financial Services," by Raji Chockaiyan. Capital One rolled out a Chaos Engineering program over many years. Raji documents the development of the discipline, from small, manual actions to coordinated Game Days, to sophisticated internal tools that they now support. All of this is set within a backdrop of highly regulated processes and outcomes: "Observability and audit trail are as important as the ability to design customized experiments in banking."

By opening up the dialog to these five use cases, we hope to show that Chaos Engineering is simultaneously old enough to have a track record of value and common industry practices, and young enough to be flexible and diverse in its interpretation and implementation.

CHAPTER 4

Slack's Disasterpiece Theater

Richard Crowley

How do you get into Chaos Engineering if your team and tools weren't born with it? It can seem like an overwhelming and insurmountable task to retrofit chaos into systems designed with the mindset that computers can and should last a long time. Complex systems born from this mindset tend to be less accommodating of extreme transience in the underlying computers than their cloud native successors. Such systems probably perform very well in optimal conditions but degrade quickly and sometimes catastrophically in case of failure.

You may be the proud owner of just such a system. It wasn't designed to accommodate chaos, but whether you like it or not, chaos is coming as its scale increases and ongoing development asks it to do more, faster, and more reliably. There isn't time for a rewrite—the system is under duress already. Applying new Chaos Engineering practices to old systems is liable to make the situation worse. You need a different strategy.

This chapter describes one strategy for safely and systematically testing complex systems that weren't necessarily designed with Chaos Engineering in mind by introducing failures and network partitions in a thoughtful and controlled manner. This is a process, not automation, that helps your team understand how your software is vulnerable, motivates improvements, and validates that systems tolerate the faults you can anticipate. This process has been in active use at Slack since the beginning of 2018. Through more than twenty exercises it has discovered vulnerabilities, proven the safety of systems new and old, and affected the roadmaps of many engineering teams.

The first step, though, is ensuring the systems in question are even theoretically ready to tolerate the kinds of faults you expect them to encounter.

Retrofitting Chaos

The tools and techniques you might use to make a system more fault tolerant are the same as you might use to modernize it, make it cloud native, make it more reliable, or make it more highly available. Let's review.

Design Patterns Common in Older Systems

Existing systems, especially older existing systems, are more likely than new systems being built today to assume that individual computers last a long time. This simple assumption is at the heart of many systems that are fault intolerant. We made this assumption in an era in which spare computers were to be avoided—that was wasteful—and it has lingered in our systems design since then.

When computers were scarce they were likely to be provisioned with an operating system and all the trimmings approximately once, shortly after they were purchased, and upgraded in place throughout their useful life. The provisioning process might have been heavily automated, especially if many computers showed up on the loading dock all at once, but initiating that process was probably manual. In smaller installations it wasn't uncommon for much more of that provisioning process to be manual.

Failover, too, was commonly a manual action taken by a human who judged that to be the appropriate response to some fault or deviation from normal operations. In particularly old systems, the period between the fault and the failover was an outage inflicted on customers. Failover was thought to be rare so automation and, in some cases, even documentation and training weren't obviously worthwhile.

Backup and restore is another area in which existing systems may trail behind the state of the art. On a positive note, backups are almost certainly being taken. It's not as certain, though, that those backups can be restored or that they can be restored quickly. As with failover, restoring from backup was at one time a rare event for which automation wasn't obviously worthwhile.

We more readily accept the potential impact of unlikely events—maybe they'll never happen at all! Existing systems built to accept these risks have a tough time coping when the rate of faults increases with scale or when the impact becomes less acceptable to the business.

For completeness, I want to address monoliths briefly. There is no precise threshold a system crosses and becomes a monolith—it's relative. Monolithic systems are not inherently more or less fault tolerant than service-oriented architectures. They may, though, be harder to retrofit because of the sheer surface area, difficulty in affecting incremental change, and difficulty limiting the blast radius of failures. Maybe you decide you're going to break up your monolith, maybe you don't. Fault tolerance is reachable via both roads.

Design Patterns Common in Newer Systems

By contrast, systems being designed today are likely to assume individual computers come and go frequently. There are many consequences of this new mindset but perhaps the most important is that systems are being designed to run on n computers simultaneously and to continue running when one fails and only $n - 1$ remain.

Health checks that are deep enough to detect problems but shallow enough to avoid cascading failures from a service's dependencies play a critical role. They remove failing computers from service and in many cases automatically initiate replacement.

Instance replacement—individual computers tend to be called instances by cloud service providers—is a powerful strategy employed by modern systems. It enables the fault tolerance I just described as well as steady-state operational patterns like blue–green deployment. And within systems that store data, instance replacement provides capacity and motivation to automatically and frequently test that backups can be restored.

Once again, I want to emphasize that a system being more monolithic does not preclude it taking advantage of these design patterns. However, it is a tried-and-true architectural choice to expose new functionality as a service that cooperates with an existing monolith.

Getting to Basic Fault Tolerance

Chaos experiments should be run in production (in addition to development and staging environments) and you should be able to confidently assert that the impact on customers will be negligible if there is any at all. These are a few high-leverage changes you can make should any of the systems you operate align with the design patterns common in older systems.

First and foremost, keep spare capacity online. Having at least an extra computer around during normal operation is the beginning of fault tolerance (and covers more kinds of hardware failures than RAID, which only covers hard disks, or application-level graceful degradation, which may not be possible in your particular application). Use that spare capacity to service requests that arrive while one or a few computers are malfunctioning.

Once you have spare capacity available, consider how to remove malfunctioning computers from service automatically (before you dive into Chaos Engineering). Don't stop at automatic removal, though. Carry on to automatic replacement. Here, the cloud provides some distinct advantages. It's easy (and fun) to get carried away optimizing instance provisioning, but a basic implementation of autoscaling that replaces instances as they're terminated to hold the total number constant will suit most systems. Automated instance replacement must be reliable. Replacement instances must enter service in less than the mean time between failures.

Some systems, especially ones that store data, may differentiate between a leader and many followers. It's easy (and fun) to get carried away with leader election and consensus, but here too an implementation that merely keeps human actions off the critical path is likely sufficient. The introduction of automated failover is the perfect time to audit the timeout and retry policies in dependent services. You should be looking for short but reasonable timeouts that are long enough to allow the automated failover to complete and retries that exponentially back off with a bit of jitter.

Tabletop exercises, in which your team talks through the details of a system's expected behavior in the presence of some fault, are useful for convincing yourselves a system is ready. This academic confidence is far from enough in a complex system, though. The only way to earn true confidence is to incite failure in production. The rest of this chapter introduces Slack's process for doing this safely.

Disasterpiece Theater

I call this process Disasterpiece Theater. When you're competing with other valuable concerns for your fellow engineers' time *and* asking them to change the way they develop and operate software systems, a memorable brand really helps. Disasterpiece Theater was first introduced as a forum on the topic of system failure. It is an ongoing series of exercises in which we get together and purposely cause a part of Slack to fail.

Goals

Every Disasterpiece Theater exercise is a bit different, digging up different hacks from our past, rekindling different fears, and taking different risks. All of them, though, can be walked back to the same fundamental goals.

Outside of the most extreme devotees to crash-only software, most systems are deployed more often than their underlying network and server infrastructure fails. When we design a Disasterpiece Theater exercise we pay very close attention to how faithfully the development environment matches the production environment. It's important that all software changes be testable in the development environment but it is *critical* for failures to be able to be practiced there. The benefits of Disasterpiece Theater forcing deviations to be rectified pay dividends during every test suite run and every deploy cycle.

More obviously, a marquee goal when we incite controlled failures is to discover vulnerabilities in our production systems. The planning that goes into these exercises helps mitigate (though never completely) the risk that any unknown vulnerability cascades into customer impact. We're looking for vulnerabilities to availability, correctness, controllability, observability, and security.

Disasterpiece Theater is an *ongoing* series of exercises. When an exercise discovers a vulnerability we plan to rerun the exercise to verify that remediation efforts were effective in the same way you rerun a program's test suite to confirm you've fixed a bug that caused a test to fail. More generally, the exercises validate system designs and the assumptions that are embedded within them. Over time, a complex system evolves and may inadvertently invalidate an assumption made long ago in a dependent part of the system. For example, the timeout one service places on requests to a dependency may not be sufficient once that dependency deploys to multiple cloud regions. Organizational and system growth decrease the accuracy of any individual's model of the system (per the STELLA report (*https://snafucatchers.github.io*)); those individuals become less and less likely to even know about all the assumptions made in the design of the system. Regularly validating fault tolerance helps the organization ensure its assumptions hold.

Anti-Goals

So, Disasterpiece Theater is meant to promote parity between development and production environments, motivate reliability improvements, and demonstrate a system's fault tolerance. I find it is also helpful to be explicit about what a process or tool is *not* supposed to be.

One size doesn't fit all but, for Slack, I decided that Disasterpiece Theater exercises should be planned and run to minimize the chance of causing a production incident. Slack is a service used by companies small and large to conduct their business; it is critical that the service is there for them all the time. Stated more formally, Slack does not have sufficient error budget to accept severe or lengthy customer impact as a result of one of these planned exercises. You may have more of an error budget or risk tolerance and, if you wield them effectively, end up learning more, more quickly, thanks to the exercises they allow you to plan.

Data durability is even more of a priority. That isn't to say that storage systems are not exercised by this process. Rather, it simply means the plans and contingencies for those plans must ensure that data is *never* irrecoverably lost. This may influence the techniques used to incite failure or motivate holding an extra replica in reserve or manually taking a backup during the exercise. Whatever benefit of Disasterpiece Theater, it isn't worth losing a customer's data.

Disasterpiece Theater is not exploratory. When introducing a little failure where none (or very little) has been experienced before, planning is key. You should have a detailed, credible hypothesis about what will happen *before* you incite the failure. Gathering all the experts and interested humans together in the same room or on the same video conference helps to temper the chaos, educates more engineers on the details of the systems being exercised, and spreads awareness of the Disasterpiece Theater program itself. The next section describes the process from idea to result in detail.

The Process

Every Disasterpiece Theater exercise begins with an idea. Or maybe, more accurately, a worry. It could come from the author and longtime owner of a system, from a discovery made during some unrelated work, as a follow up to a postmortem—anywhere, really. Armed with this worry and the help of one or more experts on the system in question, an experienced host guides us all through the process.

Preparation

You and your cohosts should get together in the same room or on the same video conference to prepare for the exercise. My original Disasterpiece Theater checklist suggests the following, each of which I'll describe in detail:

1. Decide on a server or service that will be caused to fail, the failure mode, and the strategy for simulating that failure mode.

2. Survey the server or service in dev and prod; note your confidence in our ability to simulate the failure in dev.

3. Identify alerts, dashboards, logs, and metrics that you hypothesize will detect the failure; if none exist, consider inciting the failure anyway and working backwards into detection.

4. Identify redundancies and automated remediations that should mitigate the impact of the failure and runbooks that may be necessary to respond.

5. Invite all the relevant people to the event, especially those who will be on call at the time, and announce the exercise in #disasterpiece-theater (a channel in Slack's own Slack).

I've found that most of the time an hour together is enough to get started and the final preparation can be handled asynchronously. (Yes, we use Slack for this.)

Sometimes the worry that inspired the whole exercise is specific enough that you'll already know precisely the failure you'll incite, like arranging for a process to pass its health checks but nonetheless fail to respond to requests. Other times, there are many ways to achieve the desired failure and they're all subtly different. Typically the easiest failure mode to incite, to repair, and to tolerate is stopping a process. Then there is instance termination (especially if you're in the cloud) which can be expedient if they're automatically replaced. Using iptables(8) to simulate a computer's network cable being unplugged is a fairly safe failure mode that's different from process stoppage and (sometimes) instance termination because the failures manifest as timeouts instead of ECONNREFUSED. And then you can get into the endless and sometimes terrifying world of partial and even asymmetric network partitions, which can usually be simulated with iptables(8).

Then, too, there is the question of where in the system one of these techniques is applied. Single computers are a good start but consider working your way up to whole racks, rows, datacenters, availability zones, or even regions. Larger failures can help us discover capacity constraints and tight coupling between systems. Consider introducing the failure between load balancers and application servers, between some application servers (but not all) and their backing databases, and so on. You should leave this step with very specific steps to take or, better yet, commands to run.

Next, make sure to ground yourself in what's really possible to safely exercise. Take a close, dispassionate look at your development environment to determine whether the failure you want to introduce can actually be introduced there. Consider, too, whether there is (or can be) enough traffic in your development environment to detect the failure and to experience any potential negative effects like resource exhaustion in a dependent service with poorly configured timeouts, in remaining instances of the degraded service, or in related systems like service discovery or log aggregation.

Pretend for a moment that your development environment tolerates the failure just fine. Does that give you confidence to incite the same failure in your production environment? If not, consider aborting the exercise and investing in your development environment. If so, good work on having a confidence-inspiring development environment! Now take a moment to formalize that confidence. Identify any alerts you expect to be triggered when you incite this failure, all the dashboards, logs, and/or metrics you hypothesize will detect the failure plus those you hypothesize will hold steady. Think of this a bit like "priming" your incident response process. You're not planning to need it but it's a worthwhile contingency to ensure your time to detect and time to assemble will be effectively zero should the exercise not go as planned. I hope that, most of the time, you instead need these logs and metrics to confirm your hypothesis.

What is that hypothesis, though? Take some time to write down precisely what you and your cohosts expect will happen. Take several perspectives. Consider the operation of health checks, load balancers, and service discovery around the failure. Think about the fate of the requests that are interrupted by the failure as well as those that arrive shortly after. How does a requesting program learn about the failure? How long does this take? Do any of those programs retry their requests? If so, how aggressively? Will the combination of these timeouts and retries push anything close to the point of resource exhaustion? Now extend your model of the situation to include humans and note any points in which human intervention may be necessary or desirable. Identify any runbooks or documentation that may be necessary. (This, too, serves to "prime" the incident response process.) Finally, try to quantify what customer impact you expect and confirm that it is sufficiently minimal to proceed.

Conclude your preparation by working out the logistics of the exercise. I recommend scheduling at least three hours in a big conference room. In my experience, it's rare to actually use all three hours but it would be a distraction to have to move during an exercise that's not going according to plan. If there are any remote participants, use a video conferencing system with a good microphone that picks up the entire room. Convene the cohosts, all the other experts on the system being exercised and its clients, anyone who's on call, and anyone who wants to learn. These exercises are expensive in human hours, which underscores the importance of thorough preparation. Now that you're prepared, it's time for Disasterpiece Theater.

The Exercise

I try to make something of a spectacle of each exercise to maximize awareness of Disasterpiece Theater across the company. This program competes for people's time; it's very important for everyone to understand that spending time in Disasterpiece Theater results in a more reliable system with a more confidence-inspiring development environment.

You should designate a note taker. (I have historically played this role during Slack's Disasterpiece Theater exercises but there is no reason you couldn't decide differently.) I recommend they take notes in a chat channel or some similar medium that timestamps every message automatically. We take notes in the #disasterpiece-theater channel in Slack's own Slack.

If at any point during an exercise you find yourself deviating uncomfortably from the plan or encountering unanticipated customer impacts, abort. Learn what you can, regroup, and try again another day. You can learn quite a lot without crossing the threshold into incident response.

My original Disasterpiece Theater checklist continues into the exercise itself and, as with the preparation checklist, I'll describe each step in detail:

1. Ensure everyone is comfortable being recorded and, if so, start recording the video conference if possible.

2. Review the preparation and amend it as necessary.

3. Announce the dev exercise in #ops (a channel in Slack's own Slack where we discuss production changes and incidents).

4. Incite the failure in dev. Note the time.

5. Receive alerts and inspect dashboards, logs, and metrics. Note the time when they provide definitive evidence of the failure.

6. If applicable, give automated remediations time to be triggered. Note the time they are.

7. If necessary, follow runbooks to restore service in dev. Note the time and any deviations required.

8. Make a go or no-go decision to proceed to prod. If no-go, announce the all clear in #ops, debrief, and stop. If go, go.

9. Announce the prod exercise in #ops.

10. Incite the failure in prod. Note the time.

11. Receive alerts and inspect dashboards, logs, and metrics. Note the time when they provide definitive evidence of the failure.

12. If applicable, give automated remediations time to be triggered. Note the time they are.

13. If necessary, follow runbooks to restore service in prod. Note the time and any deviations required.

14. Announce the all clear in #ops.

15. Debrief.

16. If there is one, distribute the recording once it's available.

I like to have an audio recording of the exercise to refer back to as insurance in case something important isn't captured or isn't captured clearly in the notes taken in real time. It's important, though, to be sure everyone who's participating is OK being recorded. Get this out of the way first and, if possible, start recording.

Begin with a thorough review of the plan. This is likely some of the participants' first exposure to it. Their unique perspectives may improve the plan. Incorporate their feedback, especially when it makes the exercise safer or the results more meaningful. We publish plans ahead of time in shared documents and update them with these changes. Be wary, though, of deviating too far from the plan on a whim, as this can turn a safe and well-planned exercise into an obstacle course.

When the plan is ratified, announce the exercise in a very public place like a chat channel where updates about system operations are expected, an engineering-wide mailing list, or the like. This first announcement should say the exercise is commencing in the development environment and direct onlookers to follow along there. See Example 4-1 for what a typical announcement looks like at Slack.

Example 4-1. A typical initial Disasterpiece Theater announcement at Slack

> **Richard Crowley 9:50 AM #disasterpiece-theater** is on again and we're about to mostly unplug the network cables on 1/4 of the Channel Servers in dev. Follow along in the channel or await my announcement here when we're moving on to prod.

Now for the moment of truth (in the development environment, at least). One of your cohosts should run the prepared command to incite the failure. Your note taker should record the time.

This is the time for all the participants (except the note taker) to spring into action. Collect evidence of the failure, the recovery, and the impact on adjacent systems. Confirm or disconfirm all the details of your hypothesis. Make specific note of how long automated remediations take and what your customers experienced in the interim. And if you do need to intervene to restore service, take especially detailed notes on the actions of you and your fellow participants. Throughout, make sure the note taker can capture your observations and post screenshots of the graphs you're examining.

At this time, your development environment should have returned to a steady state. Take stock. If your automated remediations didn't detect the failure or they otherwise malfunctioned in some way, you should probably stop here. If the failure was too noticeable to customers (however you extrapolate that from your development environment) or was noticeable for too long, you may decide to stop here. If you assess the risk and decide to abort, announce that wherever you announced the beginning of the exercise. See Example 4-2 for what such a rare retreat looks like at Slack.

Example 4-2. An aborted Disasterpiece Theater announcement at Slack

> **Richard Crowley 11:22 AM** Disasterpiece Theater has ended for the day without even making it to prod.

When the exercise in your development environment goes as planned, you get to announce that the exercise is moving on to your production environment. See Example 4-3 for what a typical announcement looks like at Slack.

Example 4-3. A typical announcement when Disasterpiece Theater moves on to prod

> **Richard Crowley 10:10 AM #disasterpiece-theater** did two rounds in dev and is done there. Now we're moving on to prod. Expect a bunch of channels to be redistributed in the Channel Server ring in the near future. I'll post again when all's clear.

This is the *real* moment of truth. All the preparation and the exercise in the development environment have led you to this moment in which one of your cohosts should incite the failure in the production environment using the steps or command prepared ahead of time. This will feel like nothing during some exercises and be truly terrifying during others. Take note of these feelings—they're telling you where the risk lies in your systems.

Once again, it's time for all the participants (except the note taker) to spring into action gathering evidence of the failure, the recovery, and the impact on adjacent systems. The evidence tends to be much more interesting this time around with real customer traffic on the line. Confirm or disconfirm your hypothesis in production. Watch the system respond to the fault, noting the time that you observe automated remediation. And, of course, if you need to intervene to restore service, do so quickly and decisively—your customers are counting on you! Here, too, make sure the note taker captures your observations and post screenshots of the graphs you're examining.

When your production environment has returned to its steady state, give the all clear in the same place you announced the exercise in your development environment and the transition to your production environment. If you can make any preliminary comment on the success of the exercise, that's great, but at a minimum the announcement keeps teammates making changes in production situationally aware.

Before all the participants scatter to the winds, take time for some immediate sensemaking. That is, take time to understand or at least document any lingering ambiguity about the exercise.

Debriefing

Shortly after the exercise while memories are still fresh and high fidelity, I like to summarize the exercise—just the facts—for a wide audience. It helps to form a narrative around the summary that explains why the failure mode being exercised is important, how systems tolerated (or didn't) the failure, and what that means for customers and the business. It also serves to reinforce to the rest of the company why doing these exercises is so important. My original Disasterpiece Theater checklist offers the following prompts:

- What were the time to detect and time to recover?
- Did any users notice? How do we know? How can we get that to "no"?
- What did humans have to do that computers should have done?
- Where are we blind?
- Where are our dashboards and docs wrong?
- What do we need to practice more often?
- What would on-call engineers have to do if this happened unexpectedly?

We capture the answers to these questions in Slack or in a summary document shared in Slack. More recently we've started recording audio from exercises and archiving them for posterity, too.

After the summary, the host offers conclusions and recommendations on behalf of the exercise. Your job, as host of the exercise, is to draw these conclusions and make these recommendations in service of the reliability of the system and the quality of the development environment based on the evidence presented dispassionately in the summary. These recommendations take on elevated importance when the exercise did not go according to plan. If even the most expert minds incorrectly or incompletely understood the system before the exercise, it's likely that everyone else is even further off. This is your opportunity to improve everyone's understanding.

The debriefing and its outputs offer yet another opportunity to influence your organization by educating even more people about the kinds of failures that can happen in production and the techniques your organization uses to tolerate them. In fact, this benefit is remarkably similar to one of the benefits of publishing detailed incident postmortems internally.

How the Process Has Evolved

Disasterpiece Theater was initially conceived as a complement to the incident response process and even a forum for practicing incident response. Early lists of potential exercises included quite a few failures that were known even at the time to require human intervention. This was at least theoretically acceptable because those failure modes were also the sort that relied on assumptions that may have been invalidated as the environment evolved.

More than a year later, Slack has never run a Disasterpiece Theater exercise that planned on human intervention being necessary, though there have been cases in which human intervention was necessary, nonetheless. Instead, we have developed another program for practicing incident response: Incident Management Lunch. It's a game in which a group of people try to feed themselves by following the incident response process. They periodically draw cards that introduce curveballs like sudden restaurant closures, allergies, and picky eaters. Thanks to this practice and the training that precedes it, Disasterpiece Theater no longer needs to fill this void.

Disasterpiece Theater has evolved in a few other ways, too. The earliest iterations were entirely focused on results and left a lot of educational opportunities on the table. The debriefings and, especially, the written summaries, conclusions, and recommendations were introduced specifically for their educational value. Likewise, the recent introduction of recordings allows future observers to go deeper than they can with the summary and chat history alone.

It can be tough for a remote participant on a video conference to follow who's speaking, doubly so if they cannot see the video because someone's sharing their screen. That's why I started Disasterpiece Theater recommending against screen sharing. On the other hand, it can be incredibly powerful to all look at the same graph together. I'm still searching for the right balance between screen sharing and video that creates the best experience for remote participants.

Finally, my original Disasterpiece Theater checklist prompted the hosts to come up with synthetic requests they could make in a tight loop to visualize the fault and the tolerance. This practice never turned out to be as useful as a well-curated dashboard that covered request and error rate, a latency histogram, and so on. I've removed this prompt from the checklist at Slack to streamline the process.

These certainly won't be the last evolutions of this process at Slack. If you adopt a similar process at your company, pay attention to what feels awkward to smooth it out and who's not getting value to make the process more inclusive.

Getting Management Buy-In

Once again, a narrative is key. You might begin with a rhetorical device: "Hi there, CTO and VP of Engineering. Wouldn't you like to know how well our system tolerates database master failure, network partitions, and power failures?" Paint a picture that includes some unknowns.

And then bring the uncomfortable truth. The only way to understand how a system copes with a failure in production is to have a failure in production. I should admit here that this was an incredibly easy sell to Slack's executives who already believed this to be true.

In general, though, any responsible executive will need to see evidence that you're managing risks effectively and appropriately. The Disasterpiece Theater process is designed specifically to meet this bar. Emphasize that these exercises are meticulously planned and controlled to maximize learning and minimize (or, better yet, eliminate) customer impact.

Then plan your first exercise and show off some results like the ones in the next section.

Results

I've run dozens of Disasterpiece Theater exercises at Slack. The majority of them have gone roughly according to plan, expanding our confidence in existing systems and proving the correct functioning of new ones. Some, though, have identified serious vulnerabilities to the availability or correctness of Slack and given us the opportunity to fix them before impacting customers.

Avoid Cache Inconsistency

The first time Disasterpiece Theater turned its attention to Memcached it was to demonstrate in production that automatic instance replacement worked properly. The exercise was simple, opting to disconnect a Memcached instance from the network to observe a spare take its place. Next, we restored its network connectivity and terminated the replacement instance.

During our review of the plan we recognized a vulnerability in the instance replacement algorithm and soon confirmed its existence in the development environment. As it was originally implemented, if an instance loses its lease on a range of cache keys and then gets that same lease back, it does not flush its cache entries. However, in this case, another instance had served that range of cache keys in the interim, meaning the data in the original instance had become stale and possibly incorrect.

We addressed this in the exercise by manually flushing the cache at the appropriate moment and then, immediately after the exercise, changed the algorithm and tested it again. Without this result, we may have lived unknowingly with a small risk of cache corruption for quite a while.

Try, Try Again (for Safety)

In early 2019 we planned a series of ten exercises to demonstrate Slack's tolerance of zonal failures and network partitions in AWS. One of these exercises concerned Channel Server, a system responsible for broadcasting newly sent messages and metadata to all connected Slack client WebSockets. The goal was simply to partition 25% of the Channel Servers from the network to observe that the failures were detected and the instances were replaced by spares.

The first attempt to create this network partition failed to fully account for the overlay network that provides transparent transit encryption. In effect, we isolated each Channel Server far more than anticipated creating a situation closer to disconnecting them from the network than a network partition. We stopped early to regroup and get the network partition just right.

The second attempt showed promise but was also ended before reaching production. This exercise did offer a positive result, though. It showed Consul was quite adept at routing around network partitions. This inspired confidence but doomed this exercise because none of the Channel Servers actually failed.

The third and final attempt finally brought along a complete arsenal of iptables(8) rules and succeeded in partitioning 25% of the Channel Servers from the network. Consul detected the failures quickly and replacements were thrown into action. Most importantly, the load this massive automated reconfiguration brought on the Slack API was well within that system's capacity. At the end of a long road, it was positive results all around!

Impossibility Result

There have also been negative results. Once, while responding to an incident, we were forced to make and deploy a code change to effect a configuration change because the system meant to be used to make that configuration change, an internally developed system called Confabulator, didn't work. I thought this was worthy of further investigation. The maintainers and I planned an exercise to directly mimic the situation we encountered. Confabulator would be partitioned from the Slack service but otherwise be left completely intact. Then we would try to make a no-op configuration change.

We reproduced the error without any trouble and started tracing through our code. It didn't take too long to find the problem. The system's authors anticipated the situation in which Slack itself was down and thus unable to validate the proposed configuration change; they offered an emergency mode that skipped that validation. However, both normal and emergency modes attempted to post a notice of the configuration change to a Slack channel. There was no timeout on this action but there was a timeout on the overall configuration API. As a result, even in emergency mode, the request could never make it as far as making the configuration change if Slack itself was down. Since then we've made many improvements to code and configuration deploys and have audited timeout and retry policies in these critical systems.

Conclusion

The discoveries made during these exercises and the improvements to Slack's reliability they inspired were only possible because Disasterpiece Theater gave us a clear process for testing the fault tolerance of our production systems.

Disasterpiece Theater exercises are meticulously planned failures that are introduced in the development environment and then, if that goes well, in the production environment by a group of experts all gathered together. It helps minimize the risk inherent in testing fault tolerance, especially when it's based on assumptions made long ago in older systems that maybe weren't originally designed to be so fault tolerant.

The process is intended to motivate investment in development environments that faithfully match the production environment and to drive reliability improvements throughout complex systems.

Your organization and systems will be better on a regular cadence of Disasterpiece Theater exercises. Your confidence that when something works in the development environment it will also work in the production environment should be higher. You should be able to regularly validate assumptions from long ago to stave off bit rot. And your organization should have a better understanding of risk, especially when it comes to systems that require human intervention to recover from failure. Most importantly, though, Disasterpiece Theater should be a convincing motivator for your organization to invest in fault tolerance.

About the Author

Richard Crowley is an engineer, engineering leader, and recovering manager. He's interested in operational tooling, distributed systems, and the realities of production at scale. He tolerates computers, likes bicycles, isn't a very good open source maintainer, and lives in San Francisco with his wife and kids.

CHAPTER 5

Google DiRT: Disaster Recovery Testing

Jason Cahoon

"Hope is not a strategy." This is the motto of Google's Site Reliability Engineering (SRE) team and it perfectly embodies the core philosophy of Chaos Engineering. A system may be engineered to tolerate failure but until you explicitly test failure conditions at scale there is always a risk that expectation and reality will not line up. Google's DiRT (Disaster Recovery Testing) program was founded by site reliability engineers (SREs) in 2006 to intentionally instigate failures in critical technology systems and business processes in order to expose unaccounted for risks. The engineers who championed the DiRT program made the key observation that analyzing emergencies in production becomes a whole lot easier *when it is not actually an emergency*.

Disaster testing helps prove a system's resilience when failures are handled gracefully, and exposes reliability risks in a controlled fashion when things are less than graceful. Exposing reliability risks during a controlled incident allows for thorough analysis and preemptive mitigation, as opposed to waiting for problems to expose themselves by means of circumstance alone, when issue severity and time pressure amplify missteps and force risky decisions based on incomplete information.

DiRT began with Google engineers performing role-playing exercises[1] similar to the Game Days practiced at other companies. They particularly focused on how catastrophes and natural disasters might disrupt Google's operation. Google, despite having a globally distributed workforce, has a disproportionately large footprint in the San Francisco Bay area, a location particularly prone to earthquakes. The centralization of so much internal infrastructure in a single area raised the intriguing questions, "What would realistically happen if the Mountain View campus and its employees became

---

1 Andrew Widdowson, "Disaster Role Playing," in Betsy Beyer, Chris Jones, Jennifer Petoff, and Niall Murphy, eds., *Site Reliability Engineering* (Sebastopol, CA: O'Reilly, 2016), Chapter 28.

completely unavailable for several days? How might this disrupt our systems and processes?"

Studying the impact of disrupting services hosted in Mountain View inspired many of Google's original disaster tests but as familiarity (or maybe infamy...) increased, teams interested in increasing their reliability began using company-wide DiRT events as an opportunity to probe their own services in depth. Purely theoretical and tabletop exercises gave way to service owners injecting real, but controlled, failures (adding latency, disabling communication with "noncritical" dependencies, exercising business continuity plans in the absence of key individuals, etc.). Over time, more teams participated and more practical tests were run; as tests grew in scope it became apparent just how much there was to learn about and improve in Google's overall architecture: unacknowledged hard dependencies, fallback strategies misbehaving, safeguards outright not working, shortcomings in planning small and large that become obvious after the fact but are practically invisible beforehand or that only expose themselves given the "just right" (or wrong, depending on how you look at it) combination of unfortunate conditions.

The program has continually grown since its early days and at this point many thousands of DiRT exercises have been run by teams all over Google. Large-scale coordinated events occur throughout the year and teams proactively test their systems and themselves regularly. Some level of participation in DiRT is mandatory from SRE teams and highly encouraged for service owners everywhere in the company. A significant portion of participation comes from more than just software engineering and SRE organizations: physical security, information security, datacenter operations, communications, facilities, IT, human resources, and finance business units have all designed and executed DiRT tests.

There has been a focus in recent years on providing a standardized suite of automated tests for network and software systems. Engineers can use pre-constructed automated tests out of the box to verify their system's behavior given failures in shared infrastructure and storage systems. Automated tests can be run continually to prevent reliability regressions and validate service-level objectives in extreme or unusual conditions. These tests lower the barrier to entry and provide a springboard into more intricate architecture-specific failure testing. The power of automating even the low-hanging fruit is manifest in the fact that the count of automated test executions has exceeded the total number of traditional DiRT tests by an order of magnitude, reaching several million test runs in only a few years.

Google properties are known for their high degree of reliability at scale, but the dependability that Google is known for isn't magic. Pushing the envelope for reliability means challenging assumptions about your system and becoming familiar with and preparing for uncommon combinations of failures (at Google's scale failures with one in a million odds are occurring several times a second). Merely hoping a system behaves reliably in extreme circumstances is not a good strategy. You have to expect things to fail, design them with failure in mind, and constantly prove that those designs are still valid.

Legends: Code Search Breaks When the Tech Lead Goes on Vacation

A very senior software engineer at Google once built an indexing pipeline and search utility for Google's source code repository along with a few specialized internal tools that relied on this search tool to do cool things. Everyone was happy with the cool things the tools did and they worked quite reliably for several years until inevitably something changed. The security authentication systems at Google were beefed up and one aspect of this was giving user login credentials a significantly shorter time-out. Engineers began to notice that any time the lead engineer was away from the office for a few days the code search utility and related tools would stop working.

It turns out the indexing jobs supporting these tools had run for years as regularly scheduled tasks on the engineer's workstation. The new changes to the security policies made it such that their production authorization tokens would expire if not renewed roughly daily. Even after moving these indexing pipelines off workstations and onto redundant productionized setups there were still hidden dependencies on network-mounted directories that were demonstrated to be unavailable when the Mountain View campus was taken offline. The issue was eventually exposed by a disaster test simulating an internal network failure.

It is a seemingly trivial example, but it really goes to show how a small but useful service's popularity can quickly outgrow its productionization considerations and that a changing technological landscape (in this example, the new security policy) can introduce novel critical dependencies to a well-established and otherwise stable service.

Life of a DiRT Test

Every (nonautomated) DiRT test starts with a test plan document. Google uses a standard document template for this that has evolved over time and captures the most important information necessary to assess the risks and potential benefits of a given test. The document includes the specific execution procedures, rollback procedures, well-known risks, potential impacts, dependencies, and learning goals for a test. The plan is collaboratively developed by the team that will run the test, and after they consider it complete the test is reviewed by at least two engineers from outside the team. At least one external reviewer should have technical expertise in an area related to the system under test. High-risk and high-impact tests are thoroughly scrutinized and are likely to have many more expert reviewers involved than the minimum of one. Typically, there are a few rounds of back-and-forth communication as the reviewers ask clarifying questions and request more detail. The standard aimed for is that both the test procedure and rollback steps are covered in enough detail that anyone with moderate familiarity in the system under test could conduct the necessary operations.

After the reviewers have approved the test, it is scheduled, communications (if part of the test plan) are sent out, and the test is executed. After the test is over there is another templated document that captures a brief retrospective on the test's results. Again, this document is collaboratively constructed by the team that ran the test. The results document captures anything noteworthy or unexpected that was learned from this test, records action items (also placed in our issue tracking system) and asks the originating team to assess the value of the experience.

The templates for both the original plan document and the results document are in a semi-structured format that was designed to be programmatically parsed. After a test is completed these documents are digitally indexed and made accessible through an internal web UI. The archive of previously run DiRT tests and results can be searched and referenced by any Googler. This repository of prior tests is frequently utilized to design new tests or just when engineers are interested in learning about tests their team may have performed in the past.

The Rules of Engagement

There are a handful of disaster testing guidelines that Google has come to by hard-won experience and having done the wrong thing a time or two. We've found that higher-quality tests are created by sticking to a few pre-established and well-communicated rules. A shared baseline of expectations between testers and the rest of the company will yield a smoother testing experience for everyone involved. Test designers know what is explicitly over the line and people subjected to tests know the rough limits of what might be thrown at them.

These rules of engagement are the foundation of the philosophy that defines Google's unique brand of Chaos Engineering, and took years to grow. They were by no means obvious at the outset of our journey. If your organization is interested in establishing a disaster testing program, it would be wise to take the time to write a charter document establishing overarching guidelines for your tests. The following sections present a consolidated version of the rules used at Google; they will be referenced later to highlight how pragmatic test designs are emergent when following these guidelines.

DiRT tests must have no service-level objective breaking impact on external systems or users

This rule of engagement does not mean that there needs to be *absolutely* no hint of an issue for external users, only that service levels should not be degraded below the standard objectives already set by the owning teams. If your service is trending toward going out of SLO in a way that will impact external users, the test has been a huge success but it doesn't necessarily need to take things further. DiRT tests are not an excuse to throw SLOs out the window. Your SLO should be an important guiding factor when designing and monitoring a test.

A key point of Google's approach to Chaos Engineering is that we prefer "controlled chaos" when possible. This means your test should have a well-thought-out and quickly executable rollback strategy. Having a safety net or "big red button" will allow you to halt the test when appropriate. Given that the test was soundly designed to begin with, tests cut short this way are counterintuitively the most rewarding. You have the most to learn from analyzing tests that subvert your expectations and have more impact than anticipated.

Infrastructure and internally consumed services can in extreme situations cause internal consumers to go out of SLO even when operating within expected limits. Consumers of a service inevitably grow to depend on a system based on the service level they experience on average rather than the tolerances and specifications that are actually guaranteed. We disaster test large infrastructure and shared services to specifically uncover these misconfigurations. What can be done if a test transitively impacts an externally facing system such that its SLO is severely impacted? Stopping the entire exercise at the first sign of overly impacting one team would prevent you from discovering other internal users that are similarly poorly configured, but who just haven't noticed or escalated yet. These situations call for a safe-list, that is to say build a mechanism into the test that allows for those affected to completely circumvent its impact. This allows you to avoid causing continued problems to services that are trending out of SLO as they identify themselves but to continue the test in general for everyone else. A safe-list is not a replacement for a "big red button" rollback strategy but should be available in conjunction with other failsafes when appropriate. See the "Gathering Results" section for more detail on learning more from a test's safe-list.

Production emergencies always take precedence over DiRT "emergencies"

If a real production incident occurs while a DiRT exercise is happening, the DiRT exercise should be halted and postponed so that focus can be shifted to the real incident. If your DiRT test is competing for attention during a real outage then it is implicitly violating the first rule of engagement, even when it didn't cause the real outage. Test proctors should have repeatedly communicated about DiRT exercises ahead of time to potential stakeholders and should monitor normal incident escalation channels for problems before, during, and after the test. When the first signs of a production incident expose themselves, test proctors should be evaluating possible relations to their tests and communicating with other on-duty responders. The production issue may be deemed minor enough to not require halting the test, but for a moderate severity issue even when not directly caused by the DiRT test it is most likely worth halting the test in order to make investigating the real issue smoother. Problems can occur before the test even starts, in which case if there is already an urgent issue being dealt with at a time originally scheduled for testing it may be wise to postpone the test to another day.

Run DiRT tests with transparency

Make it as clear as possible that DiRT "emergencies" are part of an exercise. You might consider this rule of engagement a corollary to the second rule of engagement, that real emergencies take precedence over fake emergencies. An on-caller can't effectively de-prioritize a DiRT emergency in lieu of an actual emergency if she isn't aware that one of the two emergencies is a DiRT test.

Communications that are part of your test (either leading up to or during the test) should, as clearly as possible, convey they are part of a DiRT test. Communicate about your test early, often, and unambiguously. Googlers will preface the subjects of DiRT test–related emails with "DiRT DiRT DiRT" and the message body will usually contain a preamble with the same "DiRT DiRT DiRT" token, meta-information about the test's duration, proctor contact information, and reminders to report any problems experienced through standard incident escalation channels.

Google creates outlandish themes for groups of tests: zombie attacks, sentient artificial intelligence viruses, alien invasions, and so on. Communications will invariably try to reference the theme, sometimes revealing continual information in an ongoing storyline. Artificially injected pages, alerts, errors, bad configuration pushes, and problem-inducing source code changes will make overt references to the theme. This practice serves two purposes. First off, it is fun! Coming up with over-the-top science fiction story arcs for your test is an opportunity to joke around, be creative, and frame the exercises positively. The less immediately obvious benefit of the themes is that they provide clear indicators to impacted users and test takers what is and is not part of the DiRT test, lowering the likelihood of confusing a test with an actual incident or vice versa.

Minimize cost, maximize value

Have you ever worked on a system that is always causing heartache, is the source of repeated incidents, and has the general reputation in your engineering organization of being unreliable? Systems like this need to be re-engineered; they don't need disaster tests—the disaster is already there. After the system is reworked a DiRT test is a great tool for proving the production reliability of the new design, or for recycling past outages to show former shortcomings no longer apply.

When designing a test you should weigh the costs of internal user disruptions and loss of goodwill carefully against what you stand to learn. DiRT is not about breaking things only for the sake of breaking them; its value comes from uncovering failures modes you don't already know about. If you can look at a system and see obvious shortcomings, you won't gain much by exposing these in a practical exercise. If you already know a system is broken you may as well prioritize the engineering work to address the known risks and then disaster test your mitigations later. Thoroughly consider the impact of your test. It is a good idea to continually re-evaluate this measurement as both planning and the actual test proceed; it can be a good foundation from which to make decisions about whether a particularly impactful test should be continued or not. If there is nothing more to learn from a test and it is causing larger than expected impact in disparate parts of your system, it may be reasonable to call the test off early.

Treat disaster tests as you would actual outages

We expect Googlers to continue working as they normally would, treating any disaster test–related disruptions the same as a real outage. Communications about DiRT tests frequently repeat the advice that if you are affected by a test to "escalate as normal." There is a natural tendency for people to be more lax about handling incidents when they know the "emergency" may be part of an exercise.[2] There are multiple reasons to encourage treating your exercises as similarly as possible to real emergencies. Incident escalation processes are an important pipeline for gathering information about the impact of a test and can frequently reveal unanticipated connections between systems. If a user casually disregards a problem, whether or not they know the test is occurring, you will miss out on this valuable information; therefore explicit training and communication in this regard can be helpful.

What to Test

Designing your first test can be a daunting undertaking. If you've got semi-recent outages these can be excellent reference material when deciding which aspects of a system could benefit from testing. Temporarily re-creating the instigating conditions of past outages will help prove that your system can handle previous problems gracefully and that the reliability risks causing the original incident have been mitigated.

Starting from some prompting questions will usually get you pointed in the right direction. Which systems keep you up at night? Are you aware of singly homed data or services? Are there processes that depend on people in a single location, a single vendor? Are you 100% confident that your monitoring and alerting systems raise alarms when expected? When was the last time you performed a cutover to your fallback systems? When was the last time you restored your system from backup? Have

---

2 This intriguing behavioral tendency is also exhibited in real-life physical emergencies such as building fires: see Lea Winerman, "Fighting Fire with Psychology," *APA Monitor on Psychology*, Vol. 35, No. 8 (Sept. 2004).

you validated your system's behavior when its "noncritical" dependencies are unavailable?

The areas of Google's business that have participated in DiRT have grown over time, expanding to include a wide range of systems and processes. Testing network and software systems is still the lion's share but Google promotes disaster testing in many other areas and thinking outside the box about a variety of business aspects has often proven rewarding. The following sections outline some general categories and prompts that will help get you started.

Run at service levels

Scenario: Unusually large traffic spikes degrade the mean latency of a shared internal service. To the service's credit, its degraded latency remains barely within published SLOs.

Limiting a service to operate at its published service level for an extended period of time is a phenomenal way to validate distributed system design, verify SLOs are properly set, and manage expectations of service consumers. Systems that are *too* stable are taken for granted over time. If your service continually exceeds its SLO, users may assume that the performance they experience on average is what they should expect all the time. The service level you deliver will eventually become an implicit contract regardless of your system's published specifications. This is an extension of an adage we are fond of at Google called Hyrum's Law (*http://www.hyrumslaw.com*), which is often summarized as:

> With a sufficient number of users of an API, it does not matter what you promise in the contract: all observable behaviors of your system will be depended on by somebody.

This rule isn't limited to aspects of the data returned by a service; it extends even to reliability and performance characteristics.

Run without dependencies

Scenario: Half of your "soft" dependencies start returning errors, while the other half see an order of magnitude increase in latency.

When one or more noncritical aspects of your system fail there should be a graceful degradation with the service continuing to operate within its designated SLO. Decreases in the service level of noncritical backends should not lead to cascading failures or cause runaway impact. If the distinction between hard and soft dependencies in your system is not so clear-cut, these tests can help get you to a state where that distinction is crystal. Your system's direct critical dependencies may be clear but it becomes increasingly difficult to keep track of the second and third layers of dependencies or how combinations of noncritical failures in backends buried within your stack may affect your ability to serve customers.[3]

Fault injection testing will give you a detailed and accurate picture of your system's tolerance to failures in dependencies, but this merely yields a snapshot from a moment in time. You should plan to perform this type of testing on a regular basis. A system's dependencies won't remain static over its lifetime and the unfortunate truth of most systems is that there will be a gradual accretion of critical dependencies over time. Critical dependencies can come from the most unanticipated places[4] and will work their way into complex systems like thieves in the night despite your best engineering efforts. At Google we've run some of the same fault injection tests on systems repeatedly for years and still uncover new issues as these systems evolve; don't take a particular test for granted just because it has been run before.

Start slow with fault injection testing; there is no need to "turn it up to 11" from the very start. You can begin with injecting a small amount of latency into a few dependencies. From there increase the latency values, the portion of injected dependencies, or both. Rome wasn't built in a day; create a feedback loop for improving your system and build up confidence to the point where you can readily answer "What if?" questions about any system you communicate with.

People outages

Scenario: A critical internal system starts going haywire but its senior developers are unreachable at a conference.

How bad is your lottery factor?[5] Aside from the siloing of technical expertise, leadership and business decisions should not be single points of failure. Do you have established primary and backup ways of reaching essential staff in the case of an emergency? Try running some Wheel of Misfortune[6] exercises and randomly selecting team members that will be considered unreachable.

---

3 For a great read on this topic, see Ben Treynor et al., "The Calculus of Service Availability," *Communications of the ACM*, Vol. 60, No. 9 (Sept. 2017).

4 One notorious public example (*https://oreil.ly/6MW5m*) was the removal of the `left-pad` package from the Node Package Manager repository (*www.npmjs.com*) in March 2016, which caused the builds of uncountable JavaScript projects around the globe to stop working.

5 Lottery factor is a metaphor of the risk resulting from information and capabilities not being shared among team members, as exemplified by a team member winning the lottery and quitting without notice. This is also known as "bus factor" (*https://oreil.ly/GzmyH*).

6 Many Google SRE teams regularly schedule theoretical exercises where they will guide a team member through prompts based on previously experienced outages and interesting incidents from on-call shifts. These exercises are an excellent way to share knowledge and experience within a team. See Beyer et al., *Site Reliability Engineering*, Chapter 28.

Release and rollback

Scenario: A faulty configuration, buggy binary, or server/client API mismatch has been pushed to some portion of your production infrastructure. The on-caller has been paged, and must isolate the issue and roll it back.

The Greek philosopher Heraclitus said "Change is the only constant in life." It can be tempting to think that a system can be brought to some kind of reliability steady state and left there perpetually, preventing the risks that come along with new code, architecture, and systems. The "don't touch it" approach carries its own risks: a system that does not adapt to a changing environment can be prone to eventual failure. There is implicit risk in any change to a system; rollouts of new software and configuration are frequently the vanguard of outage-inducing issues. Rollout procedures and their arguably even more critical rollback counterparts deserve significant scrutiny for teams that want to improve disaster resiliency.

The procedure for reverting changes to your production environment should be well documented and rehearsed. What types of errors do you expect to be prevented by automated testing in your release pipeline before a change reaches the production environment? Do you regularly validate that these safeguards remain effective? Your monitoring platform should be aware of both software and configuration releases in a way that readily highlights them alongside displayed metrics. When a given release proves faulty you will need the ability to halt rollouts and quickly identify the affected systems. You can design a disaster test that exercises both of these important procedures during the course of a regular release. Prove to yourself that you can pause a release, evaluate its progress, and choose to resume or cancel. At what saturation point does it become infeasible to wholesale turn off all instances affected by a bad release? Disabling or rolling back a release on a targeted subset of affected machines can prove extremely useful and could readily be performed as part of a disaster test using identical copies of a binary that differ only in their version number or release label. If your release building processes take significant time, it is critical to have a simple way to revert back to the immediately previous release without having to initiate a full build reconstructing it on demand. Being well versed in manipulating your release system can save you a lot of time and unnecessary complication in a crisis situation.

Incident management procedures

Scenario: A critical internal service has started returning 100% errors. Clearly a serious incident, your team must coordinate debugging your own service, contacting other teams to follow up on causes, as well as public and internal communication.

Google has a highly developed incident management protocol[7] based on the Incident Command System (*https://oreil.ly/Wppy1*) that FEMA uses to manage and coordinate disaster response efforts. Having a well-understood protocol and roles for incident management makes responsibilities clear, allowing for more efficient collaboration and utilization of responder resources. The roles provide well-defined channels for the bidirectional flow of information and this goes a long way toward clarifying what can otherwise become an overwhelming cacophony of signals that must be sifted through. Make sure your team knows how to organize efforts effectively in critical circumstances and that your organization has clear escalation guidelines along with hand-off procedures for extended incidents.

Datacenter operations

Scenario: There is a water leak on the datacenter floor adjacent to server racks and other high-voltage electrical equipment.

Google's datacenter teams have a long history of thoroughly testing the failovers for physical systems as well as stewarding robust incident management procedures and disaster plans. Datacenter engineers were some of the DiRT program's earliest and most vocal advocates at Google and have been instrumental in the promotion and growth of the program.

Disaster testing in the datacenter can be as simple as disabling power to a single rack or as complex as switching to backup power for an entire site. It is smart to make ample use of theoretical role-playing tests to drill procedure before progressing to small practical tests and beyond. Do you ever have situations where datacenter technicians are required to interface with product on-call engineers during emergencies that impact normal operations? Inversely, do on-callers know how to escalate to datacenter operators to aid in troubleshooting problems that might be hardware related? These are great candidates around which to develop tests. Make sure that everyone involved, inside and outside the datacenter, has experience with emergency procedures, knows what to expect, and how to communicate.

Capacity management

Scenario: There has been an unexpected loss of allocated compute resources in a region.

Owners of modern distributed services must monitor and forecast fluctuating resource demands to balance availability and redundancy against the potential wasted cost of overprovisioning. Disaster testing can be a valuable avenue through which you evaluate the baseline assumptions about resource and load distribution that

---

7 Andrew Widdowson, "Disaster Role Playing," in Betsy Beyer, Chris Jones, Jennifer Petoff, and Niall Murphy, eds., *Site Reliability Engineering* (Sebastopol, CA: O'Reilly, 2016), Chapter 14.

inform these decisions. How significant a spike in traffic would you need to see in order to consider emergency resource allocations? Precisely how quickly can you expand capacity given such a traffic spike? What if your cloud provider can't meet your resource demands in a preferred region? Could your team perform an emergency turn up in another region if it was a necessity? You should work toward a point where removing capacity from one location and turning it up in another, either temporarily or permanently, does not feel at all risky. You can try this first with fractional capacity, turning down a portion of network or compute resources in one place while turning an equivalent amount up in another with the expectation that automated load balancing adjusts itself appropriately.

Business continuity plans

Scenario: A natural disaster strikes at your primary office location; satellite offices must assess impact, attempt to reach those impacted by the disaster, and coordinate normal business operations.

Even when a disaster occurs, executive decisions still need to be made and vital business workflows need to remain intact. What are the contingencies for critical approval chains when leadership is unavailable? Emergency spending approvals? Public communications? Legal decisions? Having a well-thought-out business continuity plan (BCP) is merely the first step; you must make sure that employees are aware of this plan and know to follow it in an emergency. You might put an interesting spin on human response tests by adding conditions such as the responder being forced to operate from a laptop or having no direct connection to your corporate network. Under the DiRT banner, teams all over Google perform role-playing exercises to familiarize themselves and improve their BCPs.

Data integrity

Scenario: Data corruption requires you to restore from a system's most recent backup.

Backups are only as good as the last time you tested a restore. If you haven't reloaded data from a backup all the way into your production environment, how can you be confident that your recovery procedures are correct or that your backups are working at all? If your backup processes mysteriously stopped running, how long would it take to be noticed? Simple tests such as incrementally delaying a backup process or temporarily writing a backup file to an alternative location can be quite revealing with respect to the thoroughness of your monitoring in this area.

An application's robustness against data corruption is another important aspect of data integrity. Do you thoroughly fuzz test[8] even internal services? Fuzzing API endpoints in a microservice architecture is an outstanding way to harden services against unanticipated inputs that lead to crashes ("queries of death"). There are a host of open source tools that can help you get started with fuzz testing, including a few popular ones released by Google.[9]

How latency tolerant are your replicated data stores? Propagation delays and network splits in eventually consistent data storage systems have the potential to cause difficult-to-unravel inconsistencies. Artificially inducing replication latency can help you predict how a system will behave when replication queues back up. Adding replication delay can also reveal data race conditions that don't otherwise display themselves in less extreme conditions. If you already perform load testing in a pre-production environment, designing a replication disaster test may be as simple as running your normal load testing suite with storage replication delayed or temporarily disabled.

Networks

Scenario: A significant portion of your network goes offline due to a regional outage.

Network infrastructure issues can result in partial or total outages of a service, site, or team. The bandwidth and network teams at Google have been particularly fond of the DiRT program and have designed many tests involving temporary firewall configurations that reroute or entirely block traffic. Network failures should be tested at multiple scales covering everything from a single individual's desktop, an entire building, your presence in a geographic region, up through an entire datacenter. Regional outages are a real problem in cloud architectures but with a few well-crafted firewall rules you will be able to show that your system is tolerant to any single region failure. If your operation manages its own networking equipment, failovers and redundant equipment should be occasionally tested to prove they behave as expected when needed.

---

8 The Wikipedia definition is as follows: "Fuzzing or fuzz testing is an automated software testing technique that involves providing invalid, unexpected, or random data as inputs to a computer program," *https://oreil.ly/ Erveu*.

9 Two tools that have been open sourced by Google are libprotobuf-mutator (*https://oreil.ly/oXo_O*) and ClusterFuzz (*https://oreil.ly/6kFqI*).

Monitoring and alerting

Scenario: Inject failures into your system and turn off components until you find an action that doesn't result in a page.

If you have alerting metrics that you have never seen trigger in production then you are taking it on faith that they work as intended. You need to regularly verify that your monitoring and alerting systems actually do their job. This is the same reason smoke detectors have a test button.

Telecommunications and IT systems

Scenario: Your company's video conferencing suite becomes unavailable for a significant portion of the day.

Internal video conferencing and chat systems allow tens of thousands of Googlers to connect with each other every day during normal business operations. Tens of thousands of desktop computers are used to perform day-to-day work. These systems are very important, but they shouldn't be critical in the sense that their temporary absence is anything more than a moderate hindrance. Alternative communication mechanisms should be identified, agreed upon, and tested prior to being necessary.

Medical and security emergencies

Scenario: An employee has broken their leg in a difficult-to-access or security-restricted area.

Will emergency responders have the ability to access restricted areas of your facilities in case of an emergency? Google's datacenters are industrial workplaces and while Google prides itself on promoting a safe workplace, nowhere on earth can claim to be completely free from the risk of accidents. It is important to have a vetted and rehearsed procedure for how to respond to these situations. Determine ahead of time where to direct first responders if they are called to your facilities and have predesignated roles for who should escort them if necessary.

Reboot everything

Scenario: A critical security vulnerability requires the time-sensitive reboot of every system in your infrastructure. Everything must be turned off, but will all of it turn back on?

Completely restart a system or collection of related systems—don't let your ability to bootstrap your systems decay. You should be familiar with the bootstrapping and cold restart of any service that is critical to your business.

How to Test

Hopefully at this point you have a system or two in mind that you are interested in disaster testing, maybe even an idea for a specific aspect of this system that would be valuable to probe. There is still a bit of work necessary to grow that idea into a workable test. At Google, teams frequently consult with DiRT veterans for help iterating on their initial ideas, and guidance on honing them into practical tests. There are a handful of pragmatic concerns, derived from the rules of engagement, that will make execution more streamlined and less prone to negative repercussions. Your test should be scientific; consider disaster testing like you would a science experiment.[10] Extraneous variables within the system should be controlled to the degree possible. Your action on the system should be specific and targeted and the avenues for measurement of its impact identified well beforehand. A hypothesis for the outcome of your test can prove accurate knowledge of your system's behavior in failure scenarios or expose the unexpected. Make sure your test adds value; remeasuring well-established or well-understood failure modes is not a good use of time and effort.

Even after you decide on the action of your test, you should be specific about identifying what you are testing. Do you mean for this test to evaluate the reactions of human on-call response or the adherence to and execution of incident management procedures? Are you testing the system itself, complex failure modes, self-healing design? Are you testing that your service's consumers are properly configured and don't maintain unreasonable reliability expectations outside of what you can realistically provide? You should aim as much as possible to only be testing *one* hypothesis at a time and be especially wary of mixing the testing of automated system reactions in conjunction with human reactions.

Testing a single hypothesis does not imply that you need to avoid injecting simultaneous failures into your system. In the real world, interactions between co-occurring failures which individually may not have posed significant problems can lead to devastating outages. Uncovering negative feedback loops and disastrous bug combinations is one of the most rewarding outcomes of DiRT testing. As always, the usual safety controls apply: have a way to halt your test and be clear how you anticipate the system under test to behave.

When you are stressing a system to see if it gracefully handles failure conditions it is wise to make sure the on-call engineer is aware of your test. Not communicating with the on-caller limits your awareness of other issues that might be ongoing and will make it difficult to distinguish automated system mitigations from those the on-call engineer might perform. This is a good example of the application of the "Rules of

---

10 It is no coincidence that the Principles of Chaos (*https://principlesofchaos.org*) reflect the scientific method— the universe being the original large-scale, distributed system.

Engagement"; having the on-caller know about a test ahead of time will not impact or alter its technical merit and indeed increases the ability to monitor it and collect information from disparately impacted teams (the on-caller being the likely point of contact when an affected team notices something wrong in their own system).

Err on the side of overcommunicating unless you can identify an explicit reason why your test needs limited communication. If the goal of a test is to measure the human elements of an incident response, a small bit of surprise can be beneficial, but even in these cases pre-announcing a window of time when the test could occur will be helpful for avoiding scheduling conflicts and being notified sooner rather than later if a real incident rears up during the time you were intending to test. Send a reminder or two to relevant parties and potentially affected teams in the weeks and days ahead of the actual test; this will keep you from unintentionally surprising anyone and also serves to prime the awareness of a larger group of people to be vigilant for impact during the test.

Deciding when and for how long to run a test can have a huge impact on the quality and quantity of what you learn. Run a certain test for an unduly extended period of time and you may find you've unintentionally created an external customer-facing outage. Run the same test for not enough time and you might not have any measurable results; interruptions will be written off or ignored if inconsistent or ephemeral. Ideally, as system issues are uncovered and addressed, the duration of larger shared infrastructure tests can increase. Starting small is probably a good idea, but don't start so small that it becomes a waste of time and effort. You might choose to initially run the test at off-peak hours to gather data with the intent of increasing intensity gradually. Generally, at Google, we avoid testing during times with peak traffic patterns.

Keep your company's corporate calendar in mind when planning your test. Coinciding disaster tests with major holidays and significant cultural events (major sporting events, shopping holidays, etc.) should be avoided. Be wary of interfering with your business' supporting monthly or quarterly processes, unless these are specifically what you are intending to test. Finance, accounting, and business intelligence reports may not be the first things that come to mind when you are considering impact beforehand, but you don't want to be the person that took out the payroll system the night before payday.

The common advice at Google is to "look both ways" before kicking off a DiRT test. Immediately before the test starts do your best to watch out for unplanned coincidental events that might impact your test, being especially wary of ongoing production issues that your test may exacerbate. You can always postpone the test for a few hours, days, or even weeks.

Gathering Results

After planning and outreach are complete and your test is running smoothly, you must set yourself up for success recording what you find. While a test is running it is a good idea for proctors to keep a log with periodic notes on actions they perform as well as anything standing out as interesting or unusual. For every DiRT test run at Google, a lightweight analysis document is written, inspired by the "postmortem" documents we use for real incidents. Any issues brought to light by the test are specially labeled as having been found during DiRT testing and Google occasionally sponsors internal bug closure bounties on DiRT bugs to prevent lower-priority issues from stagnating. Finally, the results document contains a section for feedback on the logistic and organizational aspects of the test execution. The team of volunteers responsible for DiRT program management use this feedback to iteratively improve the program's operation year over year.

Less conventional approaches to disaster testing yield results that are still worthy of write-ups. For large infrastructure tests that offer a safe-listing mechanism to those impacted, reviewing safe-list requests can be a rewarding endeavor. At Google we require any team requesting exemptions via safe-listing to provide a short write-up explaining why they were unable to participate in the test and identify high-priority action items that will unblock their participation in the next round of testing. There are occasions when broad communications about a test will generate substantial outcry or enough safe-listing requests that the actual test becomes unnecessary, the threat alone having been enough to expose a significant amount of necessary work.[11]

Scope of Tests at Google

Google's internal infrastructure is quite large and any one individual can only reasonably be aware of so much of it at a time[12]—we're all only human after all. Disaster testing provides a scalable means to explore the interactions between systems in depth. Over time tests can grow in intensity, duration, and scope. Large tests of core infrastructure have a lot of notoriety but these are supported by a foundation of hundreds and thousands of lower-risk, isolated experiments. If you dig deep enough, most of

---

11 There is a phenomenon at Google known as the "DiRT curse" where on the occasions that a particularly major test is canceled or postponed there will shortly be a real incident uncannily similar to the originally planned test. There have even been situations where the real incident even coincided with the originally scheduled time for the fake incident. One of the things we say about DiRT is that "if you don't test it, the universe will." It is good to know the universe has a sense of humor.

12 This sentiment is succinctly expressed by Woods's Theorem: "As the complexity of a system increases, the accuracy of any single agent's own model of that system decreases rapidly." Found in the STELLA Report (*https://snafucatchers.github.io*) from the SNAFUcatchers Workshop on Coping With Complexity.

the suggested tests from the previous section can be approached at more than one scale.

Core service providers for critical infrastructure such as compute, network, storage, and locks have an implicit incentive to steward their customers into robust configurations. For these services a customer misconfiguration or underprovisioning can result in the service provider being paged despite the service working as intended. The need for worst-case service levels to be well understood by users is key to the operational success of both the service provider and consumers.

Occasionally, teams at Google will artificially limit large services to their minimum SLO within a region for extended periods of time. These tests are scheduled several times a year and the regions selected are rotated to guarantee at least some minimum exposure to the test regardless of where a particular job is running. The exact duration of the experiment is determined based on an "error budget" of SLO that the service provider is willing to burn through in order to fund it.[13] If your service is consistently exceeding its SLO then you are accumulating an "error budget" and disaster testing is an opportunity to spend it. When we run tests like this at Google we try to extend them for as long as we reasonably can. Some teams may anticipate being affected and adopt a strategy of waiting out the storm and allowing an outage rather than escalating. Extending a test into the multiple-day range helps motivate positive action and longer-term solutions from those who might be willing to endure shorter outages. Extending the test helps to shake out internal customers who have unwittingly underprovisioned themselves for the service level and reliability their applications actually require. Launch and design reviews alone are not enough to guard against these types of problems, as dependencies that start out noncritical may progress through a slow creep to criticality over time. Practical testing is one of the few ways to alleviate risks from slowly progressing reliability regressions.

A well-designed, long-running, large infrastructure test will have a safe-listing mechanism and will use this as a guide for improving any applications that requested safe-listing. The ideal test will also provide a path for users to test their services in isolation independent of the large-scale test; for example, building in the ability to artificially inject latency or errors to a service's client library. This allows teams that depend on the service under test to run their own isolated disaster tests, validating ahead of time an application's robustness under the same conditions as might be experienced in a global test. The client-side versions of the large infrastructure tests are even more useful after issues are uncovered in a particular application; they can

---

13 One Googler would refer to this practice as "taking the nines out for a spin." The concept of error budgets and their application at Google is discussed at length in Mark Roth's article "(Un)Reliability Budgets: Finding Balance between Innovation and Reliability," *login:*, Vol. 4, No. 4 (August 2015), as well as in Marc Alvidrez, "Embracing Risk," in Beyer et al., *Site Reliability Engineering*, Chapter 3.

be used as a way to prove problems have been resolved and can prevent regressions by being automated to run continuously.

Some large tests that we run at Google:

- Temporarily disabling log storage services in a region in order to ensure users requiring high-availability log writing have configured their systems with proper failovers.
- Occasionally taking our global lock service offline so that it doesn't significantly exceed its SLO.[14]
- Large-scale RPC service fuzzing. Google has automated tools that can fuzz the inputs of services and monitor for subsequent crashes; these are run continuously against development and staging jobs.
- Large network splits isolating entire campuses.
- Disallowing nonhuman account (robot and service accounts) access to our source control system for several hours.

Isolated, lower-risk tests are happening continuously at Google; teams use automated tooling to create mini-disasters in staging environments on a regular schedule. Making sure that extreme conditions are guaranteed in environments well ahead of production serves as a not-so-gentle reminder of what the real world is going to throw at systems. Standard black box monitoring of the staging environment helps to highlight regressions when an injected fault disrupts the serving path.

We try to automate everything we can at Google and disaster tests are no exception. It became clear that in order to keep pace with the massive growth of Google as an organization that the DiRT program would need to provide a common platform of ready-to-use disaster tests related to shared services. To meet this need we developed a suite of turn-key fault injection tests that are highly configurable and can be executed from a single command-line tool. This tool provides ready-made disasters-in-a-box that lower the barriers to entry for teams seeking to get started with technical disaster testing but who don't know where to begin. Our collection of automated tests makes the self-service versions of large infrastructure tests available in one easy to find place and adds a few additional tests to the mix. We have automated tests related to load balancing, regional task terminations, storage replication delays, total and partial cache flushing, as well as RPC latency and error injection. Standardizing a framework around automated disaster tests has allowed us to share first-class support for important features such as global and partial aborts of all automated tests via a

---

14 Marc Alvidrez, "The Global Chubby Planned Outage," in Beyer et al., *Site Reliability Engineering*, Chapter 4.

common "big red button" mechanism, well-thought-out rollbacks, auditing, and pre-drafted automatic communications.

Borg Eviction SLO: A Case Study

Borg[15, 16] is Google's cluster management system for scheduling and managing applications across datacenters. Users configure a priority for their jobs to be scheduled on Borg, with real-time workloads taking precedence over batch processing.[17] A Borg task "eviction" occurs when a task is terminated by the Borg master process. This can happen for a number of reasons, including needing to upgrade operating system kernels, physical equipment moves, disk replacements, or just needing resources for higher-priority tasks. Borg SRE publishes an eviction rate SLO (based on the task's priority) to provide an upper-bound specification on task evictions that users should engineer against when designing systems.

Under normal operation a task will never experience anything close to the published eviction rate SLO, but during some types of planned maintenance tasks the eviction rate increases. This type of maintenance is roughly evenly distributed across Borg cells, so it appears infrequent from the perspective of a single cell, but is a certainty given a long enough time horizon. Borg users were becoming surprised on occasions that the eviction rate got near its SLO.

Borg SRE wanted to help their users to improve the reliability of their systems by becoming more aware of the eviction rate SLO. A few dedicated engineers from the Borg SRE team developed a plan to rotate through all the Borg cells and force evictions of production tasks at the SLOs for their respective priorities. The test runs for several days during which artificially evicted tasks are labeled with a warning message referencing the test and pointing users to more detailed information on an internal website. Users can safe-list themselves while the test is running, since there is no use in rubbing it in once the point is made. In conjunction with the cell-wide testing mode, Borg SRE developed a self-service mode where users can run the test targeting specific groups of tasks in isolation. Borg users target their own jobs using the self-service test in order to prepare for scheduled cell-wide tests and know with confidence that their processes will not be disrupted.

---

15 Niall Murphy with John Looney and Michael Kacirek, in Beyer et al., *Site Reliability Engineering*, Chapter 7.

16 A. Verma et al., "Large-Scale Cluster Management at Google with Borg," in *Proceedings of the European Conference on Computer Systems*, 2015.

17 Dan Dennison, "Data-Processing Pipelines," in Beyer et al., *Site Reliability Engineering*, Chapter 25.

Conclusion

How to best prepare for the unexpected? This seemingly paradoxical question gave rise to Google's Disaster Recovery Testing program. Complexity will over time make most continually growing systems appear chaotic, and rather than rejecting this, advocates of Chaos Engineering embrace it. Disaster testing offers a means of verifying conjecture and proving a system's behavior empirically, leading to deeper understanding and ultimately more stable systems. As engineers we are frequently unaware of the implicit assumptions that we build into systems until these assumptions are radically challenged by unforeseen circumstances. Regular, formalized, and carefully crafted disaster tests will allow you to probe a system for such harmful assumptions in a controlled manner. While disaster testing is not completely absent of risk, its risk profile can be tuned to match your tolerances and pales in comparison to the risk of being caught off guard by complex multifaceted system failures in the wild.

Imagine that you have somehow magically gained the power to precisely schedule your system's next production incident. You'd put the incident on everyone's calendar and profusely communicate it in order to make sure no one is left unaware. When the scheduled time came you'd have the best engineers eagerly waiting to record and analyze the problem while it is happening. Of course this team of responders will have bolstered their knowledge of the incident source and potentially affected systems ahead of time, making them even more well equipped to interpret the data they are presented with. Once you have had enough, you exercise yet another new superpower, calling the whole incident off. The system returns to normal within minutes. The wealth of data collected is operated on, the uncovered problems fixed, and your systems are that much more reliable for it. These superpowers would swiftly and drastically increase the reliability of your system. Could you imagine choosing not to use them?

About the Author

Jason Cahoon is a full stack software developer and site reliability engineer at Google. Aside from writing software and analyzing technology systems, he enjoys woodcarving, spending time with his dogs, and being bad at chess.

CHAPTER 6

Microsoft Variation and Prioritization of Experiments

Oleg Surmachev

At Microsoft we build and operate our own Chaos Engineering program for cloud infrastructure at scale. We find that experiment selection in particular has an outsized impact on the way you apply Chaos Engineering to your system. Examples of different failure scenarios in real production systems illustrate how a variety of real-world events can affect your production system. I'll propose a method for prioritizing experimentation of your services, and then a framework for considering the variation of different experiment types. My goal in this chapter is to offer strategies you can apply in your engineering process to improve the reliability of your products.

Why Is Everything So Complicated?

Modern software systems are complex. There are hundreds, often thousands, of engineers working to enable even the smallest software product. There are thousands, maybe millions, of pieces of hardware and software that make up a single system that becomes your service. Think of all those engineers working for hardware providers like Intel, Samsung, Western Digital, and other companies designing and building server hardware. Think of Cisco, Arista, Dell, APC, and all other providers of network and power equipment. Think of Microsoft and Amazon providing you with the cloud platform. All of these dependencies you accept into your system explicitly or implicitly have their own dependencies in turn, all the way down to power grids and fiber cables. Your dependencies combine together to create a complex black box with a lot of moving parts, on top of which you create your own system.

An Example of Unexpected Complications

In the early part of my career I worked on algorithms used in submarine sonar equipment. In those days I could literally name who was responsible for every single component that my code depended on, for both software and hardware: each library, each driver, every machine we were running on. A submarine is a very contained environment, so there are only so many computers involved in processing the task, only so many wires and hard drives. You have a limited number of sensors and usually just one user in the system. Even so, I remember seeing tome after tome on these components, thousands of pages of documentation.

Every meeting included at least a dozen people: each component was endlessly scrutinized, each use case documented, and each situation reviewed. The module my team worked on involved some signal processing, and we put up the most rigorous testing in the lab that we could envision. We used recorded signals from other subs, tried different weather and location simulations. Everything was extremely thorough.

When I booked a plane ticket to conduct the first test aboard an actual ship, I was confident that the trip would not take more than a couple days. How hard could it be? Install, check, celebrate, take off. Unfortunately, nothing went as planned. It was my first trip to northern Russia. My wife who grew up in that area advised me to pack more clothes than I needed. Of course I told her, "No worries, it's just a couple days. It's August after all, still summer, you know." It was snowing when the plane landed. A half day was lost to the inclement weather and a minor cold was my friend for the rest of the trip.

When I was finally able to install our module and try it out, it simply did not work. The first attempt to make the system work end to end took 40 days. We encountered dozens of problems that we did not see coming, ran into combinations of factors that we did not consider, and faced new challenges that never showed up on the drawing board. The wiring of connections from antennae to the signal processor involved over 200 connections—none of which were done right. We had to go back and retrace every single one to adjust programmatically for the mechanical mistakes.

All of that thorough preparation and effort was invested in planning, yet there was still such a mess during the first test. What did we do wrong? We did not consider the entirety of the realm of events that would happen to our system in the real world. We focused on mathematical and computer science problems of signal processing, but we did not consider bad wiring, extreme temperatures, or quality of user input as the ship rolls over the waves in bad weather. We learned all of those after the fact and at great expense: project delays and time away from our families.

One of the advanced principles of Chaos Engineering (*https://principlesofchaos.org*) is to vary real-world events in the experiments. If we had dedicated time to explore real-world effects both inside and outside the system instead of planning thoroughly for the happy path, perhaps we would have had a more successful installation and been home with our families sooner.

A Simple System Is the Tip of the Iceberg

Let's consider for a moment a small website that I created for my wife's art school. The site is hosted on Azure. Let's consider what it depends on: I used IIS, Windows, IaaS VMs, Hyper-V, another OS on the host, Azure infrastructure, Azure storage for my data, hardware for the development and deployment machine, power and network equipment in datacenters, and servicing teams in those datacenters. All told, these systems encompass a few hundred software components and about twenty thousand engineers. For customers to see the website I also depend on a CDN, DNS, global backbone network, my customer's choice of browser and internet service provider, and so on. Even a very simple website is not so simple at all when you take into account the living systems underneath it.

All of these additional layers of software and hardware, abstractions and service providers, are part of a bigger picture that impacts the behavior of the system that concerns us. Even in the submarine system, a contained environment where I could tell exactly what components I depended on and I could literally pick up the phone and call every single person involved, I was still not in control. It was impossible to foresee many kinds of outcomes that being in the field exposed me to. Varying real-world events in Chaos Engineering is exactly what we're concerned about here.

Designing and building our products while thoughtfully considering interfaces, component contracts, and service-level agreements is already a complex task. It is even more complex when we consider our entire dependency chain. Events will happen to our system and to our black box dependencies that will affect the way they perform: hardware failures, software bugs, badly documented or ignored procedures, and acts of God. And then there are events purposefully imposed: software updates, OS patches, regular hardware and facility maintenance. There are many more that go unmentioned, unconsidered, and even unimagined. Any of them might or might not critically affect our product performance, availability, and success. Using techniques from this book you can experiment on your system for unknowns to understand how components within and outside your control can interact in real-life scenarios.

Categories of Experiment Outcomes

As you deliver your chaos solution to production you will encounter various situations that can be roughly broken into the following categories:

Known events/expected consequences
> These are experiment strategies playing out exactly as expected. You should be able to control the situation at all times. This is where you make the most progress with your Chaos Engineering program, build up correct coverage, and get comfortable with the tools that let you understand the performance of your system, whether those be metrics, logging, or observability tooling.

Known events/unexpected consequences
> This is when the experiment did not follow the expected scenario. You're still in control of the triggering event, but the outcome is not the expected one. This might be as simple as your monitoring/tracing strategy not reflecting your event properly or could be a complex problem involving recovery behavior. In any case, you should execute your plan for interrupting the experiment, record the event, and follow up. If there is tooling in place to interrupt the experiment automatically, even better. You can learn a lot from this outcome about how your system fails and how to recover from such failures.

Unknown events/unexpected consequences
> This is when failures start compounding and you're at risk of losing control of the situation. It is likely that this is the case when you need to engage human attention and use available failover and recovery plans. This is where you learn the most valuable things about your system in the long term, because your Chaos Engineering program is teaching you where your blind spots are and where you need to spend more time and planning to protect your system in the future.

The first is a self-evident consequence of planning, but the latter two warrant more discussion.

Known Events/Unexpected Consequences

When Chaos Engineering, fault injection, or disaster recovery is pitched to leadership or explained to stakeholders, it often focuses on high-profile, large-scale issues. Indeed, there is a set of problems that will manifest as a large-scale disaster. However, there are many other failure scenarios. For example, consider other threats that commonly occur. Think of all events that regularly and routinely happen in our systems: new version deployments, OS patches, credential rotations, daylight saving time changes, and others. These activities can create scheduled or otherwise well-understood disturbances like failover or downtime of a service even when things work exactly right. However, such events also create two additional risks:

- As with all things in life, things can go wrong in practice. A system can be damaged by the change introduced during an event no matter how well it is planned, like if an incorrect certificate is used during credentials rotation or a new network card driver version causes performance issues. Any such issue can cause an incident, create longer downtimes and reduced failover capability, or lead to other problems.

- Some changes are not controlled by your system, or any system. This might be related to clock changes like daylight savings time or credentials expiration, for example. Daylight savings time happens regardless of your level of readiness. Certificates will expire on a certain date. GPS can only count weeks up to 1024. Mandatory security updates can be imposed by external organizations. These external events can significantly limit the way your system is able to respond. For example, if you're already working on an issue that limits your system capacity and therefore your failover ability, you can delay CI/CD deployments. You cannot, however, delay certificate expiration.

Let's consider an example of a regular CI/CD deployment of a service. Here are some of the ways a routine update can go wrong:

- New service version has a bug and has to be rolled back or rolled forward.

- Service has a bug and corrupted your persistent state, so you cannot roll it back and go to the last known good state.

- Deployment process is broken, and the new service version does not get applied.

- Deployment process is broken and applies the new service version too fast, creating too high failover toll.

- Any combination of the above.

An example from my own recent experience involves applying security patches. With any security threat discovery, you're always working against the clock. The entire process is rushed, corners are often cut in deference to safety, testing is sometimes skipped. Unintentionally, the effort to provide safety quickly can dramatically *increase* the chance of failure.

During the Meltdown/Spectre event (*https://meltdownattack.com*) we anticipated countless failure modes during the patch deployment: startup failures, performance degradations, broken functionality, and so on. We were able to avoid many of these issues as they were already expected. However, if we had failed to experiment against such events there would be no way security patching would finish in a reasonable time. We regularly practice rushed change delivery specifically for cases like this. Over time, we have learned and adapted well enough that now dramatic shifts in maintenance and delivery schedules are transparent to the customers of the platform.

As these examples illustrate, we get progressively better at things we do often if we practice regularly. Even large-scale issues can be harmless when we prepare for them by design.

Unknown Events/Unexpected Consequences

A few years back I worked on the Bing infrastructure team. One day my Outlook application stopped working. I was not too concerned at first, as our IT department had its own sense of when to mandate updates, but Outlook did not work after restart either. Then I noticed Skype stopped working too and a few other tools. Something felt "off." That's when I heard the sound of someone running through the hallway.

People running in the office is usually a bad sign. High-level managers running is even worse. This manager stopped at my door and said, "Grab your laptop and come with me." We picked up more folks on the way and landed in a meeting room, where we finally got some briefing on what was happening. It appeared as though we could not get access to anything, even our own telemetry. Everything was down.

This type of event creates a stressful and demanding environment. The group mobilized and brainstormed potential solutions: irregular communication channels, points of manual intervention, ways to access the control plane of the platform. Twenty very stressful minutes, a couple dozen phone calls, and a handful of great ideas later, we were able to receive a correct assessment and engage the right team to mitigate. The problem was a culmination of multiple small-scale failures that ultimately led to improper DNS configuration. HQ got isolated from the world. We were very fortunate that customer traffic was not interrupted.

Why did we get into this situation? Because we did not expect it. We were siloed. We had been so focused on simulating events inside the datacenter that we completely shut our eyes to possible issues in HQ. Complexity of large-scale infrastructure lies in understanding interactions and dependencies between components. Changes in a single component lead to complex cumulative effects in upstream and downstream peers. Network isolation left us blind and helpless. Understanding the exact effect and scope of the problem was the key to inventorying potential contributing factors and eventually resolving the situation.

Could we have done something to prevent this situation before people started running through hallways? Certainly we can say so with the perfect knowledge of hindsight, but that isn't helpful to prevent future incidents for which we will never have perfect knowledge ahead of time. We missed certain failure scenarios outside our design realm that were related to HQ connectivity failure. The lesson here is that we need to be open to unexpected consequences, and practice recovery as best we can.

Prioritization of Failures

There is no way to identify all possible incidents in advance, much less to cover them all with chaos experiments. There are just too many variables at play within any reasonable-sized software system. To maximize the efficiency of your effort to reduce system failures you should prioritize different classes of incidents. Identify scenarios that are more important for your product and cover them.

Let's look at prioritization approaches as three different properties:

How often does this happen?
> What will regularly happen? Look at the events that are guaranteed or more likely to happen first, such as new version deployments, credentials rotation, daylight savings time changes, traffic pattern changes, and security threats. Think about the variety of failure modes that correspond to each such event. You want to discover failure before the actual event happens, so prioritize the ones for events happening more often than others.
> Let's take credentials rotation as a case study. You must do it some time, so do it often. In fact, do it as often as you can reasonably afford from a cost perspective, rather than dictated by the actual security need. Keep in mind that we get good at things we do often. The opposite is also true. If you have not used your credentials rotation story for half a year or more, how can you be confident that it will work when you need it?

How likely are you to deal with the event gracefully?
> What types of failures do you think you can handle? Try to understand the risks you cannot avoid. There are some failure modes that will take your service down globally and there's not much you can do about it. That will depend on your service architecture and tolerances. For a neighborhood restaurant website, it could be a local power issue. For Microsoft cloud it could be a global-scale natural disaster. In either case, there will be events that you don't need to investigate, since you accept total loss. On the other hand, there will be events you certainly won't allow to take you down. Prioritize experiments against those to make sure your assumptions on reliability and robustness are being met conscientiously and continuously.

How likely is this to happen?
> What are the imminent threats? One-off scheduled events like elections or the Super Bowl, known security vulnerabilities—these are different from regular events in that they do not happen often enough to gain the priority to be regularly checked on. However, once the event is imminent, you must prioritize testing against such events ahead of anything else. An example could be a compromised security cipher. In the past there were a few events where well-known ciphers were compromised by attackers. Looking back at incidents like

that, you can ask: How dependent is your system on communications secured by specific ciphers? What would it take for you to update ciphers used by all components of your system? How would you persist functionality during changeover? How would you communicate with customers? How long would it take? Or should you accept such risk as total loss?

Your answers to these questions should be based on the business needs of your product or service. The satisfaction of reliability goals with respect to business needs should match expectations set with your customers. It's always best to explicitly check with stakeholders whether your plans for reliability land within acceptable margins.

Explore Dependencies

Once you make a list of events that might affect your system, go through the same exercise for your dependencies. In the same way as you did for your product, you need to consider expected events, limits of tolerance, and one-off upcoming threats for the entire dependency chain of your service. It helps if you can reach out to your dependencies' owners and agree to use similar threat modeling and design models. That is not always a possibility, but it is helpful when dependency owners are involved.

Consider that all of these various failures might be experienced by more than one of your dependencies at once. Moreover, some of the dependencies also depend on each other, which might lead to compounded and cascading failures within the system. Compounded failures are harder to diagnose through end-level monitoring and are often overlooked during the design phase. Uncovering the possibility of such failures and charting actual effects on production systems is one of the capabilities of Chaos Engineering. Prioritizing events that have potential compounding impact or unknown impact is one more way to prioritize events in your Chaos Engineering system.

Degree of Variation

Chaos Engineering serves as an instrument to discover real systems behavior and real dependency graphs. While you understand the way your system functions and the value of your dependencies, you might not be able to see the full picture of end-to-end customer experience. With the current rise of microservice architectures often forming dependency clouds[1] too complex for a human to understand, it might be a futile effort to understand all potential variations of dependencies and failover plans at play. Decisions made by component developers in isolation can lead to unforeseen consequences in the grand scheme of things. Classical modeling strategies call for

---

[1] See Chapter 2 for more about the implications of complexity.

design reviews and architectural board meetings; however, this is nowhere scalable, not to mention that a lot of components could be outside of your organization's control altogether.

This makes using combined and compounded failures an important tool in designing Chaos Engineering for your product. By introducing a variety of failure modes, you can discover unknown connections, dependencies, and design decisions. Consider introducing such failures as a research task where you study alien, undocumented, and unfriendly systems that you depend on.

Varying Failures

As you enumerate and prioritize events it is a good idea to consider the degree of variation that you introduce with each experiment. Constraining variation to a single component or a single configuration setting can provide clarity to the setup and outcomes. On the other hand, introducing larger scope changes in the system can be beneficial in learning more complex system behaviors.

For instance, if your goal is to simulate network failure for your component you might be able to introduce such failure at the application protocol layer. Say you can drop connection on the other side, or within the library framework you're using. This provides you with an isolated understanding of cause and effect on your service. However, if network failure happens in real life it is just as likely to happen due to a different level of the ISO-OSI model, a hardware malfunction, a driver failure, or a routing change.

Compare two different routes for injecting failure: on the transport level through shutting down the TCP stack at the machine or plain pulling the wire out of the network card. The latter would be more realistic from a simulating cause-effect perspective. However, it would fail *all* components at the same machine at the same time thus causing combined failure of multiple components. In this case for instance your monitoring component could lose connectivity and would not register any telemetry you're trying to send from this machine, thus making diagnostics of impact harder. Or your load balancer component might behave unpredictably, etc. Combined failures create greater negative impact in the system but can yield greater understanding of actual system interaction.

In addition to combined failures, we should consider compounded ones. These are failures caused upstream or downstream from the subject of your experiment. Compounded failures can be extremely dangerous, as they rapidly increase the blast radius of your experiment. This could expand beyond the control of the experiment framework, breaching the original safety considerations and design assumptions. Don't rely on things working as designed during a drill or Game Day. Analyze your drill plan presuming any part of it might fail. Chaos Engineering assumes controlled experiments that can be reverted, with things brought back in good state. If possible, plan and test your recovery plan before executing an experiment.

Finally, you should consider failures outside of your design realm, for which you accepted total loss. Systems are not expected to cope with such failure. In the best case you expect to fail fast and notify the proper audience. But, you might also be expected to recover. Coming back online after power loss, recovering connections after fiber repair, re-instantiating storage replicas—all of those events should happen properly. Required automated procedures must work, personnel should be trained as needed, and so on. This type of drill is often difficult to automate, and so delayed or put off for that reason. However, these exercises are important because we often incur more damage via failure to recover than during the triggering incident. Experimenting on the global catastrophic failures is often expensive and invasive, but being able to recover efficiently reduces your overall risk and provides greater freedom to experiment with combined and compounded failures.

Combining Variation and Prioritization

When designing your Chaos Engineering system and choosing between isolated, combined, and compounded failures you can apply the same prioritization approach as you took for choosing scenarios to experiment on your own service and your dependencies against:

- What will happen if you opt for compounded failures? Your component performance could certainly fluctuate outside limits allowable by SLA. What else could be impacted? If you are dependent on specific hardware components, does your onsite team provide support at night? Over weekends or holidays? If you depend on upstream service, does it allow complete global failures? If you use an external CDN or traffic shaper, which additional failure modes do you get from that? Do those fit into your failure modes? Do you need to handle any new ones? Only you are responsible for your product. Customers might not care if Microsoft, Amazon, or Akamai made the news; they just want their service back.

- What failures do you think you can handle? Which dependencies can you afford to lose completely? Which can you afford to have in a degraded state and for how long?

- What is an imminent threat? Assume that each of your dependencies will fail at least once, but you also can look at imminent events, such as planned dependency changes. A few examples could be changing a cloud provider or updating to a newer operating system version. If you decided to move to a different dependency, you should run that experiment first.

Expanding Variation to Dependencies

Once you start making progress to cover your dependencies in isolation, you can begin to consider the whole system in motion: each moving part inside and outside your control performing differently and failing at random points in time. This is what the world throws at you. As an example, you know what your dependencies are, so consider what it would look like to have all of your dependencies alternating between the following variables:

- At sustained performance rate within SLA (normal situation). Obviously you should survive this.

- At reduced performance rate but still within SLA (reduced network throughput, increased request drop rate, occasionally unavailable services). You should be able to sustain this for an extended period of time and possibly forever.

- At exactly SLA. This is similar to the preceding point but interesting from the perspective that if such quality of service is not sufficient, you should renegotiate the contract or redesign your system. For instance, if you provide a database service and your upstream provides replica availability of 80% you will not be able to guarantee availability of three replica systems better than 99.2%. The chance for all three to fail simultaneously is a multiplication of probabilities of individual failures, so your availability comes up at $1-0.2^3$. You have an option to renegotiate higher instance availability (say at 90% you could guarantee 99.9%) or add another replica (to get to 99.84%). Depending on your goal and cost your decision may vary.

- Outside of SLA. You must decide if upstream performing outside of SLA or being unavailable constitutes a critical failure for you. Depending on the business case you can decide to consider this a fatal issue, or you might be able to design your system to sustain it for some period. With the database example you might get by using a local cache for a while before giving up.

Combining multiple events of various magnitude, you can learn a ton about the performance of the system under these conditions and reduce surprises in the future.

Deploying Experiments at Scale

Now that your plan is ready to go, you get to put it to work. As noted in other chapters you should start small and minimize the blast radius, as stated in "The Advanced Principles."[2] Keep in mind your prioritization and start by executing the highest priority experiments. Have action plans ready for emergencies. Remember you're not

---

2. See "Advanced Principles" on page 29 in Chapter 3.

doing anything that would not happen in real life. You are accelerating the natural course of events in order to remove surprises.

It is important to understand what type of event you're dealing with. To this end it is crucially important to build up your monitoring and tracing capabilities. There are two parts to that:

- Understanding the system subjected to failure. This will tell you if your experiment is receiving the expected reaction. A key part of this understanding is to make sure that the experiment remains in predefined boundaries. You might define those as a specific failure domain, a specific component, or a specific customer (test account).

- Understanding the overall state of your product. Failures can combine and compound outside of the scope you're looking at, in ways you could not predict and much faster than you anticipated. Any anomaly deserves a second look in this circumstance. It is not uncommon to receive escalation calls and emails during experiment runs. Distinguishing between expected and unexpected outcomes is important.

At Microsoft, the most successful strategy for rolling out a new series of experiments was to assume that once we defined the experiment boundary, we might lose everything inside that boundary at once. At the same time the definition of the boundary had to be rooted in some design assumption that took into account potential cascades. For example, experimenting with multi-replica storage systems you should consider the scenario of complete data unavailability acceptable for accounts included in the experiment. We do not anticipate getting into that situation, but it's not outside the realm of possibility. However, we do not anticipate any impact on other instances of storage.

Suppressing on-call engagements during experiments is a potential tactic to explore systemic effects, but I would advise against it. Exercising the process end to end is important to understand how well it works. If calls are part of the process (of failover, or recovery), they should happen too.

Rolling the chaos experiments from staging to production will introduce multiple new risks. Keep in mind that your Chaos Engineering system is itself a system and is susceptible to the same flaws and failures as the systems under study. You are at risk of losing state, lacking capacity, and generally failing your customer promise of not being too invasive. Subject your own system to the most rigorous experiments of all. Not only will that help to ensure the quality and stability of your product, it will also set the bar for others and supply your own examples of why Chaos Engineering is important.

Conclusion

Foreseeing all possible future events is impossible. The way events will affect your product is unpredictable. We get good at things that we do regularly so plan to run experiments repeatedly in short timeframes. List events that will happen every week. Experiment on those first. If something happens monthly, experiment on it weekly. If it happens weekly, try it daily. If it fails, you'll have six days to figure out a solution. The more often you exercise any scenario the less concerning it becomes.

Known events with expected consequences is the best situation we can hope for. The purpose of varying events in Chaos Engineering is to reduce surprises down the road. Power losses might happen, so let's try emulating power loss daily to make it less scary. OS updates happen monthly, so let's try a version forward or backward a few times a day to see how we handle it. We did all of this in cloud service infrastructure and we became more resilient to failure because of it.

Consider all major challenges for your product with a three-month forecast; for example, traffic spikes, denial-of-service attacks, or customers using a really old client version. Try those today. Plan for all the events you're adding to the system. Plan for recovery from those. Make a plan to use when recovery fails and you need to restore state.

The variability of events in your system will be much higher than you anticipate. The way your dependencies will behave in the face of various triggers is only discoverable through research and experimentation. Prioritizing the right events will make all the difference in the usefulness of Chaos Engineering for your product.

About the Author

Oleg Surmachev spent years working in the Azure cloud infrastructure team, providing toolchain and support for global-scale services in Microsoft. He is an early supporter of the effort to make Chaos Engineering an industry standard. At Microsoft he owns one of the internal Chaos Engineering tools, providing fault injection and a reliable experimentation platform at cloud scale.

CHAPTER 7

LinkedIn Being Mindful of Members

Logan Rosen

Whenever you run a chaos experiment in production, you have the potential to impact users of your product. Without our loyal users, we wouldn't have systems to maintain, so we must put them first while carefully planning our experiments. While some minor impact may be inevitable, it's very important that you minimize the blast radius of a chaos experiment and have a simple recovery plan that can get everything back to normal. In fact, minimizing the blast radius is one of the advanced principles of Chaos Engineering (see Chapter 3). In this chapter, you will learn best practices for adhering to this principle along with a story of how it was implemented within the software industry.

To put this theme in context, let's briefly shift gears to the automotive industry. All modern vehicles undergo rigorous crash testing by manufacturers, third parties, and governments to vet the safety of passengers when they get into accidents. To perform these tests, engineers leverage crash test dummies that simulate the human body and have several sensors to help determine how a crash would impact an actual human.

Automotive crash test dummies have evolved significantly over the past decades. In 2018, the NHTSA came out with Thor, which has been called the most lifelike crash test dummy ever developed. With around 140 data channels, Thor gives engineers rich data on how accidents would impact real humans, and dummies like it are able to give manufacturers and governments confidence in the vehicles that are being put on the market.[1]

---

1 For more information about Thor, see Eric Kulisch's article, "Meet Thor, the More Humanlike Crash-Test Dummy," *Automotive News*, Aug. 13, 2018, *https://oreil.ly/tK8Dc*.

This may seem self-evident: why subject real humans to intentional crashes that test the structural integrity and safety mechanisms of vehicles when you could simulate the impact instead? This same idea carries over to Chaos Engineering for software.

Just as with Thor's several sensors that determine crash impact, engineers have developed several ways over the years to instrument deviations from steady state. Even with limited-scale failure experimentation, we have the ability to see if it causes perturbations in the metrics and impact to the user experience. Experiments should be designed to impact as few people as possible, at least until you're confident enough in your system to handle these failures in similar ways at scale.

Even if you take all of the necessary precautions (and more) to minimize harm to your users during a chaos experiment, there's still the potential for unforeseen impact. As Murphy's law states, "Anything that can go wrong will go wrong." You need a big red button to shut the experiment down if it's causing your application to start misbehaving in ways beyond what is acceptable for your users. It should be as easy as one click of the mouse to return to a steady state.

Learning from Disaster

It's useful to look back at famous incidents of safety experimentation that went awry to help draw conclusions about how we should plan and execute our own chaos experiments. Even if the medium being experimented on is different, we can draw insights from how these experiments went sideways in order to try to prevent us from making similar mistakes and ending up with undesired effects.

The Chernobyl disaster of 1986 is one of the most infamous examples of a catastrophic industrial failure. Workers at the nuclear power plant were carrying out an experiment to see whether the core could still be sufficiently cooled in the event of a power loss. Despite the potential for grave consequences, safety personnel were not present during the experiment, nor did they coordinate with the operators to ensure that their actions would minimize risk.

During the experiment, what was supposed to just be a shutdown of power led to the opposite; the power surged and led to several explosions and fires, leading to radioactive fallout that had catastrophic consequences for the surrounding area.[2] Within a few weeks of the failed experiment, thirty-one people died, two of whom were workers at the plant and the rest of whom were emergency workers who suffered from radiation poisoning.[3]

---

[2] World Nuclear Association, "Chernobyl Accident Appendix 1: Sequence of Events" (updated June 2019), *https://oreil.ly/CquWN*.

[3] World Nuclear Association, "Chernobyl Accident 1986" (updated February 2020), *https://oreil.ly/Bbzcb*.

Postaccident analysis indicates that the system was in an unstable state without appropriate safeguards, and there weren't "adequate instrumentation and alarms to warn and alert the operators of the danger."[4] This multitude of factors led to the disaster we know of today, and there are clear analogues between them and what's involved in planning and executing experiments with software.

Even when the stakes are lower, injecting errors into a website rather than reducing electric power at a nuclear plant, we still need to put our users first in every experiment we perform. When we're performing chaos experiments, we must learn from what happened at Chernobyl and make sure we plan our experiments in a safety-first way that minimizes potential impact to users.

Granularly Targeting Experiments

Chances are, especially if you are only starting to explore implementing Chaos Engineering at your company, you associate the practice with engineers at Netflix shutting down servers or entire datacenters with Chaos Monkey and Chaos Kong. However, they only got to this point by building sufficient robustness into their infrastructure to generally handle these types of failures.

When you're running failure experiments for the first time, it's important to start small. Even shutting down one server can be hard to recover from if your systems aren't built for high availability. Try to architect your experimentation in a way that lets you have a high level of granularity, and target the smallest possible unit, whatever that is in your system.

There are several possible permutations of units of disruption, and they all depend on the software on which you are experimenting. Let's imagine a very simple ecommerce site that sells widgets, which has a frontend that makes REST calls to a backend service that talks to a database (Figure 7-1). If you'd like to perform application-level disruption, you'll probably want to see what happens when your frontend has issues with specific calls to your backend.

Let's say the backend exposes APIs for products, carts, and orders, each with their own methods (GET a product, POST to add to a cart, etc.). For each of these calls that the frontend makes to the backend, there should generally be a context of a customer, which can be anything from a person to a company that is shopping for widgets.

---

4 Najmedin Meshkati, "Human Factors in Large-Scale Technological Systems' Accidents: Three Mile Island, Bhopal, Chernobyl," *Industrial Crisis Quarterly*, Vol. 5, No. 2 (June 1991).

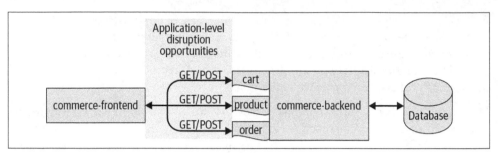

Figure 7-1. Diagram of simple ecommerce application

Even in this very simple application, there are multiple ways you could trigger a disruption—combinations of API call failures with combinations of users. Taking the start-small approach, though, you can begin to investigate the failure paths of your system without invoking mass disruption for all of your users.

Ideally, you can start experimenting with failures for just API calls with your user in the context. This way, you can validate failures on a small scale without the fear of wide-scale impact.[5] Let's say that you want to see what the user experience is when your frontend cannot make a GET call to the backend cart API. First, it helps to think about what the optimal experience should be for the customer when this happens; do you want to show an error page that asks the user to try again? Maybe you want to retry the call automatically, or you possibly want to show a fallback experience containing products that the customer might want to look at in the meantime while you fix your API.

You can invoke a failure for your user with this context and see what happens when you try to add a widget to your cart and the API call times out. It might match what you think should or does happen when this failure occurs, or it might show you an opportunity to improve robustness or the quality of the customer experience.

This is, of course, a contrived example based on a simple system where you might engineer or leverage a chaos experimentation framework that allows you to disrupt REST calls on a very targeted level. That's not always possible, especially depending on how much you're willing to invest in your Chaos Engineering or the limitations of the system on which you are experimenting.

Maybe the granularity you can choose is all communication to or from a specific port on a given host. Even at this level, you are still avoiding greater-scale consequences from your experiment, since the worst that will happen is that a single host is not responding to requests. As long as you stay small, you minimize your blast radius.

---

5 Ted Strzalkowski, an SRE on the Waterbear team, gave an informative presentation (*https://oreil.ly/eu44v*) on how to trigger disruptions in a small Flask application.

Experimenting at Scale, Safely

So, you've verified your system's robustness against a wide array of failures, or maybe just a particular failure about which you were specifically concerned. What's next? Naturally, the inclination will be to start running these failure experiments at scale and seeing if your system still reacts in a healthy way. It makes sense to experiment with failures at scale; sometimes, depending on how your system is architected, it may react in a different way to one request failing than to a multitude experiencing the same failure.

Maybe your cache is picking up the slack when you cause a timeout for calls to your database, but you want to make sure it can handle *all* calls to the database failing. Or maybe your system might respond differently to one failure happening at scale versus multiple disruptions impacting different parts of it. Certain disruptions may lead to cascading failures throughout your system that you weren't able to reproduce when just causing failures for your experiment user.

It's clear that experimenting at scale is important—but this comes with significant risks that should be accounted for before experimentation occurs beyond your small subset of requests. Whenever you're experimenting with failures at any scale, it's important to be aware of your system's steady state and consequently any deviations from it, but it's of utmost criticality when failures could lead to catastrophic effects for the users of your system. The key takeaways of the steady-state principle are that you should always have an eye on your metrics and be able to quickly terminate an experiment if anything seems to be going wrong in unexpected and impactful ways. By having planned criteria for when to abort your experiment, you can mitigate impact more quickly and reduce the time to resolve any incidents caused.

If there's a way to automate your chaos experimentation to immediately stop if there's a deviation in your metrics leading to issues with your system that would impact users, all the better to help ensure safety. Although a chaos experimentation framework may not be able to catch all unanticipated issues caused by an experiment, adding logic to terminate based on clear signals can lower the frequency and length of customer-impacting incidents.

Regardless of the automation built into your framework, the big red button to shut down experiments immediately, as mentioned earlier, is a key component of any chaos experimentation. This "button" can come in many forms, depending on how you're performing your experiments. It could be anything from a kill -9 command to a series of API calls; as long as it's able to return your environment to a steady state, it fits the bill.

If the failure you've injected into your system is causing real issues, you need to shut it down before it leads to significant user impact or revenue and trust loss. Some impact is okay, but lengthened impact can drive people away from your software.

Of course, there's some nuance in terms of what qualifies as a degraded experience for users that should lead to the termination of your experimentation, depending on factors including the size of your userbase that's impacted and how much it inhibits core functionality. Finding this threshold will likely involve collaboration between several teams, including product owners and engineers. It's important to have these discussions before starting experimentation so that you know how to weigh different kinds of failures against the user experience.

In Practice: LinkedOut

As a site reliability engineer (SRE) at LinkedIn who has worked on bringing Chaos Engineering to our organization, I've spent a significant amount of time trying to engineer our failure experimentation framework to adhere to the Principles of Chaos Engineering (*https://principlesofchaos.org*), especially minimizing the blast radius via granular experimentation capabilities. Our request-level failure injection framework, LinkedOut,[6] as part of the Waterbear project,[7] has led to significant changes in how engineers at LinkedIn write and experiment on their software, but they are only comfortable using it because they know that they can easily avoid wide impact to users.

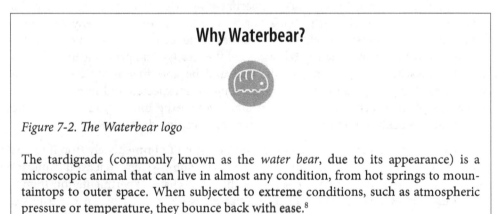

Why Waterbear?

Figure 7-2. The Waterbear logo

The tardigrade (commonly known as the *water bear*, due to its appearance) is a microscopic animal that can live in almost any condition, from hot springs to mountaintops to outer space. When subjected to extreme conditions, such as atmospheric pressure or temperature, they bounce back with ease.[8]

They represent well the robustness that we'd like to see in our services and can experiment on with tools like LinkedOut.

---

6 Logan Rosen, "LinkedOut: A Request-Level Failure Injection Framework," LinkedIn Engineering, May 24, 2018, *https://oreil.ly/KkhdS*.

7 Bhaskaran Devaraj and Xiao Li, "Resilience Engineering at LinkedIn with Project Waterbear," LinkedIn Engineering, Nov. 10, 2017, *https://oreil.ly/2tDRk*.

8 Cornelia Dean, "The Tardigrade: Practically Invisible, Indestructible 'Water Bears,'" *The New York Times*, Sept. 7, 2015.

In building a request disruption framework for LinkedIn, we had the benefit of a standardized, open sourced REST framework, Rest.li (*https://oreil.ly/7k1c_*), used in most production applications at the company. Having predictable interservice communication simplified the design of LinkedOut and allowed it to have significant impact across our stack. Also of extreme benefit is Rest.li's pluggable architecture, which has customizable filter chains that are evaluated on every request and response.

Within these chains, an engineer or service owner can add a filter that has complete context on what is going in and out of the client or server and manipulate the request or response as needed. This context includes what service made the call, what resource the call is targeting, what method is being used, and other relevant data.

It seemed fitting, given this, to write a Rest.li disruptor within the default filter chain that can inject failures into requests on the client side. The disruptor allows us to have all of the context provided by the Rest.li framework in choosing when and how to disrupt requests, which helps us minimize the blast radius by granularly targeting our experiments.

We chose to start with client-side disruption because it lowers the barrier of entry to chaos experimentation—instead of causing failures in a downstream service, you have total control simulating them in your client—and it also minimizes risk. If you were to add a delay to several requests in the downstream servlet, you might tie up all of its threads and cause it to fall over completely. Instead, simulating disruption in the client, while it might not give the entire picture of what delayed requests would do to all services involved, allows for validation of the client-side impact while reducing potential harm to the services you rely on.

Failure Modes

In choosing failure modes for the disruptor, we focused on those that are indicative of the failures that we see day to day as on-call SREs and would represent most issues with which internet-scale companies contend. We intentionally stayed away from modifying response bodies (e.g., changing the response codes or creating malformed content) since we knew that is better suited for integration test territory and presents a security risk. These failure modes, conversely, are simple but powerful and are great predictors of how LinkedIn's applications would respond to real failures.

We consequently built three failure modes into the disruptor:

Error
> The first mode is *error*. Coming in all shapes and forms, errors are probably the most prevalent issues that are dealt with by on-call SREs. The Rest.li framework has several default exceptions thrown when there are communication or data issues with the requested resource. We trigger a generic Java exception within the

filter to mock unavailability of the resource, which bubbles up as a `RestliResponseException`.

LinkedOut users can also set an amount of latency to inject before throwing the exception. This functionality allows for the simulation of the time it might take for a downstream service to process a request before throwing an error. This also allows engineers to avoid odd deviations in their client-side latency metrics, where the downstream service suddenly starts processing requests in no time at all.

Delay
The second failure mode is *delay*; you can pass in an amount of latency, and the filter will delay the request for that much time before passing it on downstream. This is also a common on-call issue, where a downstream service slows down, potentially due to database or other dependent service issues. Delays can cause cascading failures in a service-oriented architecture, so it's important to understand their impact on the stack.

Timeout
Last but not least is *timeout*, which holds the request for a configured amount of time until the Rest.li client throws a `TimeoutException`. This failure mode leverages the configured timeout setting for the endpoint being disrupted, which allows LinkedOut to expose timeouts that are overly long and could be tuned to improve the user experience.

Being able to choose between the error, delay, and timeout failure modes in Linked-Out gives engineers significant control over their experiments in a way that can accurately simulate real production incidents. We know exactly how these modes behave and can consequently have confidence in the magnitude of the blast whose radius we are limiting.

Using LiX to Target Experiments

Having the LinkedOut disruption filter in the Rest.li filter chain allows us to hook into our internal experimentation and targeting framework, LiX (Figure 7-3). This framework allows us to have very high granularity in choosing who is affected by our experiments and provides APIs that allow for a first-class targeting experience via a custom UI, including the ability to terminate experiments on-demand via a "big red button."

This integration was the first mechanism we built to trigger failure experiments, since the LiX framework allows us to specify whom should be affected by any given experiment. We built a schema that ties into the concept of LiX "treatments" and describes how exactly a failure should occur, and for whom (Figure 7-3).

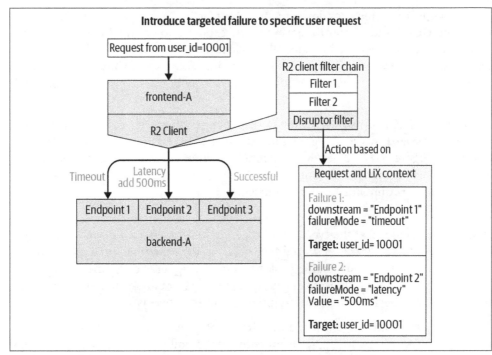

Figure 7-3. Diagram of LiX-based disruption mechanism in LinkedOut

LiX is an extremely powerful platform. It can use what are called selectors to target segments of our member population, from one individual member to all members who live in the United States and speak English, to specific percentages of all of our members. With this power comes great responsibility and the necessity of extreme caution in setting up experiments, since a misplaced digit or letter might lead to impact that you did not intend from ramping your experiment.

It became clear to us very quickly that a good UI matters in terms of ensuring that we provide ease of mind to those using our platform. In early 2018, a nuclear missile alert was sent erroneously to residents of Hawaii, causing widespread terror. In what was supposed to be a routine drill, a real alert was sent out instead of a test one. While later reports indicated that the worker legitimately thought there was an inbound missile,[9] investigations into the incident revealed a user interface that was designed in a way that could easily lead to false alarms.

In screenshots provided by Hawaii government officials that emulated the real UI used by workers, the link for sending a test alert was placed right above the link for

---

9 Cecelia Kang, "Hawaii Missile Alert Wasn't Accidental, Officials Say, Blaming Worker," *The New York Times*, Jan. 30, 2018.

real alerts, in the same dropdown menu.[10] By placing these items so close to each other, the UI failed to support the way people expected to use the interface. Regardless of whether the worker intentionally clicked the link to send a real alert to residents or not, there's a clear lesson here: user interfaces should make sense to the people using them, especially for critical work. Clarity in user experience goes a long way.

Even though LiX had its own UI for targeting experiments, we determined that the best path forward was to design a LinkedOut-specific failure experiment targeting interface (Figure 7-4). It provides intentionally limited options in terms of how widely you can ramp an experiment, specifically only to employees who have signed into our tool and provided explicit consent to have failure experiments targeted to them.

If someone decides that they've verified a LinkedIn service's robustness against specific failures at a small scale and would like to ramp the experiment to a greater population, it requires manual editing of the underlying LiX experiment and close collaboration with the Waterbear team. We believe it's important to have checks and balances here, especially when the happiness of our members is at stake.

We consciously limit targeting to LinkedIn employees in the UI, even though the underlying LiX framework supports targeting real members, because we believe that product owners can get significant value from internal experiments without risking production-impacting incidents. Furthermore, if we were to allow employees to target members via our UI, we'd want to build in protections to automatically terminate experiments when there are clear deviations from steady state. Technology like this is available in the Redliner capacity experimentation tool at LinkedIn,[11] so there may be an opportunity for collaboration in the future if this feature is prioritized and requested by our customers.

There is, of course, the possibility for smaller-scale experiments to go wrong as well; as such, we leverage the LiX framework's ability to immediately terminate any given experiment and give LinkedOut users the power to do so within our UI. With the click of a button, an employee can instantly send a signal to terminate the LiX experiment across our production stack, which converges within minutes. Even though the blast radius is already inherently quite small for the experiments we permit by default, our "big red button" allows for easy termination when there's unintended impact.

---

10 Colin Lecher, "Here's How Hawaii's Emergency Alert Design Led to a False Alarm," *The Verge*, Jan. 28, 2018, *https://oreil.ly/Nqb59*.

11 Susie Xia and Anant Rao, "Redliner: How LinkedIn Determines the Capacity Limits of Its Services," LinkedIn Engineering, Feb. 17, 2017, *https://oreil.ly/QxSlJ*.

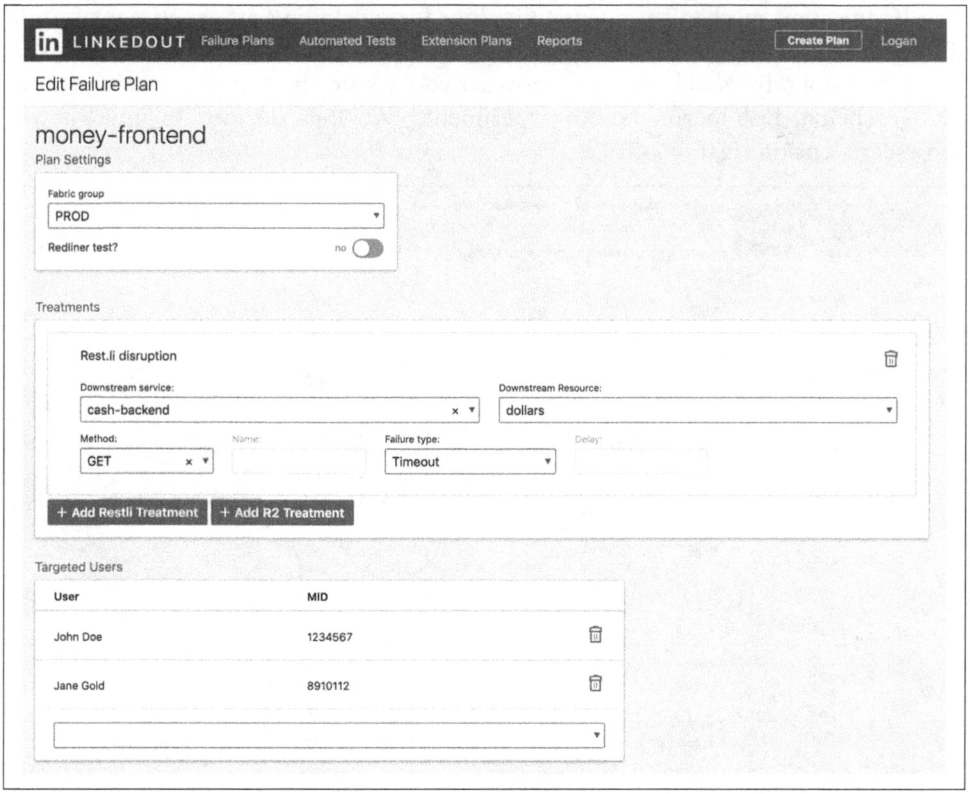

Figure 7-4. A screenshot of our custom LinkedOut failure plan targeting UI

Browser Extension for Rapid Experimentation

While our LiX-based offering is great for targeting multiple users and experimentation at scale, we realized that another component of a successful failure experimentation framework was missing: the ability to rapidly experiment on failures in your own browser, without having to wait for changes to experiments to propagate across the production stack. A big part of Chaos Engineering is exploration, or trying different failures out to see what the impact is to your system, and our A/B testing–based solution is a bit too heavy for that type of quick iteration.

We consequently added another mechanism to inject failures into requests, via the Invocation Context (IC). The IC is a LinkedIn-specific internal component of the Rest.li framework that allows keys and values to be passed into requests and propagated to all of the services involved in handling them. We built a new schema for disruption data that can be passed down through the IC, and then failures would instantly happen for that request.

The IC injection mechanism opened the door for quick, one-off experimentation in the browser by injecting IC disruption data via a cookie. But we took a reasonable guess that nobody would want to construct cookies on their own, adhering to our JSON schema, just to run failure experiments. We thus decided to build a web browser extension (Figure 7-5).

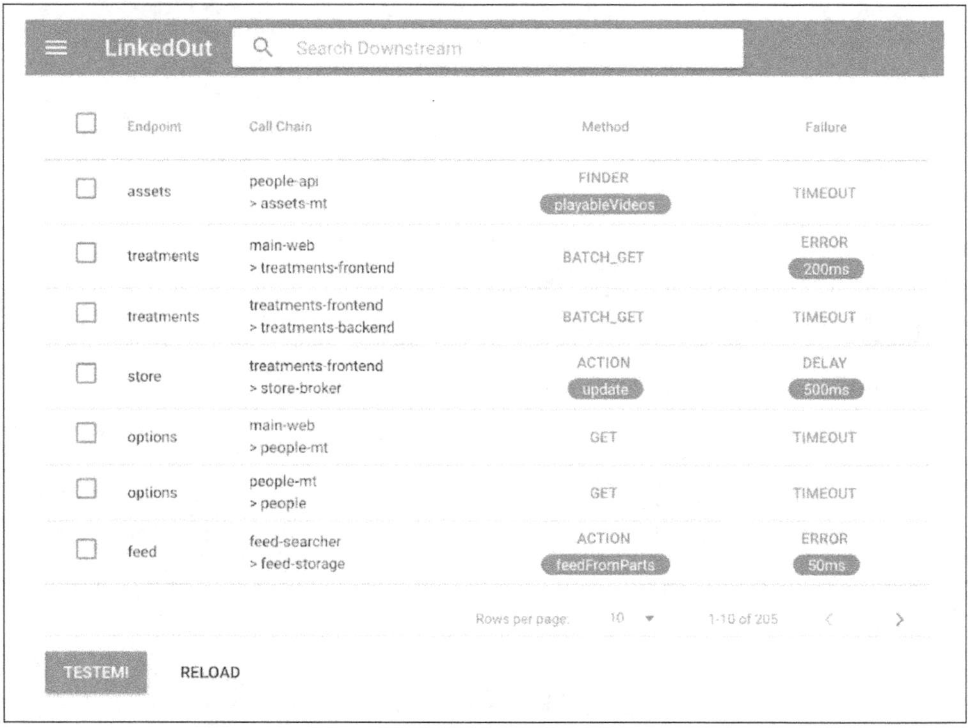

Figure 7-5. The LinkedOut browser extension

We developed a simple flow for experimenting with failures, given how we envisioned people would want to quickly run chaos experiments in their browser:

1. Click a button to discover all of the services involved in the request.
2. Select the services for which you want to inject failures.
3. Click a button to refresh the page with those failures injected.

To discover the downstreams, we leverage request tracing via an internal framework called Call Tree, which allows engineers to set a grouping key as a cookie with their requests, linking together all the downstream calls it discovered. Consequently, we designed the browser extension to refresh the page with the Call Tree grouping key cookie set, discover the downstreams involved, and then display them in the UI (Figure 7-6).

There can be several services involved in a request at LinkedIn—in fact, there can be hundreds. So we added a search box that lets the user quickly filter to the endpoints/ services that they care about. And, due to the granularity in the disruption filter, users are able to, for a given endpoint, inject a failure for only a specific Rest.li method.

Once the user selects failure modes for all applicable resources, the extension creates a disruption JSON blob for these failures, sets a cookie to inject it into the IC, and then refreshes the page with the failure applied. It's a very seamless experience with little work required on behalf of the user.

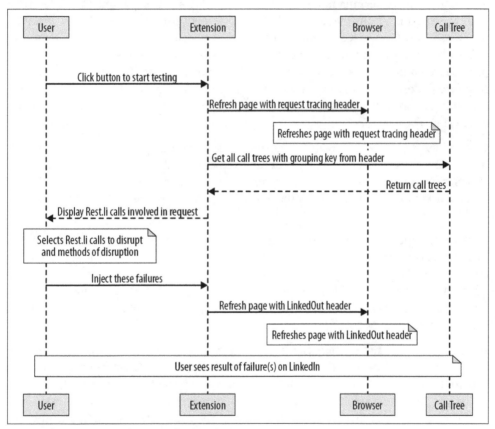

Figure 7-6. Sequence diagram for browser extension

The best part of the browser extension is that the blast radius is essentially nonexistent—by only allowing employees to target request-level failures in their own browser, it limits the impact of said failures to just them. If they fail a request from our homepage to the API that serves the LinkedIn feed, it will only break their experience in their session, not anyone else's. It's simple to reverse the impact by clicking a button in the extension.

Automated Experimentation

On top of the aforementioned methods of triggering failures in LinkedOut, our platform also provides an automated experimentation framework that limits the blast radius in a similar way to that of the browser extension, with one slight twist. While the browser extension involves experimenting on your own session and affects your user only, our automated experimentation solely affects a service account, or synthetic user, to validate the effects of triggering failures.

The automated experimentation in LinkedOut allows a user to put in a URL they wish to experiment on, the failures they wish to apply to each downstream involved in the call tree, the service account to use for the experiment (in case they need to use one with special permissions), and criteria for matching failures. While LinkedOut provides default criteria for matching against "oops" pages, blank pages, and bad response codes, which indicate a severe degradation in site functionality, there's also the ability to specify exactly what constitutes a degradation in your product's experience via DOM selectors.

Once an automated experiment is triggered, there's absolutely no impact to real members. It first discovers all of the services involved in the call tree for the requested URL at this moment, as the call graph can change over time, and then it tells a pool of Selenium workers to log in as the synthetic user and inject failures on this request via a cookie.

When the experiment finishes, the user is provided with a report containing the injected disruptions and whether they caused the page to fail against the specified criteria (Figure 7-7). It also provides screenshots of the disrupted experience to show what a real member would see if the failure occurred in production; employees find this feature extremely useful for validating the failure criteria they've chosen for their experiments.

In this report, product owners can mark certain downstreams as known critical: this is done if graceful degradation of their data is counter to product requirements and should lead to an error state if not received as expected. Sometimes, it's next to impossible to give a member a good experience when a critical service fails. In this scenario, we want to give product owners the ability to mark these edges in the call graph as critical and exclude them from the failures in future reports.

Our experimentation is also automated in the sense that it can be scheduled to run on a regular basis: daily, weekly, or monthly. By scheduling these experiments, product owners can become aware of any regressions or fixes when it comes to robustness against downstream failures in their services. On the roadmap is the ability to trigger automated tests upon a release of new code, which will give developers further signal into how their changes are impacting resiliency.

Automated Test - https://www.linkedin.com/testendpoint/				
Hide Known Critical Downstreams	Off		Total Endpoints	50
Hide Passed Tests	Off		Incompatible ⑦	2
			Critical ⑦	3
			Total Tests	58
			Failed Tests	2
			Passed Tests	56

Client Service	Resource ⑦	Failure Type ⑦	Result	Critical ⑦
books-frontend	authors-mt / authors	Timeout	Passed	🔵
authors-mt	libraries-backend / libraries	Timeout	Failed	🔵
authors-mt	locations-backend locations	Timeout	Passed	🔵

Figure 7-7. An example automated experiment report

LinkedOut's automated experimentation is a key component in how it allows for low-touch investigation of the robustness of our services on a regular basis with intuitive reporting capabilities. In limiting the experiment to a service account or test user, it minimizes the blast radius and avoids impact to LinkedIn members.

Conclusion

Even the most carefully planned experiments can have unintended consequences, so you must have the right safeguards in place to terminate an experiment and limit impact to users. The safest option is always to experiment on a small scale, especially when the potential ramifications of your experimentation on users are unknown.

Hopefully the examples of how LinkedOut does this—via limited targeting with LiX, rapid in-browser experimentation with the browser extension, and automated experimentation against service accounts—can inspire you to try similar ideas within your own system. By emphasizing the targeting of only employees, we're still able to get a high signal in our failure experimentation without risking bad experiences for our members.

LinkedOut's ease of use and features have helped lead to a shift in emphasizing robustness in writing new software at LinkedIn, and it continues to help validate the failsafes that engineers build into their applications. Our current and planned automated experimentation features can assist product owners in making sure that their services continue to be robust against failures throughout the stack.

Experimenting at scale is important as well, once you've validated robustness against failures within a smaller radius. When you have the potential to impact many people with your experiment, you should keep a close eye on your metrics and be able to terminate your experiment quickly if there's any deviation from steady state. If you are to run several experiments at scale, it's strongly encouraged to build in automatic protections to terminate experiments when there's unexpected impact to your business metrics and member experience.

About the Author

Logan Rosen is a staff site reliability engineer at LinkedIn in New York. As one of the founding members of the Waterbear project, he helped implement LinkedOut, a request-level failure injection framework, and introduce Chaos Engineering to the organization.

CHAPTER 8

Capital One Adoption and Evolution of Chaos Engineering

Raji Chockaiyan

Chaos Engineering provides a point of view of embracing failure and learning about the system's weakness from those failures. In the cloud native environment, this way of developing software cannot be ignored. Cloud native systems accept that failure can happen at any time and we will need to engineer and build robust systems that can withstand a full range of failures. Compared to industries that have less regulation, software in the financial services sector comes with a few more layers of complexity to take into consideration. During a system failure, a single parent could be applying for a loan for their first house, another customer might be trying to transfer funds using their mobile device, and a student could be applying for their first credit card to start building credit history. Depending on the size of the failure, the impact would range from a mild annoyance to bitter detachment to the brand, negatively reflecting on the reputation of the financial institution and potentially affecting the business.

Additionally, there are governing bodies related to how banks do their business. Necessary audit trails need to be maintained and submitted periodically to financial regulators, including the Office of the Comptroller of the Currency (OCC), the Consumer Financial Protection Bureau (CFPB), FinCEN, the Federal Trade Commission, and the Department of Justice. The effect is any change in the production environment has to have a clear audit trail on why, how, and when. Banks have put in required governance processes and tools in collecting and submitting this evidence to the appropriate authorities. That process has legal implications and must not be affected by efforts or tooling like Chaos Engineering.

On the other hand, with the rise of digital banks and neobanks,[1] the way customers interact with their money is changing. Financial capabilities powered by blockchain, AI, machine learning, and business intelligence has exposed the need for highly robust and scalable systems that the cloud infrastructure provides. This drives an evolution in software development methodologies and the need to bake in the right engineering practices into their way of working. Just like automated deployments have improved feature velocity, and immutable infrastructure makes sure the deployed servers are never altered, the systems need to be continuously validated for reliability. This provides an entry point for Chaos Engineering. There are multiple approaches to getting started. For some it could be reactive and for others it could come from the inside out, built in the company's DNA. This chapter covers how Capital One embraced and evolved Chaos Engineering, and discusses factors you must take into account during such endeavors; we'll review things to watch out for while designing an experiment for FinTech, how tooling plays an important role in creating necessary audit trails, and necessary metrics to capture while running an experiment.

A Capital One Case Study

Capital One, the largest direct bank[2] in the United States, is known for being a data and tech pioneer in the financial services industry and is seven years into a massive digital transformation. They have solved challenges nearest to the hearts of American enterprises: how to harness digital technologies, real-time analytics, and machine learning to transform the business and customer experience. They have comprehensively reinvented their talent, culture, and technology infrastructure by building cloud native apps and building tools to bake in sophisticated engineering practices like CI/CD pipelines, templated frameworks with built-in compliance and regulations standards, secret management, and Chaos Engineering.

Blind Resiliency Testing

Chaos Engineering has been in practice at Capital One since before the cloud journey started in full swing. One of the core API platforms that serves mobile and web portals adopted this practice and mindset when it was still hosted in physical datacenters. Speaking with Geetha Gopal, the technology leader at Capital One, the motivation for implementing a Chaos Engineering program started with a need to fully understand all the factors—internal, external, application, hardware, integration points—that could affect the service uptime. They called it "Blind Resiliency Testing." In 2013, they

---

1 A *neobank* is a type of direct bank that is entirely digital and serves its customers only through mobile apps and computer platforms

2 A *direct bank* is a bank that provides its service remotely. Its online presence is larger than its physical branches.

formed two groups who would be responsible for the orchestration: the *disruption group* and the *response group*.

Interestingly, neither of these groups is an application team supporting the core API platform. Cybersecurity and monitoring teams are also invited to participate in these exercises, held at regular intervals, once a month or after every release. The intent was to make sure the exercises are done and observed objectively. They started with a list of around 25 experiments. The disruption team picked two at random and executed them while the response team simply monitored, responded, and documented the results. The experiments were triggered from the DMZ using multiple synthetic accounts that generated load. This was all done in a nonproduction environment. Over the next few years, the number of experiments would increase, and the group started seeing tangible results: a smaller number of incident-inducing changes in production and the ability to react to external and hardware failures quickly. Their focus was always on the backend services where they saw potential failure points.

Transition to Chaos Engineering

Fast-forward to 2018. This same team from the core API is running their platform exclusively on the cloud and experiments are running in the production environment. This time around, they are called chaos experiments. They use a homegrown chaos experiment tool that helps them schedule recurring experiments and trigger them automatically at the scheduled time and interval. They run every single experiment in their nonproduction environment making sure all the failure points are discovered and fixed before moving everything into production. Because of this, most of their learning outcomes come from running nonproduction experiments.

Oftentimes companies and engineering teams struggle with prioritizing these engineering excellence goals against the business capabilities that have direct commercial ROIs. One of the success metrics is reduction of call volume. The more experiments the platform passes, the fewer incidents in production, leading to fewer calls due to things like login issues. This is easily converted into a dollar value (for instance, number of customer service representatives that get involved, the time spent by the on-call developer in troubleshooting and resolving the issues) and thus a tangible success measure to monitor. As a result, business partners within Capital One now have a vested interest in performing these experiments. For the developers, fewer support calls serve as an incentive to prioritize chaos experiments. Some of the other metrics that matter in this case are latency, service error rate, failover time, autoscaling duration, and resource saturation like CPU and memory.

This core API platform team has an interesting take on alerting and monitoring. Receiving an alert during an experiment means their system failed the experiment, because the expectation of the robust system is such that the requests should have been failed over to the alternate cloud region or autoscaling should have kicked off.

These experiments and results are also reviewed periodically with regulators and auditors, due to the criticality of the learnings from these experiments. This has become a fundamental part of their reliability journey. They also started a community of practice for Chaos Engineers in the enterprise. This is a forum for all the teams that are already looking into performing these experiments to come together as a group and share what they are learning.

Chaos Experiments in CI/CD

There are other teams who have taken Chaos Engineering and integrated it into their normal software development life cycle as well. For them, keeping it as a cool new technology to play with was insufficient. Some of these services are serving more than ten thousand transactions per second on any given day. Some act as integration layers between two core systems at Capital One. Highly resilient, scalable, available systems and APIs are a basic necessity. These teams adopt Chaos Engineering to gain confidence that their systems are resilient and can meet their business objectives.

They start with an in-depth analysis of their design decisions looking for potential failure points. They then verify those utilizing chaos experiments that are triggered as part of their CI/CD pipelines. Capital One has a very mature pipeline process with baked-in compliance and regulation requirements like the Sarbanes-Oxley Act (SOX) and security. The teams who provide recorded evidence that they are meeting these requirements are pre-approved to release their code to production without any manual intervention.

Some teams trigger the experiments for their infrastructure as part of their CI/CD process. They test the reliability of the new infrastructure stack as soon as it is provisioned and before the traffic is switched over to the new codebase, which allows them to make sure the infrastructure is scalable and robust to the conditions in the experiment. Another team incorporated the experiments as part of the performance testing tool, so that they can validate the robustness at peak load. Their main intention with this approach is validating their autoscaling and region failover design decisions. With this, their p99 metrics (commonly used percentile metric) are collected and validated before switching the traffic over completely.

Capital One's platform team provides necessary support and tooling capabilities for these teams and their varying use cases. The customers (both our internal development teams and our end consumers of the bank's services) are the North Star, and every decision is made with an intention to make things better for them. These teams have adopted Chaos Engineering in their own way to achieve highly resilient systems ultimately for the sake of customer experience.

Things to Watch Out for While Designing the Experiment

Designing a thoughtful chaos experiment often takes more time and resources than developing a feature. Until the system is ready to take chaos experiments in production, running this in the lower-level environment that mimics production can also incur additional costs. Tasks such as setting up a production-like environment with needed capacity and making sure the dependent services are available take time and effort. Accounting for that in planning is important in the early stages of adopting this practice. The ability to create templates for basic disruption and design experiments based on that template helps tremendously in successive runs, though it does take significant upfront investment. For example, if bringing down a host machine to test the autoscaling setup is one of the most commonly and frequently run disruptions, then providing a configurable template for the teams to use can save time and effort.

When designing the experiments during the early stages, having a good understanding of and documentation on the following will help the team gain confidence in running the experiment:

- Clear documentation of the expected behavior
- Potential/possible failures
- Impact to in-flight transactions
- Monitoring of the infrastructure and application
- Criticality of that specific failure point you are trying to validate
- Risk score for each experiment

Once the experiments run, documenting the observed behavior both from the system and business perspective is critical.

In a nonproduction environment, it is normal to perform these experiments during the day so that the entire team is available if something goes wrong. In financial services companies, the stakes are high for any failure, induced or not. If the experiments are being performed in production, it is important to pick a time that is suitable for your application where the impact is minimal or nonexistent, in case a new failure point is identified during the experiment.

Maintaining a clean audit trail of events is very important for any experiment involving synthetic customer information or business transaction, such as: who scheduled this experiment, whether it was approved to be executed in that specific environment, whether the system subjected to the experiment fails as a result, what notification and escalation procedures are set up to handle the issue and avoid customer impact, and so on. This helps with the holistic picture. This is in addition to logging and/or tracing, which are more informative of application health and state.

When teams start experimenting with Chaos Engineering, they start small, like yanking an instance inside an autoscaling group in a nonproduction environment. It is usually done manually with some team members monitoring and documenting the entire process. As they scale up, the support can take a toll. The change management pain points can be alleviated by:

- Automating these experiments with a reliable tool.
- Setting up proper monitoring and alerting.
- Developing a support plan for the teams as they progress in their journey.

Tooling

There are three major operational steps involved in Chaos Engineering:

1. Design experiments that can validate a very specific design assumption that you have made architecting your system.
2. Execute (scheduling and triggering) those experiments as per the plan.
3. Observe the results of the experiments.

All of these steps can very well be done manually. But the benefit of Chaos Engineering comes when it is done repetitively and at scale. For that, having a proper tool that simplifies these three procedures is necessary.

There are both open sourced and licensed enterprise tools available that can do the job. The majority of them focus on infrastructure and network-related disruptions that can be injected into the environment of choice. Some of them also provide a dashboard to understand what happened when that experiment is triggered. A benefit of reusing an existing tool is not to reinvent the wheel and instead focus the energy and time on building business capabilities.

Some companies choose to build their own tools for a number of reasons and requirements. Having the right talent, budget, and core competency are a few of the factors that need to be considered. Capital One has also built its own tool for Chaos Engineering. An all-in approach to microservices architecture required a higher level of enterprise-wide resiliency than that offered in third-party tools. Resilience is a necessary core competency for Capital One, as is security and risk management. Bringing this competency in-house helped them build a Chaos Engineering platform that can meet these requirements as well as address compliance. The intent, execution, and observation all can be controlled in-house completely so any risk of data leaving their network is prevented. Also, if there is any specific audit reporting required after the experiment is run, that can be built in to the tool.

Using an internal SaaS tool, the data does not leave their enterprise. All the integrations stay within their enterprise network. This helps to mitigate some security risks such as exposure of encrypted data that might come up. Customized experiments that are specific to banking functionality (such as those that could disrupt some core transactions) can be added on top of basic network saturation, server shutdown, or a database lockdown. Since both the tooling and the application teams work with the same goal, prioritizing these customizations can be done quickly with a shorter feedback loop in contrast to when they have to interface with external third-party companies.

Observability and audit trail are as important as the ability to design customized experiments in banking. In fact, this is extremely critical even in a nonregulated environment. A failure due to experimentation has to be known and tracked for troubleshooting and learning. Collecting necessary data from the tool and the applications' logs and traces before, during, and after the experiments helps teams to meet the compliance needs (ability to differentiate between real and induced failures), create reports on the health of the infrastructure, and identify the difference between the observed and expected behavior and potential impact to the inflight transactions for further analysis.

In summary, choosing the right tool for Chaos Engineering that aligns with your company's business and operational objective is important. Once the tool is in place, supportability of that tool with the right team structure becomes critical for the adoption and success of the practice.

Team Structure

If an organization decides to build their own tools, it is crucial that the structure of the Chaos Engineering team closely aligns with the company's culture and way of working, as this will contribute heavily to the success and adoption of the tool and practices. The most commonly adopted model by enterprise teams is to have a core Agile team of full stack engineers and a product manager to build the tool. This team is well equipped with Chaos Engineering concepts and experiment designing skill sets. There are some caveats with this model, however: for example, only the core team is responsible for building all the capabilities, and there could be a backlog of capabilities that would not get prioritized due to limited number of person hours. In addition, this team lacks expertise in the functional and business domain of the system. While they can read logs and traces, they may not be able to accurately observe the business context of how the system reacted to the disruption.

Establishing a consistent working channel with other stakeholders (including cybersecurity, cloud engineering, compliance, auditing and governance, and monitoring and observability teams) is critical to a successful Chaos Engineering journey. This is often overlooked and must be implemented from the beginning.

Some companies who are further along in their Agile journey try to experiment and come up with creative and sustainable structure. Capital One, for example, believes in co-creation of software. Besides having a core team, they also have a dedicated engineer or group of engineers from an application team who can be assigned to work with the core team on understanding the onboarding and usage of the Chaos Engineering platform. They would be working with the core team experts in identifying the failure points of their application architecture and designing the experiment according to what they want to uncover. This can be done via various channels such as Game Days, community of practice meetings, or simple one-on-one workshops. Once the experiments are scheduled, the dedicated team members observe and analyze the system for anomalies and document their takeaways. If any tool support is needed, then the core tooling team is contacted.

If there are any capabilities specific to their architecture that they need from tooling, they would develop that feature and create a pull request for the tooling team to merge. This way, the application teams are not stuck waiting for the tool to be updated, and at the same time, they can innovate and make their contributions available for enterprise use. This also prevents another major pitfall: tool duplication. In large enterprises, however well connected the teams are, due to the innovative nature of today's software engineering skill sets, the same problem is bound to be solved by multiple teams simultaneously, resulting in tool proliferation, which incurs further cost and management issues. Having teams contribute their innovations helps with tool consolidation. Their work can also involve templated experiments that other teams can use and benefit from.

Evangelism

As with any successful technology or a development practice, there will always be notable interest at the grassroots level. Turning this into a scalable and consistent momentum takes influence, clear strategies across both horizontal and vertical levels, tooling to simplify the process, and a platform to share the success stories among the engineering, business, and compliance teams. Conducting focused Game Days, workshops, and webinars are some ways of evangelizing the practice.

In the community of practice that one team in Capital One started within the organization, they pulled in engineers with the same interest from different divisions. They created a knowledge base with a collection of information, including "how to get started" guides, available tools, Game Day samples, resilience best practices, and ideas on automation. They formed working groups of volunteers to take ownership of each of these items. This group meets frequently to share what they are learning, and has grown considerably in size. With this kind of grassroots-level knowledge sharing, we saw an increased interest and willingness to give Chaos Engineering a try. We saw several examples of teams convincing their managers to bring in chaos experiments as part of their development best practices.

Lastly, compliance and regulations can be used as levers in evangelizing Chaos Engineering practice. They help the financial services companies govern their business. One of the important goals for these policies is to maintain the integrity of the process and data. Chaos Engineering helps uncover system and infrastructure resilience gaps that could potentially impact this goal. Promoting this practice as part of any such risk management process, or a change governance process to provide evidence for the resilience of the system, can also help with widespread adoption.

Conclusion

Like every large industry, the financial services sector has unique requirements when it comes to software engineering practices. This is especially true when considering something such as Chaos Engineering, which can potentially disrupt end consumer experience. Building reliable systems demands practices that help validate that reliability. Chaos Engineering fits this role, with proper tooling, a carefully considered approach in designing experiments and identifying metrics, and a team structure aligned with the organization's culture. Using governance and compliance as levers to evangelize this practice can help achieve the reliability objectives of the company. Within Capital One, we found ways to implement this practice that best fit our company's core values and mission. After all, tools and practices are for enabling engineers to do their best, and not the other way around.

About the Author

Raji Chockaiyan is a senior director of software engineering at Capital One Bank. She leads enterprise framework and container management platforms that bring continuous journey to the developer's laptop. Along with her team, she creates strategies, roadmaps, and platforms to test and improve the reliability of Capital One's microservices.

PART III

Human Factors

Resilience is created by people. The engineers who write the functionality, those who operate and maintain the system, and even the management that allocates resources toward it are all part of a complex system. We call this a sociotechnical system.

By the end of this part, we hope to convince you that successfully improving your resilience requires an understanding of the interplay between the human and nonhuman actors who authorize, fund, observe, build, operate, maintain, and make demands of the system. Chaos Engineering can help you better understand the sociotechnical boundary between the humans and the machines.

Nora Jones opens this part of the book with Chapter 9, "Creating Foresight." With a focus on learning as a means of improving resilience, she explains how sometimes the most important part of Chaos Engineering happens before an experiment is even run. She also ties in the relationship between controlled experimentation and unplanned incidents: "Incidents are an opportunity for us to sit down and see how one person's mental model of how the system worked is different than another person's mental model of how the system worked."

Andy Fleener explores the application of Chaos Engineering to the "socio" part of sociotechnical systems in Chapter 10, "Humanistic Chaos." He asks, "What if we could apply the field of Chaos Engineering not only to the complex distributed technical systems we know and love, but to the complex distributed systems known as organizations?" What happens when an organizational change is implemented through the lens of a chaos experiment?

In Chapter 11, "People in the Loop," John Allspaw explores the context-dependent relationship between people and the tools built to make our systems more available and secure. Regarding Chaos Engineering specifically, he argues that "we should view the approach as one that can *augment* the flexible and context-sensitive capacities that only people possess as they continue to cope with the complexity that necessarily comes with successful software."

Contrast that with Peter Alvaro's position in Chapter 12, "Experiment Selection Problem (and a Solution)," where he argues for increased reliance on automation. In particular, he proposes an original algorithm for exploring the solution space of potential system failures. This algorithm was developed in the service of "training computers to replace the role of experts in chaos experiment selection."

As with prior parts of the book, we present here a diverse selection of viewpoints on human factors to both reinforce the value proposition of Chaos Engineering, and to demonstrate its flexibility as a nascent discipline within software engineering.

CHAPTER 9

Creating Foresight

In order to determine and envision how to achieve reliability and resilience that our customers and businesses are happy with, organizations must be able to look back unobscured by hindsight bias. Resilient organizations don't take past successes as a reason for confidence. Instead, they use them as an opportunity to dig deeper, find underlying risks, and refine mental models of how our systems succeed and fail.

There are key components of Chaos Engineering beyond building platforms for testing reliability and running Game Days. Understanding the concerns, ideas, and mental models of how the system is structured for each individual and learning where your organization excels in technical and human resilience are things that can't be automated away by code. This chapter will address the three different phases of Chaos Engineering and the hidden goals within each phase that might be the greatest benefit of all: using Chaos Engineering as a way to distill expertise.

The chronically underinvested stages of Chaos Engineering in our industry are the Before and After phases—and these tend to fall on a single individual to complete, usually the facilitator. This is someone who can act as a third party during the experiment, but prior to that will educate themselves on what the team is going through, their systems, and how it all works. If we only optimize for finding issues before they become incidents, we miss out on getting the most out of the main Chaos Engineering goal, which is refining the mental models of our systems.

In this chapter we focus on the Before and After phases of developing Chaos Engineering experiments (whether they be Game Days or driven by software) and develop important questions to ask with each of these phases. We will also dig into some of the "Ironies of Automation"[1] present with Chaos Engineering today.

---

[1] Lisanne Bainbridge, "Ironies of Automation," *Automatica*, Vol. 19, No. 6 (1983).

As an industry, we have been placing too much attention on just how to make things fail and break them, and miss out on the value that the setup (the Before phase) and dissemination of learning outcomes (the After phase) can bring us. I will be drawing on both research from simulation exercises in other industries, as well as personal experience of what has (and hasn't) worked while executing chaos experiments across multiple companies with vastly different business goals. It is important to note, each phase of the cycle requires a different skill set and different types of roles to maximize success. We will go through these skill sets and mindsets (both of which can be trained and aided) in order to make these pieces most effective.

Chaos Engineering and Resilience

Before we review the phases of the Chaos Engineering cycle, let's set some common ground for the goals of the practice. As already discussed in previous chapters, the goal of Chaos Engineering is not to break things. The goal is also not to leverage tools to stop issues or find vulnerabilities. Let's pause there for a minute, because I want this to sink in—*Chaos Engineering is not about finding or surfacing vulnerabilities*.

Because Chaos Engineering is new and exciting, there has been a significant amount of focus on Chaos Engineering tools, rather than all the other reasons that we do Chaos Engineering. Why do we do Chaos Engineering? What is it all about then?

Chaos Engineering is about building a culture of resilience in the presence of unexpected system outcomes. If tools can help meet this goal, then that is excellent, but they are only one possible means to an end.

> Resilience engineering is about identifying and then enhancing the positive capabilities of people and organizations that allow them to adapt effectively and safely under varying circumstances. Resilience is not about reducing negatives [errors].
>
> —Sidney Dekker[2]

Chaos Engineering is just one means to help us enhance these adaptive capabilities of resilience.

Steps of the Chaos Engineering Cycle

In this section, we will focus on the different phases of Chaos Engineering (Before, During, and After an experiment). We will specifically focus our attention on the Before and After phases. Why? Because the During phase gets a lot of attention; there is as much (if not more) insightful data and pieces to explore in the Before and After phases.

---

2 Sidney Dekker, *Foundations of Safety Science: A Century of Understanding Accidents and Disasters* (Boca Raton: Taylor & Francis, CRC Press, 2019).

The goal of the Before phase of chaos experiments is to get teammates to discuss their differing mental models of the system in question. A secondary goal is to develop strategies behind how to design the failure, prior to executing it, in a structured and less ad hoc way. In this section we will discuss various design techniques and how these mental models come to light.

Designing the Experiment

> All [mental] models are wrong, but some are useful.
>
> —George Box[3]

Incidents are an opportunity for us to sit down and see how one team member's mental model of how the system worked is different than another member's understanding of how it worked. Incidents give us this opportunity because, at some level, they disprove our assumptions about how the system operated and handled risk.

Hypothetically, let's say Josie thought she could expect 100% uptime from their service discovery infrastructure, whereas Mateo, the designer of the service discovery infrastructure at your company, predicted that users of this infrastructure would never even make that assumption.

Mateo, given his lengthy experience as an operator, assumed that no one would expect 100% uptime from a system and both retries and fallbacks would be configured by services using the service discovery infrastructure. He never put this in the documentation, nor did he set up things in the service discovery infrastructure that would mitigate the risk if someone *assumed* 100% uptime.

Meanwhile, Josie had been using the service discovery infrastructure for various things for a while and has loved it. It has saved her a lot of time and energy on storing important key–value pairs, and the flexibility to quickly change them if needed. It did exactly what she wanted—until it didn't.

A massive outage occurred, partially as a result of these mismatched expectations and the lack of opportunity to discuss inherent assumptions. The assumptions made by both parties were *completely reasonable* given the context they individually had about how the service discovery infrastructure worked. Josie and Mateo never explicitly had this conversation about support. Why would anyone discuss what is obvious? You can't, really, until you have an incident.

This is where chaos experiments come in. While they do serve as a chance for us to find vulnerabilities in our systems, even more importantly they serve as an opportunity for us to see how our mental model and assumption of what will happen when X

---

3 G. E. P. Box, "Robustness in the Strategy of Scientific Model Building," in R. L. Launer and G. N. Wilkinson (eds.), *Robustness in Statistics* (New York: Academic Press, 1979), pp. 201–236.

part of the system fails is different from our teammate's mental model and assumption of what happens when X fails. You'll actually find people are more open to discussing these differences than they are during an incident, because well, an incident hasn't happened and as a result, there is an element of psychological safety present that cannot be overstated. Knowing we experimented on this in a safe setting removes any sense of shame or insecurity for the resulting behavior of the system. And that emotional foundation lets everyone focus on what we can learn without distraction about who's gonna get in trouble for what happened.

Tool Support for Chaos Experiment Design

How teams decide what to experiment on is just as revealing as the experiment itself. When I joined Netflix back in early 2017, the team I worked with was building a tool called ChAP (see Figure 9-1). At a high level, the platform interrogates the deployment pipeline for a user-specified service. It then launches experiment and control clusters of that service, and routes a small amount of traffic to each. A specified failure-injection scenario is applied to the experimental group, and the results of the experiment were then reported to the person that created the experiment.

ChAP took advantage of the fact that applications used a common set of Java libraries and annotated the incoming request metadata that a particular call should be failed. The metadata is then passed along as the call propagates through the system. ChAP would look for that metadata as the requests propagate between services, calculate a percentage of traffic small enough to limit the blast radius but large enough to get a statistically significant signal, split that percentage in half, and route the traffic into two clusters—an experiment (canary) cluster and a control (baseline) cluster.

Pretty neat, right? Many organizations roll their own versions of this tool and vendors came out with similar tools shortly after we announced ChAP.

However, after months went by with our four backend developers doing nothing but heads down coding, I couldn't help but notice our specific team had all this unique expertise about the system and its failure modes. By spending time architecting how to safely fail specific places in the Netflix system, you naturally start to develop a specific expertise in how it's all wired together, without having "deep" expertise in any particular area of the system.

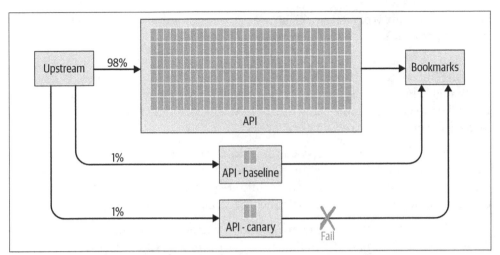

Figure 9-1. ChAP experiment injecting failure into bookmarks from API[4]

We would use this expertise not only to build and architect chaos experiments but also to coach teams on how they could best leverage the tool; we showed them how to use it and asked probing questions that got them thinking in terms of how their services could fail. While this expertise was amazing and undoubtedly needed, I began to notice that most teams would not run experiments of their own volition. They'd usually run them when (a) we asked, or (b) before a major event (like the holiday season at Netflix). I started to wonder if my theory was accurate: "Were the Chaos Team members themselves running most of these experiments? Was this a bad thing?"

As part of the ChAP UI, we had created a "Runs" page where any user could view previous experiments, and understand when they ran, how long, what they failed, and, most importantly for my purposes, *who* ran them. Being curious, I started doing an analysis of who was running the experiments. What did I find? Well, I realized that one of the questions I had posed earlier was true: it was mostly just us, the Chaos Engineers, running these experiments. But, was this a good idea? After all, the Netflix ecosystem was huge; how were we supposed to know where to experiment all the time?

Here we were, so proud of this amazing technical feat we had accomplished—we could safely fail and add latency to calls in production—but what good is that functionality if the only people using the tool are the four people who created it? On top of that, while the four of us were good engineers, we couldn't gain expertise in every

---

4 Ali Basiri et al., "Automating Chaos Experiments in Production," International Conference on Software Engineering (ICSE), 2019, *https://https://arxiv.org/abs/1905.04648* (*https://arxiv.org/abs/1905.04648*).

area of the Netflix ecosystem, which meant we could not individually devise meaningful experiments that spanned the entire system.

Additionally, when we tried encouraging people to run experiments, we found that they were nervous about potentially triggering a production issue. "But it's so safe!" we thought; however, they didn't have quite the same context we had. In order to make them feel comfortable using the tool, we allocated time to spend with them and help them construct a "safe" experiment.

It was quite a bit of work on top of a full-time day job of programming—a job where we were expected to be programming most of the time. Naturally, we attempted to solve the problem in a very common software engineer way: we automated it! We thought we would just create and run these experiments for the teams, *automagically*.

In order to do that, I had to develop a whole new understanding of different pieces of the ecosystem—enough that I could develop algorithms to apply to different places of the system to create meaningful experiments. How did I do this? I had to collect several pieces of information on what it meant for a service to be safe to run a chaos experiment on, how to prioritize experiments, and how to find the necessary information to create them. I, along with my team, did this by interviewing about 30 people across the organization and studying what they knew about their systems and how they knew it. Once we felt we had enough information on how to do this in several different places, we then moved on to collecting that information automatically. Now we couldn't develop different algorithms for the whole Netflix ecosystem, so we developed something that was similar across a number of services. Based on the results of the interviews with experts throughout Netflix, we determined that *at least* the following information was needed in order for a call included in a particular service to be considered safe or unsafe to run experiments on:

- Timeouts
- Retries
- Whether or not the call had a fallback associated with it
- Percent of traffic it regularly served

This brings me to my next point—many teams developing chaos experiments need to go and talk to their users. This can be aided by a Product Manager or Engineering Manager, but ultimately the engineers should be getting out and doing this as well. As mentioned, the best way to gather the information I needed was to partner with these service owners and get an understanding of their perspectives and respective mental models. So, let's talk about how to do that in a judicious way.

Effectively Partnering Internally

Incident investigation techniques in other industries (aviation, medicine, maritime) involve a third party (the facilitator) who conducts cognitive interviews as a means to extract details about what teammates believe happened during and leading up to the incident. This is not done as a way to get the one canonical story; instead, trained interviewers recognize that all accounts are important to collect because the gaps in these mental models reveal where the real problems are. We can also use cognitive interviews to inform chaos experiments.

Though this can be a time-intensive activity, it is important (at least in the design of the chaos experiment phase) to gather the mental model of different teammates and develop a hypothesis. This hypothesis should *not* come from the facilitator. The facilitator should interview teammates in a group setting (for roughly 30 minutes to an hour) and give each teammate a chance to talk about their understanding of the system and what happens when it fails.

Why is a group setting important? You get the *most* value out of Chaos Engineering when multiple people, from different teams involved in the experiment, are in a room together discussing their expectations of the system. Distilling the explicit information about what you learned during this phase is equally as important (if not more important) than executing the experiment.

Next, let's talk through some questions to ask (as a facilitator) to get the most value out of a chaos experiment. Each question represents a path of inquiry to draw out the mental models from experts and to get the team contrasting their different points of view.

Understand Operating Procedures

The facilitator should guide and seed the group of participants by asking a series of questions, starting with "What behaviors and interactions are you concerned about in the system?" If comfortable to do without repercussion, this question should first be posed to a less-tenured person to the company on the team, and then to a person more tenured (or more of an expert in the particular area). Then, each person in the room should contribute, ultimately leveling up the expertise. Let's quickly touch on David Woods's Law of Fluency, which states that once experts become so skilled in their own expertise, they cannot recognize, nor fathom their expertise as a thing.[5] Expertise hides the effort involved in work; your role as a facilitator understanding operating procedures in preparation for a chaos experiment is to uncover and ultimately disseminate what that effort looks like.

---

5 Robert R. Hoffman and David R. Woods, "Beyond Simon's Slice: Five Fundamental Trade-Offs That Bound the Performance of Macrocognitive Work Systems," *IEEE Intelligent Systems* (Nov./Dec. 2011).

Another reason for this ordering is that new employees have a fresh eye for the system and unobscured hindsight bias. Cognitive psychologist Gary Klein has extensively studied differences between the mental models of newer and more tenured employees:

> The new employee can see the times when the system *broke down* not the time when it worked.[6]

The facilitator should draw their understanding of the system based on the description team members are providing.

The facilitator should also capture how the behaviors and interactions people are concerned about varies among teammates. Identify expertise, as well as gaps, and treat this part of the exercise as a learning experience. Team members will most certainly have different answers to this question.

Next, the facilitator should ask "What things do you assume your teammates know about the system?" This question is asked so we can find things like common ground breakdown:

- Are there downstream services you are worried about?

- What happens to upstream services if something goes wrong with your service(s)?

- What happens when something goes wrong with your service(s) now? Do you have fallbacks in place (or something else)? What do those fallbacks do? How do those fallbacks change the behavior of the service? How could those fallbacks impact the user experience?

- Are there recent changes to your system (either in your service or in your upstreams/downstreams) that could have introduced new vulnerabilities in the system? Who knows the most about these changes?

- Is it possible for your service to get into a bad state? What could lead to that happening?

- How confident are you in the settings for various configuration parameters of your system? That is, do you understand the implications of configured timeouts, retries, and other hardcoded values on your system?

- What (in so many words) scares you most about the day-to-day operations of the system?

---

6 Gary Klein and Robert Hoffman, "Seeing the Invisible: Perceptual-Cognitive Aspects of Expertise," in M. Rabinowitz (Ed.), *Cognitive Science Foundations of Instruction* (Mahwah, NJ: Lawrence Erlbaum Associates, 1993), pp. 203-226.

The confidence, or lack thereof, that people possess is a sign of an uncertainty about their own mental model, or perhaps a lack of confidence in the operating procedures.

Once everyone involved in the experiment design is aligned on these questions, only then should you move to discussing the scope of the experiment. Note that it is entirely reasonable, and may frequently be the case, that you decide to not move past this section based on the answers to the preceding questions.

Discuss Scope

Once you've chosen an experiment, it's important to discuss the scope and align everyone's mental models by asking the following questions (this should be done before the day that the experiment is actually run):

- *How* do you define a "normal" or "good" operation?
- *How* are we establishing the scope (where we are injecting the failure) of the experiment?
  - What is the reasoning for determining this scope?
  - Does everyone in the room understand the reasoning—and how do you know?
  - Is this fear-driven? (Are we doing this experiment because this thing has bitten us in the past? If so, link the "postmortem" and relevant conversations related to these incidents.)
  - Is this experiment generated by a lack of understanding on what *would* happen if X failed? (Meaning, has this failure rarely, if ever, happened and we're just not sure about it?)
- *What* do we expect to happen with this failure? *(Be explicit)*
  - What do we expect from individual components?
  - What do we expect from the system as a whole?
- *How* do you know if the system is in a bad state?
  - Which metrics are most important for us to measure during the experiment?

    When asking yourself these questions, consider the following quote from Hollnagel and Woods:[7] "Observability is *feedback that provides insight into a process* and refers to the work needed to extract meaning from available data."
  - With this in mind, how are we *observing* the system?

---

7 Erik Hollnagel and David D. Woods, *Joint Cognitive Systems: Foundations of Cognitive Systems Engineering* (Boca Raton, FL: Taylor & Francis, 2005).

- *How* are we limiting the blast radius?
- *What* is the perceived business value of the experiment (to the service team)? What is the perceived value to the rest of the organization?

Note that the answers to these questions might be different, and that's okay.

Hypothesize

Next, take some time to formulate and restate your collective hypothesis of the experiment:

> If we fail X part of system, then Y will happen, and the impact will be Z.

- Write down what the "steady state" is.
- What is the expectation of the deviation from the steady state? (Do this for *all* of the metrics you decided you should monitor.)
- Then write down what you expect (if anything) from the user experience.
- Follow up by writing down what you expect (if anything) the downstream impact will be.
- Finally, share the document with all of the stakeholders.

Determine Roles

If you are running a Game Day–type experiment, identify the people involved and their roles in the experiment. Note that not all these roles are needed for automated experiments, but they are still overall very beneficial if you can get the time and resources to temporarily staff them. Before we have automation in place to limit the blast radius and automatically create failure, each facilitated experiment preparation should have the following roles:

- Designer/Facilitator (the person leading the discussion)
- Commander (the person executing the commands)
- Scribe (takes notes in a communication tool, such as Slack, on what is occurring in the room)
- Observer (looks at and shares relevant graphs with the rest of the group)
- Correspondent (keeps an eye on #alerts-type-channel and makes sure the current on-call is aware of the experiment occurring and what the expected impact is)

List all additional folks that are present in the design and running of the experiment as well as their stake in the experiment.

Once all of these questions are answered and roles are in place, the designer/facilitator should share their understanding of the experiment and what was discussed and learned in this meeting with the rest of the group in an easy-to-consume format that clearly states the methods they used and areas where attention should be directed.

Let's quickly summarize what we've learned to ask and think about in these phases:

Before the experiment

How do you learn about deviations of understanding and assumptions of steady state among teammates by asking questions?

Where do these differences derive from, and what do they mean? How do you define a "normal" or "good" operation?

What's the perceived value of experimenting on this piece of the system?

How do you encourage people to draw out their mental models in a structured way—either through a visual representation or a structured hypothesis about how they think the system operates?

In order to get to the During process, there may be some things you decide to automate—how do you decide what these things should be? How do you determine what scale you can safely execute your experiments on? What should and should not measuring effectiveness of a resilience experimentation platform be used for? How do you separate signal from noise and determine if an error is the result of the chaos experiment or something else?

After the experiment:

If the experiment found an issue, you'll want to ask the following questions afterwards:

- What did you learn?
- How do you use the information you learned to restructure understandings and repeat?
- How did teams gain confidence in running the experiment before they ran it?
- How did the team communicate with each other about what was unfolding in the experiment?
- Did anyone that was not present in the design or running of the experiment need to be called into the experiment or pinged during it because they had a specific expertise?
- Did any incidents occur during the experiment (related or unrelated)?
- How do we start classifying *what* the result of the experiment was?
- Which parts of the experiment behaved differently than expected?

- Based on what we have learned and what we still do not understand, what experiments should we consider for the next cycle?
- How do we disseminate these learnings in a way that everyone in the organization can see and read through?
- How do we make sure we can understand themes across different experiments over time? And how do we tie these themes to incidents and other surprises our organization experiences?

Conclusion

The questions just listed are tools a facilitator can use to guide the discussion. However, the point of these discussions is to help the team of experts discover and share their hidden expertise about the components of the system. Remember: you as the facilitator are not and should not be the expert in this situation—you are there to uncover expertise, not display it. All of this work to uncover expertise is in service of developing the best hypotheses that will guide an experiment to discovering things that surprise us.

We're looking for the surprises.

Let's go back to the Netflix story from earlier in the chapter. All of the guiding principles around the Before and After phases of chaos experiments came from that experience of *trying to automate experiments in production* and *trying to remove the user "burden."* While we succeeded in synthesizing all of this information to build an algorithm that created, prioritized, and ran chaos experiments, the biggest value we achieved from all of this was that we helped people refine and hone mental models of their systems.

By gathering all of this information to automatically create experiments, we had developed a new expertise and wanted to share it with the world. All of the things we learned in the process of developing this automation we shared in a dynamic dashboard. This was a side effect of the project of automating experiments, of course; our main goal was not to develop a dashboard. However, this dashboard gave so much insight into the system: it showed users whether or not our algorithm thought that their service was safe to fail, before we ever ran an experiment on it. My favorite thing to do with this new dashboard was to take it to teams and show them which parts of their system were safe to fail. The results? Every time I showed this dashboard to someone, they were surprised. They always learned something new, whether it be that one of their services was "unexpectedly critical," they had a timeout that was a bit too high, or their retry behavior logically did not make sense. That look of amazement on users' faces each time I showed them the dashboard: I could see them grokking what we had actually been trying to do the whole time, to give them a better understanding of their system. While we turned the automation on, and it worked, we ultimately turned it off after a few weeks of it running. Why? Well, we honestly got most of the value out of the dashboard and the *process* of automating these experiments, rather than the automation itself, and adoption skyrocketed, but not in the way we had originally intended. Go figure.

This whole experience led me to recognize that facilitation, cognitive interviewing, and disseminating expertise is not only very important to the success of Chaos Engineering in organizations, but it is chronically underinvested in. Automating the indicators mentioned here ended up reducing the depth of learning by the other teams and once again increased the depth of learning for our team. Only after sharing our methods for developing this automation and the results would we achieve what we were looking for: a better overall understanding among individuals on how their systems worked and failed. Teams ultimately learn more from facilitated experiment design and resulting comparison of their mental models.

CHAPTER 10

Humanistic Chaos

Andy Fleener

I'm faced with a question that has been bothering me for quite some time. How can I apply what I know about Chaos Engineering to human systems? When I first learned about the emerging field of Chaos Engineering, to say I was intrigued would be putting it lightly. Injecting failure into a system purposefully to help you better understand your system? I was sold right away. As a "new view" safety nerd and systems thinker, I can get behind a paradigm that acknowledges the systems we use every day are inherently unsafe. My initial hypothesis was if Chaos Engineering practices were designed to run against distributed web systems, then they could also be applied to other distributed systems we interact with on a daily basis—systems that are all around us, systems that form our daily lives.

What if we could apply the field of Chaos Engineering not only to the complex distributed technical systems we know and love, but to the complex distributed systems known as organizations? An organization is one giant system of systems, so why shouldn't the same rules apply? In this chapter I will lay out three real-world case studies of putting Chaos Engineering principles into practice within the Platform Operations team I lead, as well as the greater Product Development organization at SportsEngine, and hope to give you the tools to apply these same techniques within your own organization.

Humans in the System

In an organization, the fundamental unit or actor in the system is a person. The truly hard problems lie within the interactions between those actors. We're frequently faced with questions like "How can we create software that people can effectively operate to achieve a goal?" Notice that people are central to both the problem and the solution. They are simultaneously the reason there's a need and the solution to solve that need.

Putting the "Socio" in Sociotechnical Systems

As technologists, we are drawn to technical solutions for human problems. Technology has made a massive impact on our lives. It's in everything we do. The "monolith-to-microservices" stories are a dime a dozen, and many of those journeys are centered around solving very real organizational scaling problems. But changing the technology we use will not magically create the culture we desire. We consistently neglect the social side of the sociotechnical systems we weave in and out of every day. It's clear that the most effective way to improve technical systems is to map them. Gary Klein talks about how we gain these insights in his book *Seeing What Others Don't*. He states that stories are "anchors" within an organization and those stories are how we interpret details. We do this in a number of ways, like architecture reviews, system designs, and documentation, and at a higher level with retrospective activities like incident reviews. We're constantly trying to adjust our mental model of how the system functions. But how are we doing this with the socio side of the system? When was the last time you mapped out your incident response escalation flow? Does that map include what to do when the Level 2 person is on vacation? Does it include what to do when you don't get an acknowledgment that someone is working on an issue? Does it include how to decide if something even is an incident? Awesome, you've got all of those things mapped, have you ever tried to monitor these systems in action? Remember to mind the gap between work-as-imagined versus work-as-done. What we say we do, and what we actually do, are very different. The impact of this gap can be described as "dark debt," a term first used in the SNAFUcatchers' STELLA report.[1]

We can think of components or actors of a system as being designed to handle a certain capacity; what happens when that capacity is exhausted can be extremely uncertain. In the technical side of the system this can show up as big ripples like cascading failures. On the human side of the system we often think of this in terms of things like burnout, or dropping the ball. But the impact of that burnt-out engineer, or a manager dropping the ball, can be incredibly difficult to reason about without actually seeing it happen.

Organizations Are a System of Systems

What's so fascinating about an organization for me is that there are systems everywhere. Some of those systems are written down—for example, you might have a vacation policy that allows you to take x number of days off per year. Or you have a week-long on-call shift that rotates between six people. But other systems aren't written down at all, they're just well-known tribal knowledge, like only communicate with George via Slack because he never checks his email. Or Suzi knows the most about

---

1 SNAFUcatchers, "Dark Debt," STELLA: Report from the SNAFUcatchers Workshop on Coping With Complexity, March 14-16, 2017, *https://oreil.ly/D34nE*.

this service, because she wrote most of it. Tribal knowledge systems tend to be way less reliable than the explicitly stated counterparts. But nothing creates an unreliable system quite like a poorly mapped explicit system. There will always be a gap between work-as-imagined and work-as-done.[2] The way you create truly reliable systems is by actively working to shrink that gap.

Since organizations are complex systems, they adhere to Dr. Richard Cook's principles of how complex systems fail.[3] In short, they are hazardous, containing many latent failures around every corner; they are well defended against failure (catastrophe is only possible through a sequence of failures); and humans play a dual role as both defenders and producers of failure. Every action taken within a complex system is a gamble, but it's these gambles that create the safety within the system.

Engineering Adaptive Capacity

Dr. Sidney Dekker's paper on human performance[4] presents two views on safety. One (old) view "consider(s) people as a problem to control (through procedures, compliance, standardization, sanctions). Safety is measured mainly by the absence of negatives." Another (new) perspective wants to "view people as a solution to harness rather than a problem to control, and consider safety more as a presence of positive capacities." It is through this newer, refreshed lens that I've been focused on building a highly reliable, robust, and hopefully resilient team of engineers. As a manager of an team with an on-call rotation, I look at my role as searching for signals that may indicate the team may be exhausting its capacity while simultaneously looking for ways to grow the capacity boundary. What can I do, as an actor in the system, to push the system away from the edges of real impactful failure like the exit of an important engineer, a significant loss of customers, or a data breach?

Spotting Weak Signals

Focusing on maintaining a margin between normal "safe" operation and impactful failure has pushed me to seek out weak signals. Weak signals are small, barely noticeable indications of new emergent behavior in the system. In the world of web systems we use methods like USE, which represents utilization, saturation, and errors. These are monitors built on key bottlenecks in the system. They may not indicate immediate problems, but once they pass a given boundary the system starts to fail (strong signals). Within the context of an organization, Dr. Todd Conklin describes signals in

---

2 Steven Shorrock, "The Varieties and Archetypes of Human Work," Safety Synthesis: The Repository for Safety-II (website), *https://oreil.ly/6ECXu.*

3 Richard I. Cook, "How Complex Systems Fail," Cognitive Technologies Laboratory, 2000, *https://oreil.ly/kvlZ8.*

4 Sidney Dekker, "Employees: A Problem to Control or Solution to Harness?," *Professional Safety* Vol. 59, No. 8 (Aug. 2014).

his Pre-Accident Investigations podcast [5] as weak indicators that tell us when there's a problem happening, not when a problem has happened: "You'll never hear a weak signal in failure, the signal in a failure is loud." He gives a few examples like "a door that opens backwards" or a "stoplight that isn't timed long enough to safely walk across the street." To understand weak signals, you need to listen to the signals in success, and find the steady state. Organizations are so highly reliable that weak signals are often the only type of signal you can use to increase the capacity of the system.

Let's walk through some examples I've seen personally. I noticed ending an on-call shift on a Monday is more tiring than ending on a Friday. This isn't a problem, until it is. If an engineer is tired they will be less effective, perhaps making a significant error. At the time, we also used a team-wide Slack channel as a place to take requests and answer questions for other teams. This was mostly fine, but if the whole team responds to a question when only one of them is needed, or even worse no one responds, it would impact the flow of work for my team and other teams. Another super common weak signal might be "I don't know anything about this, we'll need to talk to Emma." That flag "we need to talk to x" happens all of the time; information is not and cannot be evenly distributed. But it's signaling the system is approaching a boundary. What happens if Emma decides to pursue other opportunities? Your system is signaling constantly. Finding the balance of what signal to act on versus continuing to monitor is the truly hard part.

Failure and Success, Two Sides of the Same Coin

The revelation to me about seeking out weak signals was that success and failure are not choices that we make. What makes something a success versus a failure is whether, as Dr. Jens Rasmussen describes in his dynamic safety model, the operating point of the system crosses over the boundary, a tipping point, of performance failure. Rasmussen refers to this as "going solid."[6] What was once a success can suddenly and unexpectedly drift into a state of failure. If we intentionally search for the failure states of our organizational systems we become more familiar with that boundary. It will either make the boundary more explicit, or even better, improve the system and push the boundary further away. What I've observed at SportsEngine is that through the principles of Chaos Engineering, both of these things are possible: we can make the boundary more explicit and push it further away.

---

5 Todd Conklin, "Safety Moment: Weak Signals Matter," Pre-Accident Investigation (podcast), July 8, 2011, *https://oreil.ly/6rBbw*.

6 R. Cook and Jens Rasmussen, "'Going Solid': A Model of System Dynamics and Consequences for Patient Safety," *BMJ Quality and Safety Healthcare*, 14 (2005).

Putting the Principles into Practice

Much has been written about applying the principles of Chaos Engineering to large distributed systems. There are fantastic tools built by the folks at Netflix, ChaosIQ, and others, but those tools are for technical systems. So how do you start searching for the chaos in your human systems?

What's interesting about human systems is that your position within the system greatly impacts your ability to change it. As an actor within the system you're exposed to feedback in a way that's not possible with below-the-line systems[7] like the software products we create and run. If you want to see the feedback machine in action try executing a department-wide desk move. If you got *anything* wrong someone will tell you.

As with any chaos experiment, it should be grounded on the core principles. For these case studies we will focus on three of the core principles. First, build a hypothesis based on the steady state of the system. You need to understand the current system before you'll be able to monitor the outcome. Then, define a variable that you plan to intentionally change. This is the failure injection part. And finally, monitor the outcome. Look for the new emergent behavior the system is displaying, and compare it to the previous state of the system.

Build a Hypothesis

As we know, the first step to conducting a chaos experiment is to build a hypothesis around steady-state behavior. In the classic sense we're talking about basic service-level indicators like throughput, error rate, latency, and so on. In a human system our understanding of the steady state is much different. Input/output metrics are harder to come by, the feedback loops can be shorter, and the visibility of the system is drastically different than the way we monitor our technical systems. This is where qualitative analysis can be far more impactful. Humans are feedback machines; it's what we do every day. We're in a constant state of giving feedback. If you're going to set up an experiment, it is critical that you create effective feedback loops within the experiment. This should not come as a surprise because feedback loops are at the core of how you create successful change within an organization.

If you're searching for a first hypothesis, look at your organizational limits. Where do you have single points of failure, communication bottlenecks, long work queues? Identify the systems where your gut is telling you that you're close to capacity, as this is where you will find the most value.

---

7 SNAFUcatchers, "The Above-the-Line/Below-the-Line Framework," STELLA: Report from the SNAFUcatchers Workshop on Coping with Complexity, March 14-16, 2017, *https://oreil.ly/V7M98*.

Vary Real-World Events

Once you've identified a limit, the next step is to attempt to push over the edge. Try to find the boundaries. You will likely see a variation of three different scenarios play out:

Scenario 1

You make a change to the system, and it immediately collapses under the weight of your change. Don't forget to have a rollback plan. You may not learn very much from this scenario, but congratulations you found a hard limit! Hard limits should be explicit, and the value of the experiment is that you have now made it explicit. An example of this scenario might be a change that results in important work immediately falling on the floor—work that's too critical to let slip.

Scenario 2

You've made a change, and now the limit you have been monitoring has changed but the impact on capacity is too high to sustain this change indefinitely. This feedback can be impactful for understanding your margin, and what emergent properties the system will take on in this state. Seeing that emergent behavior can help you recognize weak signals in the future, and give you leading indicators. This tends to show up with competing priorities, and is more subtle than work falling on the floor. Let's say you moved someone between teams, and it works for a while, but when there's increased production pressure for the original team you may have to send them right back to that team.

Scenario 3

You make a change to the system, and all indications are that it had no significant impact. This is the most challenging scenario. It likely either means your hypothesis was completely wrong, or you're measuring the wrong thing and don't have the proper feedback loops to understand the impact. In this situation you should generally go back to the drawing board. Much like a failed science experiment you may be missing key information about the steady state of the experiment. An example here would be you've found a single point of failure in the system (a person). But despite your attempts to share their knowledge, they continue to be the only subject matter expert for some class of incidents.

Minimize the Blast Radius

As with technical systems, cascading failures are the biggest risk to these types of activities. Be mindful of what kind of impact a particular experiment could have. For example, making a drastic capacity-limiting change to a team that many other teams rely on could send a big ripple through the organization and make future experimentation more difficult. That level of impact will likely result in Scenario #1, and you'll quickly need to undo whatever change you made.

You'll learn quickly how the system functions and where the margins are thinner than you expected. But before you attempt that experiment again, you definitely need to work on increasing the margins. The impact of the blast radius is highly dependent on the context of your business. For example, SportsEngine is very seasonal in nature. Trying something significant that would impact our customers' ability to use our products for a year has a very real impact on our business. Our next shot at acquiring that customer is on the order of a year. But if we can reduce the scope to be within the context of a product that's currently out of season, it has no impact on our customers or our bottom line.

Your planning phase should include contingency plans. This will obviously depend on the nature of the experiment, but a "rollback," rip cord, escape hatch—whatever you want to call it—should be explicit. Everyone involved in the experiment should have the ability and authority to pull it, even if it's just for them.

Playing at this level, just like with experimenting on your technical systems, means making good business decisions. Don't break a system just to prove a point. You need buy-in throughout your organization, and that means showing clear explicit value in what you're doing.

You also need to remember all of the actors in this system are humans. That means they all have their own perspectives, life experiences, and goals. That includes you, the person running the experiment. Your personal biases can have a significant impact on the experiment, the people in the experiment, and the business. Question everything, search out feedback, and be open to changing or even scrapping the whole experiment. Don't let your desire to see it succeed blind you from the feedback.

Case Study 1: Gaming Your Game Days

Putting aside culture and systems thinking, let's discover some new system boundaries. Coming from this fascination with "new view" safety led me to the belief that incidents are unplanned learning events within my organization.[8] This realization inspired me to create Game Days that fully practiced our incident response life cycle. It's a chance to throw someone new in the organization into the deep end and give them exposure to what it's like to be part of the response, in a safe, low-consequence environment. There's no immediate impact to customers or the business outside of the time investment. If you aren't doing Game Days at your organization, you should be.

---

8 John Allspaw, "How Your Systems Keep Running Day After Day," IT Revolution, April 30, 2018, *https://oreil.ly/vHVIW*.

Game Days at SportsEngine have four stages:

1. *Scheduling and planning*: At a basic level you're picking a day or an afternoon on a calendar, and identifying a diverse group of folks to be your "game runners."

2. *Game execution*: This is my personal favorite stage. Your objective as a game runner is to inject failure into the system in a methodical way, then step back and see how it ripples through your system.

3. *Incident response*: As a game runner you should observe closely here; you have the benefit of knowing the triggering event. Watching the response closely can give you tons of insight about the gaps in your processes, monitoring, and alerting.

4. *Incident review*: In the same way we hold incident reviews for production incidents, we'll hold more informal, short reviews after each game.

The cycle then repeats: you start a new game at stage 2 until you run out of games, or you run out of time.

Game Days made a significant impact in the robustness of the SportsEngine platform, but they made an even bigger impact on our ability to execute an effective incident response plan. There's so much that goes into successful incident response, like work assignment to subject matter experts, effective troubleshooting, communication with stakeholders, and customer communication through outreach channels like status pages. We view incident response as a team sport, which means you need plenty of practice to do it effectively.

The hypothesis

If incident response is a team sport, how would our process work if someone was "sidelined"? If you were to interview a player on a professional sports team about injuries to a star player, they'll give you a sort of robotic "next player up" response. I found myself identifying specific parts of our platform where we either had one or two subject matter experts. What if the biggest single point of failure for a system was that there was only one expert? This can be painfully obvious, but usually it's more gray than black and white. Two or three people might know something about a system, but there might be one person who knows a specific subcomponent. I landed on a very specific hypothesis around intentionally creating a game where "the right people" could not participate. My hunch was that this would greatly impact the amount of time it would take to respond to an issue and resolve it. I wanted to intentionally search out single points of failure within our incident response process, but I also wanted to give folks real experience in coping with that failure.

The variable

Remember in a chaos experiment you're thinking about control groups and experiment groups. Running a control in this scenario is difficult, but the most effective way I've found is to run several games normally with a full team response. Then as you start a game, declare: "[expert you think is a single point of failure] is on vacation." Run a game and break the system that engineer is most knowledgeable about. You'll also want that engineer to observe all of the communication, troubleshooting, and actions taken by the team. This will give them a whole new perspective on where they should be sharing knowledge.

Another slightly less surprising way to hold this experiment is to recruit a suspected single point of failure to be one of the game runners. It's less of a surprise because everyone knows before the game even starts they won't be able to ask them questions, but it gives you a chance to use their knowledge about that system to inject failure into it. This not only gives you the benefit of the expert not being involved in the response, but it also helps them think critically about where the weak points in their system live.

The outcome

This concept of identifying a single point of failure within our organization has been successful for us. The best we can do is actively search them out to find more of them. We are trying to uncover systemic weaknesses in the system. Those weaknesses are constantly changing, which means our work will never be done. My most effective measurement for success is seeing folks go on long vacations and never get paged about a single incident. You can also use a simple survey to gauge the confidence level of folks in the rotation, and their comfort level with handling alerts to the relevant part of the system. This culture of building humane on-call practices is one of the things I'm most proud of at SportsEngine.

Communication: The Network Latency of Any Organization

In the world of distributed systems, we spend countless hours obsessing over how to create effective communication protocols and systems. If you say the words "CAP theorem" loud enough at a tech conference you'll hear audible groans and be met with eye rolls—but you'll also see the folks, like me, who beeline to the conversation. Distributed systems are in a constant state of both success and failure, backboned by consensus algorithms like Raft or Paxos and robust delivery mechanisms like TCP. But even those highly reliable systems start to fall apart if an unexpected amount of network latency is added to the system. It doesn't take much to send you into the world of cascades, leader elections, split brains, or data loss.

Network latency failures have an analog in our human-distributed system, the organization. We create all of these reliable systems to keep track of work, like ticketing systems, asynchronous chat rooms, and frameworks like Lean, Scrum, or Kanban. These systems are designed to work well when communication is consistent and fast. They start to fall apart when it's less frequent. Generally this is when communication starts to cross boundaries, like teams or departments. The effectiveness of the structures and frameworks are based on short feedback loops between people. In fact, many of these structures are designed to shorten feedback loops, but generally they are not built to enable new communication structures. This rigidity can lead to stalled work, missed deadlines, and unmet expectations. Autonomy and effectiveness is gained through trusted relationships. Expected interrupts are handled effectively in the system, but unexpected interrupts can be lost in emails, DMs, backlogs, and the like, never pushing needed context to the right people.

Pave new pathways to communication

The problem with this is that these lost emails, DMs, and tickets were a promise to that outside actor in the system. The repercussions of a small failure in communication can cascade dramatically throughout the organization. This can take many forms, like angry customers, lost revenue, or bad public reputation. These cascading failures are all too common, especially in the software industry. All it takes is one missed estimation on the size and scope of a project. It's also why these frameworks are so prevalent and effective. Organizations are in a constant state of finding common ground between actors in the system.

In the spirit of thinking about how to reduce network latency, and create more routes for communication traffic, I wanted to find ways to pave new communication channels. Explicitly surface and define channels that have already been paved. Turn a dirt path into a paved road. These human network failures frequently fall down by flowing through single points of direct communication between two people. But simultaneously, two actors in a system who interact regularly is the most effective form of communication. So how do you avoid the pitfalls of communication breakdowns, but maintain the speed and effectiveness?

Case Study 2: Connecting the Dots

Looking at the risk of standard communication channels within an organization had me thinking about ways to expand the network. Dunbar's number[9] tells us there is a limit to the number of people, somewhere around 150, you can hold and maintain stable relationships with. That means there is a hard limit to the number of new connections you can make within an organization. Many organizations, ones that depend on high connectivity, are often built on more than 150 people. So how do we manage

---

9 R. I. M. Dunbar, "Co-evolution of Neocortex Size, Group Size and Language in Humans," *Behavioral and Brain Sciences* 16 (4), 1993.

these contradictions? The theory is that if networks can be meshed by teammates creating connections and relationships with folks on different teams, the network can be expanded.

The hypothesis

When I was thinking about this concept, I ran across a blog post[10] from the folks at Etsy about their "bootcamp" concept. Every new hire spends a short amount of time, a few weeks to a few months, with a different team in the organization, before officially joining the team they were hired onto. This time gives them a varied perspective from a different part of the organization. But it also creates natural communication channels through established trusted relationships. At SportsEngine, we're always in some state of growth, whether that's hiring new people, or acquiring new companies (15+ since I started in 2011), each with their own software and people. This near constant expansion requires new connections to be formed. The question we asked ourselves was what if we intentionally and regularly have folks spend time with different teams? What kind of an impact will this have on product delivery, availability, and scalability concerns that come along with having many software products?

The variable

Finding ways to get people out of their comfort zones and their daily routines is quite difficult. In the Platform Operations team's case, it was looked at from a few different angles. First, with a goal of creating more operational context throughout product development. Second, to create opportunities to be more in tune with upcoming projects and new emerging operational concerns. These types of conversation and communication were of course happening normally through meetings, emails, and tickets. But it was very ad hoc, and it felt important to be more intentional about creating space for these conversations to happen regularly.

Borrowing heavily from Etsy's bootcamp concept, the Ops team started a rotational program. Instead of sending Ops people to product teams, we decided to have one software engineer from each product team spend a sprint (two weeks) on the team. The initial group consisted of five engineers, so every couple of months each engineer would spend a sprint on the team., effectively creating a system where the Ops team ends up with another full-time engineer, and each product team only loses one engineer for 20% of the time. The goal here was to expand operational awareness within each of the teams. Over time, the Product teams would gain an engineer that could

---

10 Marc Hedlund and Raffi Krikorian, "The Engineer Exchange Program," Etsy Code as Craft, Sept. 10, 2012, *https://oreil.ly/sO7fK*.

act as both an expert in the product domain, and in operating the product on the platform.

The other experiment that's been refined over the last year was an inversion of this approach. Instead of training a product team engineer, I assigned a designated operations engineer to each product team to be their designated Operations Advocate. The purpose here is to create accountability for both the operations engineer and the product team. By assigning a designated person to work with a product team directly, they're more likely to reach out and ask questions. This person is also expected to attend design sessions, rollout meetings, etc., essentially acting as an operations stakeholder within the team.

The outcome

These initiatives have given us a mixture of success and failure. In the spirit of Chaos Engineering, it's injecting failure into the system by taking engineers from the teams they normally work on and sending them off to other teams for periods of time. It's a trade-off, by valuing providing operational context or product domain context over what these engineers do on a normal day.

As you might expect, production pressure is always working against these types of initiatives. "We need this engineer next sprint to finish a feature ahead of an upcoming release." Or worse, an engineer is so critical to the success of their normal team that they're now suddenly unable to work on either team effectively, being constantly pulled in multiple directions.

There were some interesting results from the bootcamp concept. Several engineers decided to do longer stints on the Ops team. One even joined the team full time for a year, before deciding to go back to their original product team. With the added capacity, and software engineering skills, the team was able to complete important projects that would have taken much longer without them. The bootcampers almost single-handedly turned SportsEngine's internal deployment service from what was just an idea into a beast that averages close to 100 deploys per day across 75 different services, and created a shared experience for developers deploying to services of all different shapes and sizes. This experiment also forced the Ops team to figure out how to onboard people to the team effectively. When you bring one new person onto a team over the course of a few months, it's a very different experience than it is to onboard five engineers with almost no operational experience onto the team.

With the advocates, the system has been harder to enforce. It's not nearly as clean of a design with built-in feedback loops like the bootcamp concept. It's difficult to know what information they're missing out on without being a member of the team. What has been interesting is that the bootcampers will often recognize when an advocate should be present and pull them in. The biggest trade-off I've noticed from the advocate concept is around resource allocation. If I have an operations engineer on an important project, and their product team is pulling them into a discussion, or a new project they need help with, it then impacts what I'm trying to do.

These deliberate attempts at increasing connections within the organization have made a significant difference in our ability as an operations team to create the platform our engineers need. As an organization we don't have unlimited resources to hire our way out of the problem, and frankly I'm not even sure that's a thing. Operational context is so critical to the success of software. Finding new ways to disseminate it throughout the organization will always be on my mind. I think more generally you could say the same thing about shared context and the value of finding common ground.

Leadership Is an Emergent Property of the System

What I find fascinating about systems thinking and complexity theory is that it applies to everything. When I realized that leadership within an organization could be looked at through this lens, it blew my mind. It's important to note that when I talk about the word "leadership" in this context, I'm not talking about people or a team of people who "lead others." Rather, I'm talking about leadership as a phenomenon that happens, in the same way that communication between actors in the system is a property of that system. Or in the world of consensus algorithms, there is a "leader" or "leader elections." These are properties of the system that change over time. That isn't to say someone in a "leadership position" doesn't contribute to these properties; in fact, they do it more frequently than others. Why is that? Many of the challenges we deal with in distributed systems can be mapped to challenges within an organization, and at some point ownership and accountability ultimately end up on the shoulders of the system's leader.

Moving your organization forward

Dr. James Barker is a professor and researcher at Dalhousie University, specializing in organizational safety, leadership theories, and complexity theory. He describes leadership as an emergent property of the system that moves the organization forward. I love this definition. It frames leadership as decision making within bounded context. A leader is one who makes a given choice that they become accountable for. This definition aligns well with pushing context and decision making out to the edges, to the "sharp end," the practitioners, the people who understand the most about the tradeoffs they make every day.

Using signals to set a direction

What happens when you push this decision making out to the edges is that, as you would expect, consensus becomes more and more difficult. Local rationality is at play. Local rationality can be described as what makes sense from one person's perspective may not make sense from someone else's. But in return you give freedom and responsibility to those who are accountable. Those who interact with a given system are the experts of that system. They will see and understand signals, or feedback, coming from that system. When they have authority to act on those signals, amazing things can happen.

Case Study 3: Changing a Basic Assumption

As technologists we often find ourselves questioning the very foundation we stand on. This is a natural state for us to live in. We often question architectural decisions (e.g., "Did we choose the right database?", "Did we select the right network topology?", "Should this be its own service?"). How frequently do you ask yourself these kinds of foundational questions at the core of how your organization works? Something that has always fascinated me about SportsEngine is my ability to change the system. It often happens slowly over time, but it's happening. This often starts when you can, as Eli Goldratt describes in *Essays on the Theory of Constraints*,[11] "Change a basic assumption and you have changed the system itself." The basic assumption of any system within an organization is that it's working. This is where empowering actors within these systems to enact change on them can make a massive impact. Help them change the organization's basic assumption of the system by raising the weak signals only they can see from their perspective.

The hypothesis

Employees are a solution to be harnessed, not a problem to control. Referring back to Sidney Dekker's paper on this topic,[12] he talks about worker-managed safety. People at the edges are the experts of the system. Secondarily, engagement is a driving factor in human performance. By creating a place where people want to work, you end up with happier and more productive employees. This set of experiments were empowering folks who were individual contributors, engineers, in the organization to make impactful change to the system.

The variable

When you start talking about organizational change and effective leadership, identifying specific acts can be difficult. Based on my personal experience, the two examples of this come from actions taken by engineers that turned into great pillars of our culture.

---

11 Eliyahu Goldratt, *Essays on the Theory of Constraints* (Great Barrington, MA: North River Press, 1998).

12 Sidney Dekker, "Employees: A Problem to Control or Solution to Harness?"

The first was an engineer that had a burning desire to improve. They were completely driven by personal growth and mastery. As an engineering manager you can only provide so much guidance into how an engineer can improve their daily work, but as a peer on the team you share so much context that identifying ways to improve can be a natural part of how you do everyday work. It was this desire and hunger that spawned a mentorship program. Our initial iteration was just a single pair of engineers, with a few loose guidelines about how to be effective, and regular feedback loops to ensure it was adding value. This structure grew into two additional mentorships, all the way up to its current state with six active mentorships. But this program only existed because of one engineer's desire to seek out more feedback, and acknowledging that if this system could benefit one engineer, it could likely make an even bigger impact on a culture of learning within the organization.

The second example started from a belief that you can be intentional about creating a culture focused on shared learning through retrospectives. An engineer read Spotify's blog post[13] on how to hold effective team health checks and wanted to see what it would be like to hold one within our Product Development teams at SportsEngine. They started small, held several of them with one team over the course of a year, and the positive feedback told them it was worth expanding the reach. This has now grown into every Product team holding regular health checks, with score cards, and fascinating discussion about where the team is effective and where it has room for growth. This is another initiative, started by one engineer as a one-off experiment, that turned into a massively productive exercise that shows real value in growth and improvement within the organization.

The outcome

The types of activities described so far are not a silver bullet. Not everyone will make a great mentor and not everyone who wants a mentor will be invested enough to get the full value of the experience. Likewise, when you have a good working relationship, the production pressure will always be battling with the importance of growth and development. In a similar vein, if your team doesn't have good communication, or leaders who aren't open to change and new ideas, health checks will create more problems than they will fix. To be effective, the health checks can't be management performance reviews, or contain a single ounce of blame and shame. They exist to facilitate a retrospective on how teams can be even more effective than they already are.

---

13 Henrik Kniberg, "Squad Health Check Model–Visualizing What to Improve," Spotify Labs, Sept. 16, 2014, *https://oreil.ly/whbiH*.

This is where minimizing the blast radius[14] is critical to success. Find a safe space to try out ideas, where there's a higher level of trust, or less risk to business outcomes. You will be amazed at the ideas people generate when they feel listened to, free to fail, and encouraged to experiment. In both of these examples, they were attempted in places that felt safe; they were treated as experiments with low consequences for failure.

There's nothing groundbreaking about these examples, but unlike most of these types of cultural initiatives, they were formed from the ground up. Built through experience, put through the paces of practitioners, they weren't top-down "management initiatives." When you think about leadership as acting on a collection of signals to move the organization forward, it's much easier to recognize and encourage that behavior.

I've found the most success with these types of activities when I'm explicitly stating that I want to "try something." By clearly setting up an expectation that this can fail, and that's okay, what you end up with is a higher likelihood of success.

Safely Organizing the Chaos

At this point you may be asking: How did you get people on board to make this happen? The answer to that question is, as Andrew Clay Shafer likes to say, "Chop wood and carry water." You have to focus on creating the right culture where these types of activities are acceptable. I like to use the model created by sociologist Ron Westrum.[15] You can use this to understand the state of your organization. An organization can fall under three states: pathological, bureaucratic, and generative. It's based on the idea of observing how your organization communicates and collaborates. For example, in a pathological organization, novelty is crushed; in a bureaucratic organization, novelty leads to problems; and in a generative organization, novelty is implemented. This model can be used as a "sniff test" to understand how ready your organization is for experimentation. If you wouldn't classify your organization as falling somewhere close to the generative side, I wouldn't even touch a larger experiment like the bootcamp concept. You can only run these experiments within a system of autonomy that favors learning and improvement over dogmas and bureaucracy. I've never been particularly great at following rules, but one thing I've had some success with is presenting data-driven arguments around a need for systemic change.

---

14 Refer back to Chapter 3 for more on "Minimize the blast radius," an advanced principle of Chaos Engineering.

15 Ron Westrum, "A Typology of Organizational Cultures," *BMJ Quality and Safety* 13 (2004), ii22-ii27.

All You Need Is Altitude and a Direction

Any experiment you run requires you to have enough margin to avoid a catastrophic failure. In the aviation industry, the literal definition of that margin is altitude. If you haven't hit the ground yet, there's still time. But that margin is pretty useless if you're not moving. Any experiment you try should have stated goals with desired outcomes and a rip cord to end the experiment before it does serious harm to any of the people involved or to the business. In all of the previous experiments I have described, there was an explicit unacceptable outcome. During a Game Day, if a team spent on the order of an hour trying to solve a problem that adding the "on vacation engineer" could solve right away, we called it. We didn't miss any learning opportunity with the scenario, we learned what we needed to. In the bootcamp example, we were flexible with the bootcampers; if they were getting hit super hard, they skipped a turn, or traded it with another engineer. The same goes for advocates: if they were unavailable for whatever reason, we could sub someone in for them, or if it wasn't a critical conversation it could happen at a later date. It's when these rip cords start to become commonplace that you should start to rethink your experiment. We eventually ended the bootcamp concept because all of our engineers were too busy, or moved teams, or changed roles. Our margin had disappeared, so it was time for the experiment to come to an end.

Close the Loops

Systems thinking revolves around feedback loops. They are like the senses, the nervous system—they carry the signal to the sense makers. Without a feedback loop, you have no idea what direction you're headed, or if you're moving at all. When "The Principles of Chaos Engineering" talks about understanding the steady state, it's talking about your feedback loops. You have enough feedback from the system to know how it works normally. It stands to reason that if you change the system you may need to implement new feedback loops to understand the impact of your change. In the case of the bootcampers, we held a retrospective with them to keep a pulse on if it was providing value, if they found the work interesting, and if they felt like it was a good use of their time. This retrospective turned out to be critical in identifying an issue with engineers in a "tech lead" role finding it difficult to be away from their team for any extended period of time. Creating feedback loops within human systems is typically quite simple. Hold interviews with the folks involved, and get a qualitative analysis of the situation. If they feel the value, you're headed in the right direction.

If You're Not Failing, You're Not Learning

Once you have these useful feedback loops in place, if everything is "just working," you aren't looking hard enough. Remember, *all* systems contain both successes and failures intrinsically. Looking at your experiment with rose-colored glasses isn't going to provide you with the value you need. Expect to get it wrong, make adjustments, and keep moving. Failure is learning in action. Experiments frequently never see the light of day, because they're either too costly, or they don't appear to add enough value. It's normal for us to try something for a period of time, and then abandon it almost as quickly as we adopted it. This is where having a team full of avid learners creates an amazing culture. When you start to have more ideas, then time to try them, you know you're headed in the right direction.

About the Author

Andy Fleener is a humanist and a "new view" safety nerd who believes software is as much about the people developing and operating it as it is the people using it. He is the senior platform operations manager at SportsEngine, where he's been building and running software-as-a-service applications for youth and amateur sports organizations since 2011.

CHAPTER 11

People in the Loop

John Allspaw

The very notion that performing experiments on a software system can be a valuable approach to better understand its behavior is an implied acknowledgment its behavior *cannot* be comprehensively prescribed at the time the system is designed. Most modern software engineers understand this; *writing* software and *understanding how it works* (and how it might fail) are two very different things.

Developing and maintaining an understanding about a system's behavior depends on people's ability to revise or recalibrate their "mental models" of its behavior.[1] The process of experimentation in production systems can be seen (alongside post-incident analysis) as a fruitful opportunity for this recalibration or "mental model updating."

Much of this book is dedicated to approaches, nuances, details, and perspectives on the *how* of Chaos Engineering. The very existence of this book and the topic's presence in the current dialogue of software engineering and operations is exciting and is likely to continue evolving. It brings to the table the notion that *confidence* can be built through more sophisticated and mature ways.

As should be expected in the world of software, new ideas and debate have arisen about how to *automate* more and more in the context of Chaos Engineering. This tendency is understandable (given that building "automation" is essentially the *raison d'être* of software engineers). Proposals in this vein can be unaware of the irony of introducing more automation to a process that exists primarily to provide confidence around the uncertain behavior of...automation.

---

1 David D. Woods, *STELLA: Report from the SNAFUcatchers Workshop on Coping with Complexity* (Columbus, OH: The Ohio State University, 2017).

As the Principles of Chaos Engineering puts it:[2]

> Chaos Engineering is the discipline of experimenting on a system in order to build confidence in the system's capability to withstand turbulent conditions in production.

What does "building confidence" look like in real-world settings?

- People are *context-sensitive* in what, when, and how they feel confident.
- A process such as experimentation is also *context-dependent* in what drives the target(s) and details of a given experiment, the rationale for when and how it should be performed, and how the results are interpreted.

These are the areas we need to explore in order to understand what "people in the loop" actually means.

The Why, How, and When of Experiments

The approach that Chaos Engineering offers to software engineers is straightforward enough: to increase *confidence* about a system's behavior under a variety of conditions and varying parameters that can move outside the optimistic "happy path" (*https://oreil.ly/g7L-P*) of functioning.

The Why

This *modus operandi* puts the approach in good company with other methods and techniques to build confidence around how software might behave, such as:

- The various forms of testing (e.g., unit, integration, functional, etc.)
- Code reviewing strategies (to gather multiple perspectives on the same code change)
- "Dark" deploys to production[3]
- "Ramp-ups" of new functionality on a per-cohort basis (e.g., on for employees only) or a percentage basis (e.g., 50% of customer traffic)

Some of these methods take their "target" as functions within a snippet of code, as contained groupings of code interacting with each other, or as connected subsystems or components. In any case, engineers can build confidence with these approaches that exist on a spectrum that includes experiments via Chaos Engineering.

---

2 Principles of Chaos Engineering, retrieved June 10, 2019, from *https://principlesofchaos.org*.

3 Deploying a change in software with its execution path gated "on" only for some portion of users is known as a "dark" deploy. See Justin Baker, "The Dark Launch: How Google and Facebook Release New Features," April 20, 2018, Tech.co, *https://oreil.ly/jKKRX*.

These confidence-building techniques are typically associated with the relatively modern paradigm known as "continuous delivery"[4,5] and it's reasonable to include Chaos Engineering as a solid approach in that paradigm.[6]

Some experiments are driven not by an absence of confidence of the team responsible for the "target" of the experiment, but by an absence of confidence on the part of *other* parties. For example, imagine a team wanting to make a significant change to their service needs to demonstrate a form of due diligence, or "production readiness" to a stakeholder. In this way, the experiment can serve as a form of implicit verification that a particular effort has been made.

The How

As mentioned in the preceding observations, these techniques are *context-dependent*, meaning that they may be more or less productive in particular circumstances.

For example, in the absence of unit or functional testing, some code changes may warrant greater scrutiny via code review. Or at particular times (maybe during a daily peak of traffic, or the holiday season experienced by ecommerce sites) a more conservative rate of "ramp-up" for new code paths may be considered. Database schema changes, search index rebuilding, lower-layer network routing, and "cosmetic" markup changes are all examples of activities that carry different uncertainties, different consequences if things go "sideways," and different contingencies to take when they do.

Chaos Engineering is no different; to experiment effectively is to be context-sensitive. The following must be considered:

- What you experiment on (and what you don't)
- When you experiment (and how long it needs to run to be confident in the results)
- How you experiment (and all the details about the experiment's specific implementations)
- Who the experiment is for
- What the experiment's broader purpose might be, beyond building confidence for the *designer(s)* of the experiment

---

4 Continuous delivery is the "ability to get changes of all types—including new features, configuration changes, bug fixes and experiments—into production, or into the hands of users, *safely* and *quickly* in a *sustainable* way." See *https://continuousdelivery.com*.

5 Jez Humble and David Farley, *Continuous Delivery* (Upper Saddle River, NJ: Addison-Wesley, 2015).

6 See also Chapter 16, which covers continuous verification.

In practice, the cheeky answer is "it depends" and *only people* can tell you more about "it depends." This chapter explores "it depends."

The When

What influences *when* to embark on a particular experiment? In practice, engineering teams have demonstrated that a variety of conditions can influence the timing of an experiment, in terms of not only when to *begin* an experiment, but also when to *end* one. When asked how common it is to turn off or pause a running experiment, an engineer remarked:

> In some cases, these experiments were frequently delayed...because there was another team that wanted to coordinate our exercise or experiment with their deployment cycle. So we would prep to fail out an entire region and then they would say, "Oh no, can you please wait? We're in the middle of a *redeploy*."[7]

Conditions that can influence the timing of experiments include:

- Responding to unexpected or surprising dynamics or behaviors observed in an *incident*
- Launching a new feature/product/subsystem with potentially surprising behavior
- Integrating with other parts of the system (i.e., introducing a new piece of infrastructure)
- Preparing for a high-demand marketing event such as Black Friday or Cyber Monday
- Adapting to external forces (stock price fluctuations, newsworthy events, etc.)
- Confirming theories about unknown or rare system behaviors (e.g., ensuring the fallback implementation doesn't bring down business-critical infrastructure)

During incidents: "Is this related to what you're running?"

Uncertainty and ambiguity are hallmark qualities of incidents that take place in software. A common heuristic used by engineers to aid their understanding of what's actually happening with their system is to reduce the number of potential contributors (without first comprehensively justifying which are worth bringing attention to) by halting the processes, stopping services, etc.[8]

---

7 Personal communication, 2019.

8 John Allspaw, "Trade-Offs Under Pressure: Heuristics and Observations of Teams Resolving Internet Service Outages" (Master's thesis, Lund University, Lund, Sweden), 2015.

Chaos experiments in production are not immune from consideration as a potential contributor to incidents, which is understandable given how often teams find themselves at a loss for understanding what's happening with their systems.

But what about automation and getting people "out of the loop"?

As mentioned before, there are questions posed about what parts of Chaos Engineering can be "automated."[9] One lens to look at this through is a description of these activities that encompass Chaos Engineering, as outlined in "The Principles of Chaos Engineering":[10]

1. Start by defining "steady state" as some measurable output of a system that indicates normal behavior.

2. Hypothesize that this steady state will continue in both the control group and the experimental group.

3. Introduce variables that reflect real-world events like servers that crash, hard drives that malfunction, network connections that are severed, etc.

4. Try to disprove the hypothesis by looking for a difference in steady state between the control group and the experimental group.

Which of these activities *could* be automated, or *should* be?

Which ones *can't* be automated and *shouldn't* be? How should automation aid?

In order to approach these questions critically, it's worthwhile to take a short detour into the topic of *function allocation*.

Functional Allocation, or Humans-Are-Better-At/Machines-Are-Better-At

Function allocation originated in a 1951 paper entitled "Human Engineering for an Effective Air-Navigation and Traffic-Control System"[11] aimed at providing guidance on what "functions" (tasks, jobs) should be "allocated" to people, and which should be allocated to machines (today often a computer). This idea was encapsulated in what's become known as the "Fitts List." See Figure 11-1 and Table 11-1.

---

9 This term deserves scare quotes when it comes to its application in software, which can't exist in any form without being described as *automation* itself. Indeed, all facets of computing-centered work is made possible by automation and is impossible without it. There can be no "non-automated" aspects of modern computing; even actions as routine as keyboard input is not possible to be done *manually,* in a literal sense.

10 Principles of Chaos Engineering, retrieved June 10, 2019, from *https://principlesofchaos.org*.

11 P. M. Fitts, ed., "Human Engineering for an Effective Air-Navigation and Traffic-Control System," 1951, Washington, DC: National Research Council.

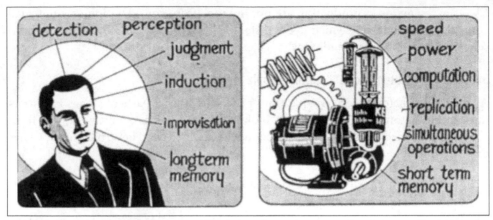

Figure 11-1. Illustrations of the Fitts list taken from the original 1951 report[12]

Table 11-1. The original Fitts list[a]

Humans appear to surpass present-day machines in respect to	Present-day machines appear to surpass humans in respect to
Ability to detect a small amount of visual or acoustic energy	Ability to respond quickly to control signals and to apply great force smoothly and precisely
Ability to perceive patterns of light and sound	Ability to perform repetitive, routine tasks
Ability to improvise and use flexible procedures	Ability to store information briefly and then to erase it completely
Ability to store very large amounts of information for long periods and recall relevant facts at the appropriate time	Ability to reason deductively, including computational ability
Ability to reason inductively	Ability to handle highly complex operations (i.e., to do many different things at once)
Ability to exercise judgment	

[a] P. M. Fitts, ed., "Human Engineering for an Effective Air-Navigation and Traffic-Control System."

Many software engineers reading this would find items in the Fitts list familiar. One could almost see some of these ideas as a sort of grand philosophical *modus operandi* for software engineering. While function allocation, beginning with the Fitts list and later coined as "HABA-MABA"[13] (humans-are-better-at/machines-are-better-at) has been core to human factors research for decades, there are some (relatively) recent critiques of the guidance stemming from empirical research in Cognitive Systems Engineering.

---

12 P. M. Fitts, ed., "Human Engineering for an Effective Air-Navigation and Traffic-Control System."

13 This coinage is modern; the original was "MABA-MABA" (*men*-are-better-at/machines-are-better-at), which reflects the state of gendered stereotypes at that time.

Exploring these critiques in a comprehensive way is beyond the scope of this chapter. However, the primary challenges to this HABA-MABA paradigm can be summarized here.

The Substitution Myth

The idea that work can be decomposed into tasks that can be identified and isolated in such a way that they can then be "allocated" to the proper agent (human or machine) is problematic for a number of reasons:[14]

> This is what Hollnagel (1999) called "function allocation by substitution." The idea is that automation can be introduced as a straightforward substitution of machines for people—preserving the basic system while improving some of its output measures (lower workload, better economy, fewer errors, higher accuracy, etc.).

> Behind the idea of substitution lies the idea that people and computers (or any other machines) have fixed strengths and weaknesses and that the point of automation is to capitalize on the strengths while eliminating or compensating for the weaknesses. The problem is that capitalizing on some strength of computers does not replace a human weakness. It creates new human strengths and weaknesses—often in unanticipated ways.[15]

When new forms of automation are proposed with this "give the bits that computers do well to computers" logic, it often comes with an assumption that:[16]

> ...new automation can be substituted for human action without any larger impact on the system in which that action or task occurs, except on output. This view is predicated on the notion that a complex system is decomposable into a set of essentially independent tasks.

> However, investigations of the impact of new technology have shown that these assumptions are not tenable (they are what could be termed the substitution myth). Tasks and activities are highly interdependent or coupled in real complex systems.

Would these perspectives hold in the case of "automating" portions of the Chaos Engineering approach?

In the next chapter of this book, Peter Alvaro proposes that experiment *selection*[17] can be automated, with the rationale being that a significant hurdle to overcome in Chaos Engineering is not just the existence of a "combinatorial space" of possible faults to

---

14 Sidney W. A. Dekker, *Safety Differently*, Second Edition (CRC Press: Boca Raton, FL, 2015).

15 Lisanne Bainbridge, "Ironies of Automation," *Automatica*, Vol. 19, No. 6, 1983.

16 Nadine B. Sarter, and David D. Woods, "Team Play with a Powerful and Independent Agent: Operational Experiences and Automation Surprises on the Airbus A-320," *Human Factors*, 39(4), 1997.

17 A necessary distinction regarding terminology might be made about experiments being "chosen" or "selected" as from a list of options, rather than an output from an exercise perhaps more accurately described as "designed."

experiment on[18] but finding an experiment that has a greater *likelihood* of being productive in revealing undesirable behavior.

At first glance, the idea seems reasonable. If we can develop and execute an application to "discover" weaknesses or items to potentially experiment on and present those to people to choose from, then this application would have potentially "solved" a challenge of the Chaos Engineering activity. The application doing this "selection" work can analyze a software system and then present the results to a person who can in turn choose which experiment to run. Such an effort would certainly be interesting on a number of fronts. Perhaps the greatest contribution of such an application might be to generate dialogue among engineers.

However, the foundational notion that such an application will "automate away" distractions is problematic. As Bainbridge notes in her seminal article "The Ironies of Automation,"[19] one irony is:

> Designer errors [in automation] can be a major source of operating problems.

Will the algorithm doing this automated experiment "selection" be bug-free? If not, how much attention will this automation require itself? Will the application itself require expertise to run effectively?

The irony (using Bainbridge's term) here may be that the automation intended to make life *easier* for people can itself be a source of *new* challenges for them to consider and handle. Indeed, automation does not come for free.

A second irony that Bainbridge notes is:

> The designer [of the automation], who tries to eliminate the operator, still leaves the operator to do the tasks which the designer cannot think how to automate.

While in theory we have relieved engineers from exploring the space of potential experiment scenarios, we have introduced new tasks that they did not have before:

- They must decide how *often* this automated experiment finder should be run, given that the system's in a continual state of change and usage.

- They will also be responsible for stopping or pausing the automation operating on production systems under certain conditions (just as with an experiment).

- They will now have another piece of software to maintain and extend, ideally introducing new improvements and fixing bugs as they arise.

---

18 Peter Alvaro, Joshua Rosen, and Joseph M. Hellerstein, "Lineage-Driven Fault Injection," *Proceedings of the 2015 ACM SIGMOD International Conference on Management of Data-SIGMOD 15*, 2015, doi: 10.1145/2723372.2723711.

19 Bainbridge, "Ironies of Automation."

Conclusion

The emergence of Chaos Engineering represents an exciting opportunity that we should expect to continue evolving. Despite claims to the contrary, this opportunity does *not* represent the potential for fewer bugs and/or incidents in software systems.

Instead, this opportunity is a new and productive way for system engineers and operators to develop richer understandings not only of their system's behaviors, but through the generative dialogue that surrounds all of the activities (hypothesis generation, steady-state definition, expression of concerns and fears about uncertainty or ambiguity) involved in taking a Chaos Engineering approach. Therefore, we should view the approach as one that can *augment* the flexible and context-sensitive capacities that only people possess as they continue to cope with the complexity that necessarily comes with successful software.

People are *the* beneficiaries of all technology, including software. The reason why *building confidence* in software systems via experiments is important is because these software systems *matter to people*, and sometimes in multiple ways.

People will *always* need to be "in the loop" with software because people are responsible, and software cannot be:

> An essential part of being human is the ability to enter into commitments and to be responsible for the courses of action that they anticipate. A computer can never enter into a commitment.[20]

Chaos Engineering's capacity to build confidence is ultimately about helping people in their responsibility to design and operate complex systems.

About the Author

John Allspaw has worked in software systems engineering and operations for over twenty years in many different environments. John's publications include *The Art of Capacity Planning* and *Web Operations* (both O'Reilly) as well as the foreword to *The DevOps Handbook* (IT Revolution Press). His 2009 Velocity talk with Paul Hammond, "10+ Deploys Per Day: Dev and Ops Cooperation" helped start the DevOps movement. John served as CTO at Etsy, and holds an MSc in Human Factors and Systems Safety from Lund University.

---

20 Terry Winograd and Fernando Flores, *Understanding Computers and Cognition* (Reading, MA: Addison-Wesley, 1986).

CHAPTER 12

The Experiment Selection Problem (and a Solution)

Peter Alvaro

It is hard to imagine a large-scale, real-world system that does not involve the interaction of people and machines. When we design such a system, often the hardest (and most important) part is figuring out how best to use the two different kinds of resources. In this chapter, I make the case that the resiliency community should rethink how it leverages humans and computers as resources. Specifically, I argue that the problem of developing intuition about system failure modes using observability infrastructure, and ultimately discharging those intuitions in the form of chaos experiments, is a role better played by a computer than by a person. Finally, I provide some evidence that the community is ready to move in this direction.

Choosing Experiments

Independent from (and complementary to) the methodologies discussed in the rest of the book is the problem of *experiment selection*: choosing which faults to inject into which system executions. As we have seen, choosing the right experiments can mean identifying bugs before our users do, as well as learning new things about the behavior of our distributed system at scale. Unfortunately, due to the inherent complexity of such systems, the number of possible distinct experiments that we could run is astronomical—exponential in the number of communicating instances. For example, suppose we wanted to exhaustively test the effect of every possible combination of node crashes in an application involving 20 distinct services. There are 2^{20}—over one million—ways that even this modestly sized distributed system could be affected by just node crashes!

Out of this massive combinatorial space, how do we choose the experiments on which to spend time and resources? An exhaustive search is not tractable—the sun would be extinguished before we performed every possible experiment given a distributed system of even modest size. The current state of the art provides two reasonable albeit unsatisfactory answers that we have already considered in this book.

Random Search

Early chaos approaches (e.g., the monkey from which the discipline borrows its name) searched the space of faults *randomly* (see Figure 12-1). The random approach has many advantages. First, it is simple to implement: once we have enumerated a fault space (e.g., all possible combinations of instance crashes, to use the simple

---

1 Haopeng Liu, et al., "FCatch: Automatically Detecting Time-of-fault Bugs in Cloud Systems," *Proceedings of the Twenty-Third International Conference on Architectural Support for Programming Languages and Operating Systems*, Williamsburg, VA, 2018.

example with which Chaos Monkey began) we can simply choose experiments by sampling from it uniformly and at random. The random approach also requires no domain knowledge to operate: it performs equally well on any distributed system.

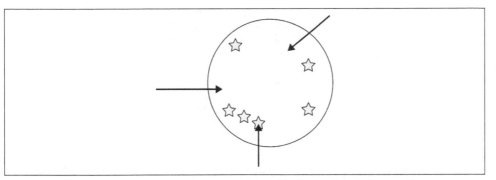

Figure 12-1. The circle represents the space of possible faults that a chaos infrastructure could inject. In random experiment selection, individual fault injection experiments (arrows) sometimes identify software bugs (stars) in which a failure that should have been tolerated by the system is not.

Unfortunately, the random approach does not perform particularly well on any distributed system. The combinatorial space of faults is vast enough that approaches that simply stab blindly into it are unlikely to identify rich software bugs and misconfigurations that are only detected when some number of independent faults (e.g., the roughly simultaneous loss of a top-of-rack switch and a node crash on a data replica) occur. Nor do random approaches give us any sense of how well the experiments we have run so far have "covered" the space of possible experiments. They tell us nothing about how long a random chaos experiment should be carried out before concluding that a system under test is adequately robust to safely release new code.

The Age of the Experts

The emerging principled alternative to random testing is the subject of much of this book: leveraging the domain knowledge of system experts to drive the search for experiments. Expert-guided experiment selection (shown in Figure 12-2) is very much the opposite end of the spectrum from random testing. At the cost of significant resources (experts are expensive) and time, this approach can zero in on system-specific weaknesses or corner cases rather than applying the same strategy everywhere. Unlike random testing, which cannot learn from its mistakes and in some sense never makes progress, expert-guided experiment selection can use the observations of previous experiments (positive or negative) to formulate new hypotheses, progressively *refining* them. This refinement process, if carried out carefully, gradually identifies "holes" in the expert's mental model of the system under study, targets these holes via experiments, and ultimately fills them, either by identifying a bug or obtaining new evidence (to incorporate into our model) of how the system tolerates those fault conditions. This sounds great! Let's do it.

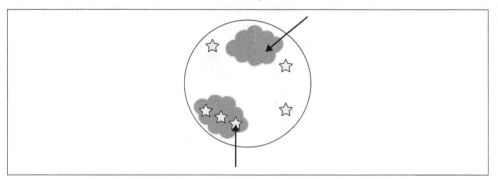

Figure 12-2. By harnessing observability infrastructure to explain executions (both successful and unsuccessful), expert-guided experiment selection can identify regions (clouds) of the experiment space in which the outcomes of experiments already performed can identify future experiments that need not be performed. In this example, some experiments (top cloud shape) do not expose a bug, and their traces reveal a bug-free region that we need not search. Others (bottom cloud shape) expose a bug and alert us to the existence of other bugs (again, experiments we no do not need to run).

Unfortunately, to begin carrying out expert-guided experiment selection an enterprise must recruit and train *experts*.

The role of the expert

Part of the expert's job is *choice* of faults: they must decide which experiments to spend time, money, and energy running. But it is more interesting to consider this problem from the other side: the expert must decide which experiments *need not be run*. Why would we choose to skip over any point in the combinatorial space of possible experiments? It would only be sound to do so if we know something about the system—specifically, because we already know what will happen if we inject that collection of faults! As you have read elsewhere in this book, if we already know that a particular fault injection experiment will trigger a bug, it is unnecessary (not to mention impolite!) to perform that experiment. Instead, we should muster resources to repair the bug before it affects our users. For example, suppose an experiment has identified a critical flaw in the fault-handling logic of a particular service. This bug needs to be prioritized for repair before we bother exploring fault injection in any of the other services upon which it depends! We are unlikely to learn anything new from this experiment, and it is likely to put a burden on our operations teams.

Again, however, the flip-side here is even more interesting: if we know an experiment *will not* trigger a bug, we should not perform that experiment either. For example, consider a service (call it X) that we have confirmed via experimentation to be a *soft dependency*—that is, all of the services that call it have been demonstrated to perform correctly even when that service is down. Now consider a service Y that X (but no other service) depends on. Any faults that we might inject in Y can at worst only be observed as failures of X, which we already know the system tolerates! Hence it is not worth exploring that region of the fault space at all.

This second example illustrates that beyond the choosing of experiments, an equally important job of the expert is deciding *in what order* to run them (in this case, our decision to experiment on X thoroughly before looking at Y saved us possibly many experiments by revealing what their outcomes would have been). Picking the right ordering, however, requires us to optimize a number of different objectives that may be at odds with each other. First, as I argued earlier, we should consider the semantics of the system under study to better understand which experiments are likely to give us new knowledge that allows us to skip future experiments. That is, we want to use our knowledge of the system to choose new experiments that most quickly increase our knowledge. Second, because we want to identify bugs before our users do, we also want to run experiments that correspond to *likely events* (e.g., a concurrent failure of a replica and a network partition between two remaining replicas) before exploring rare events (e.g., the simultaneous loss of three distinct datacenters).

Putting all of this together, an experiment selection expert must:

- Begin with semantic knowledge of the system under test (e.g., the topology of the call graph).
- Use that knowledge to *avoid* redundant experiments, whose outcomes we can already predict.
- Among the interesting experiments, choose an order that *best increases knowledge* while simultaneously exploring likely faults first.

This process is iterative: the new knowledge guides future choices and orders.

But where does the knowledge come from? In order to do their job, the expert requires that the system under study reveal information about itself during experiments (as well as during steady state). That is to say, they require some kind of *observability* infrastructure—the richer the better. Without the observability there can be no new knowledge, no refinement of the space of experiments. We will return to this subject later.

The human mind can be bafflingly good at traversing an enormous space of possibilities in an intelligent way, while simultaneously managing differing, sometimes conflicting objectives. Good Chaos Engineers are really good at what they do. However, can we characterize exactly the process that they followed to become good? If we cannot, what hope do we have of effectively training new ones?

The Communicability of Human Intuition

As you probably inferred from earlier chapters in this book, there is an ongoing debate regarding the proper role of automation in Chaos Engineering and the appropriate balance between automation and human expertise. I think everyone would agree that we want neither an all-human nor an all-automaton system. Instead, we would like to automate away all of the distracting details so that we can allow humans to do what it is that they do best, without distraction. I hope that this is an uncontroversial beginning to this sidebar.

What exactly is it that humans are uniquely good at? It turns out that this is difficult to answer, at least for me. It would sometimes appear that synthesis—coming up with a completely new idea by combining existing ideas—is what we were put on earth to do. Yet with each passing year computers surprise us with how good they are at synthesis. What about abstraction—generalizing from concrete examples to concepts? This is certainly one of the things that humans are best at. But here too machines show a great deal of promise. Maybe the best answer is creation *ex nihilo*: coming up with a completely new idea that does not involve the combination of existing, smaller ideas. Computers are not good at this yet! This should come as no surprise since after all, we cannot explain what makes people good at this. We have little hope of teaching a computer how to do it until we can.

It is tempting to say that *intuition*—the ability to think "from the gut'" without explicit reasoning—is what people are best at. Humans have an amazing capacity to rapidly make connections based on observations, and to later use those connections to efficiently make decisions. Unfortunately, humans do a poor job of explaining their intuitions to others. When we make a decision based on intuition, it is often impossible to recall the observations that contributed to that intuition (as useful as it might be to do so!). Because of this, relying on human intuition (something which in general cannot be documented or disseminated) as a key part of the business process can be risky. If a site reliability engineer (SRE), after staring at a dashboard for a few moments during an outage, begins narrowing their investigation to a particular suspect service, we might want to ask them *why* that set of signals led to that action. How often could they answer? Perhaps this is why we can train SREs so effectively to deal with incidents by putting them in front of incidents, but we aren't very good at training SREs based on the accumulated knowledge of past SREs.

In a 2015 post on the Netflix Tech Blog,[2] Casey Rosenthal (a coeditor of this book) and his coauthors describe the desire to create a "holistic understanding" of complex system behavior using a thought experiment called a "pain suit." The pain suit

---

2 Casey Rosenthal et al., "Flux: A New Approach to System Intuition," The Netflix Tech Blog, Oct. 1, 2015, *https://oreil.ly/dp_-3*.

converts system alerts and other signals surfaced by the observability infrastructure into painful sensations on the wearer's skin.

They write:

> Now imagine that you are wearing the Pain Suit for a few short days. You wake up one morning and feel a pain in your shoulder. "Of course," you think. "Microservice X is misbehaving again." It would not take you long to get a visceral sense of the holistic state of the system. Very quickly, you would have an intuitive understanding of the entire service, without having any numerical facts about any events or explicit alerts.

I imagine that a pain suit, if such a thing existed, would be just as effective as the authors of the post describe. Moreover, I think the analogy to the state of the art in SRE training is apt. In the current state of the art, in which SREs are trained as apprentices, would-be expert experiment selectors are also trained by putting them in front of a huge set of diverse signals and teaching them, by example, how to go from signal to potential cause. However, I strongly believe that this is a catastrophically wrong solution to the experiment selection problem and I hope that I will convince you of this as well.

As powerful of a human capability as intuition may be, as a general rule it is at odds with *explainability*. Decisions we make from our gut are not rational in the sense that although they may be based upon observations in some sense, we have lost the ability to connect them via an explanation. Explanations are powerful: they make the reasoning behind our decisions *communicable*. If we can explain a decision we can teach someone else to make a similar decision under similar circumstances without "overfitting" to the details of a particular example. If we can explain a decision we can encode the logic into a computer program and automate (some of) the steps that contribute to making that decision. The stated goal of Chaos Engineering is to increase our *knowledge* of the system, and knowledge implies communicability. In some important sense an SRE trained with a pain suit or its real-world equivalent does not have knowledge—they merely have reactions, or instinct.

I would like to suggest that one of the things—perhaps the most important thing— that people are uniquely good at is providing and interpreting explanations. If all we need is a body to place in a pain suit, something that can be trained by examples but cannot train others, we should probably put a computer in it! This sounds like a job for a deep neural net, not an expensive SRE.

Observability: The Opportunity

Performing Chaos Engineering experiments in the principled manner advocated for in this book requires investment not just in fault injection infrastructure but in observability infrastructure. After all, what is the point of setting something on fire if you can't watch it burn? In many cases, the same mechanisms that are used to determine *whether* a test group diverged from steady state can be used to explain *how* individual requests within a test group succeeded despite the faults introduced in the experiments.

Call graph tracing, for example, provides explanations of individual distributed system executions by revealing the causal chain of communication. Today, most request-level distributed tracing infrastructures are loosely based on the design of Google's Dapper,[3] which was published in 2010. By 2012, engineers at Twitter had implemented an open source version called Zipkin; by 2015 Zipkin clones had proliferated to many microservice-based organizations (e.g., Salp at Netflix, Jaeger at Uber). Today, OpenTracing provides an open standard for call graph tracing.

Among organizations that have call graph tracing systems, SREs and developers commonly think narrowly about the potential uses cases. In particular, in the most common use cases:

- Call graphs are used to diagnose *what went wrong* in anomalous executions—for example, to understand why a particular request failed or took so much longer than the mean time to complete. This is not surprising: the use case that motivated the development of Dapper was diagnosing tail latency issues in the massive fanout of a Google search, a problem that was not well served by the aggregate measures provided by monitoring infrastructure.

- Call graphs are consumed by human end users (a human–computer interaction problem) and hence are outside the scope of automation. A lot of recent work has gone into better visualizations of call graphs, but little work has been done analyzing them in bulk.

These use cases, however, only scratch the surface of the potential applications of the rich signals available in traces. Consider the value to an SRE-in-training of studying *what went right* rather than diagnosing what went wrong.[4] In order to formulate the problems identified in Section 1 (namely, choosing which experiments to run and in which order to run them), we need to understand what steady state looks like for the

---

3 Benjamin H. Sigelman, et al., "Dapper, a Large-Scale Distributed Systems Tracing Infrastructure", Technical Report (Google), 2010.

4 In Resilience Engineering this concept is known as Safety-II; see Eric Hollnagel's description: *https://oreil.ly/sw5KR*.

system under test. Although we tend to think of a distributed system's steady state as best represented by a collection of aggregate measures of system health, this thirty-thousand-foot view does not tell the whole story. Understanding the steady state of a system also involves understanding what individual successful or expected executions (e.g., individual request/response interactions) *look like*. As discussed earlier (see "The role of the expert" on page 164), choosing the right experiments requires semantic understanding of the system under test—in particular, an understanding of how it tolerates the faults that it was designed to tolerate. This means also understanding what the executions *in which the system tolerates some faults but nevertheless functions as expected* look like. Of particular interest to the SRE are the call graphs of these executions, which help explain how the system tolerated a particular fault or combination of faults.

Observability for Intuition Engineering

While the ostensible purpose of the observability infrastructure was to assist in forensics when something goes wrong on the site, we see that in this case the infrastructure can be used to assist the experts in building a *model* of the system under study. It is tempting to ask—especially given the research question I posed about automating intuition ("What exactly is it that humans are uniquely good at?") in the earlier sidebar—whether we could use these traces to train computers (instead of expert users) to perform intelligent experiment selection. The "pain suit" fell short of truly automating intuition: it automated how information is presented to a human expert, whose job it was to build (and later discharge) intuition. We should be thinking about how to automate this process end to end, so that those precious human cycles can be saved for those tasks that we could never automate.

Lineage-driven fault injection

While it is by no means the only possible realization of this goal, Disorderly Labs' (*https://disorderlylabs.github.io*) research on lineage-driven fault injection (LDFI) shows that with a little creativity it is possible to answer the question of whether experiment selection intuition can be automated from end to end in the affirmative. LDFI fills the role of the SRE expert that I described in the rest of this chapter, consuming the explanations provided by tracing infrastructure and formulating experiments that can be executed by the fault injection infrastructure.

The first key idea behind LDFI is that traces often reveal how a distributed system works around faults by employing *redundancy* in a variety of forms. From my perspective, fault tolerance and redundancy are of a piece: a system is fault-tolerant *precisely* if it provides *enough different ways* for the distributed computation to succeed that the partial failure of some of those computations does not rule out success! This redundancy is played out in a variety of dimensions: replication, failover, retry, checkpoints and upstream backups, and write-ahead logs. The second key idea is that this redundancy is very often manifest in the *structure* of the explanations provided by system tracing. For example, a timeout and failover to a redundant stateless service instance or a fallback to an alternative service reveals a new "branch" in the explanation. Similarly, when soft dependencies fail, a call graph gives us evidence that that subgraph was not required for a successful computation. Over time, the history of a sequence of successful call graphs can reveal a variety of *alternative* computations that are individually sufficient to make an execution succeed, as well as the *critical* computations common to all successful executions. As a rule, the former give us hints about experiments that can be skipped, while the latter tell us about which experiments to prioritize.

After this, the rest is just a matter of modeling and engineering. We chose a particular, rather simplistic way of modeling the information contained in system traces: as Boolean formulae. It is relatively straightforward to convert a collection of traces of successful executions into such a formula, and once we have done so the problem of choosing a "good experiment" (one that is likely to either reveal a bug or reveal redundancy that we have not yet modeled) is something we can pose as a decision problem to an efficient, off-the-shelf Boolean satisfiability (SAT) solver. Similarly, in order to prioritize our experiments we can encode ranking information based on the topology of graphs or the likelihood of failure of a particular service or piece of hardware. Using this ranking, we can present the same Boolean formula to an integer linear programming (ILP) solver, and ask it to find the *best* solution (experiment) that maximizes the rankings. By fine-tuning the ranking function, we can encode a heuristic such as "explore the most likely faults first, but among equally likely faults, explore those experiments that (based on topological information) are likely to rule the most out future experiments." To make LDFI work at a variety of industrial collaborators (including Netflix, Huawei, and eBay) required a certain amount of integration engineering. For example, extracting the relevant information from a particular tracing deployment is never quite the same job twice, nor do any two custom fault injection infrastructures look quite alike. Nevertheless, the process of "glueing" these pieces together can be thought of as establishing a set of abstract mappings. We describe this in a recent paper.[5]

Boolean formulae were just one possible way to build our models and it is easy to imagine others. Perhaps most appropriate to the fundamentally uncertain nature of distributed systems would be probabilistic models or trained statistical models such as deep neural networks. These are outside of my own area of expertise, but I would very much like to find collaborators and recruit graduate students who are interested in working on these problems!

---

5 Peter Alvaro, et al., "Automating Failure Testing Research at Internet Scale", *Proceedings of the 7th Annual Symposium on Cloud Computing* (SoCC 2016), Santa Clara, CA: ACM (October 2016).

It was not my intent in this section to advertise the LDFI approach per se, but rather to provide an example that shows that the sort of end-to-end "intuition automation" for which I advocated in the sidebar is possible in practice. I hope that I have convinced you that if your organization already has a mature SRE culture and infrastructure then the raw materials are already there to begin automating intuition. Instead of training SREs, via apprenticeship, to become expert experiment selectors, try putting in the time to automate the experiment selection process. Then it can chug along on its own, and when it identifies bugs, those experts can be mustered to work on a problem that seems (at least on the surface)[6] much harder to automate: tracking down and repairing bugs.

Conclusion

The current state of the art in Intuition Engineering is flawed. What we need is "intuition automation"—training computers to replace the role of experts in chaos experiment selection. While it is certainly possible to train expert experiment selectors using our community's ever-improving observability infrastructure, it can be expensive, unreliable, and difficult to repeat. If we can train machines to do even close to as good a job as these human experts we should start doing so right away, so as to save those precious human cycles for those tasks (e.g., reacting to new phenomena and providing explanations for those reactions) that humans are uniquely suited to do.

About the Author

Peter Alvaro is an assistant professor of computer science at the University of California Santa Cruz, where he leads the Disorderly Labs research group (disorderly-labs.github.io). His research focuses on using data-centric languages and analysis techniques to build and reason about data-intensive distributed systems, in order to make them scalable, predictable, and robust to the failures and nondeterminism endemic to large-scale distribution. Peter earned his PhD at UC Berkeley, where he studied with Joseph M. Hellerstein. He is a recipient of the NSF CAREER Award and the Facebook Research Award.

---

6 Lennart Oldenburg et al., "Fixed It For You: Protocol Repair Using Lineage Graphs", *Proceedings of the 9th biennial Conference on Innovative Data Systems Research* (CIDR 2019), Asilomar, CA, 2019.

PART IV

Business Factors

Chaos Engineering exists to solve a real business need. It was born at Netflix and now has adoption across thousands of companies, a large portion of which are not primarily software companies. This part of the book provides more context about how Chaos Engineering fits into the larger context of business concerns.

Chapter 13, "ROI of Chaos Engineering," addresses the most important question about the practice from a business perspective, namely: How do we prove that adopting Chaos Engineering provides more value than it costs? "Demonstrating the ROI of Chaos Engineering is not easy. In most cases, you will feel the value of experiments almost immediately, before you can articulate that value." This chapter provides a model for considering ROI and applies it to the practice.

Russ Miles takes the business considerations in a different direction in Chapter 14, "Open Minds, Open Science, and Open Chaos," by emphasizing the relationship between business domains and scientific pursuits. "Like all science, Chaos Engineering is at its most valuable when it is highly collaborative: where everyone can see what experiments are being pursued, when they are happening, and what findings have surfaced." He makes a case for open source tools, experiments, and community to get the most value out of this discipline.

One of the most common questions for organizations adopting Chaos Engineering is where to start, or how to proceed. Chapter 15, "Chaos Maturity Model," provides a map for how to evaluate an existing Chaos Engineering program. As a map, it also suggests ways to consider evolving the practice to achieve a higher level of maturity, and therefore get more value out of it: "Highly sophisticated, pervasive Chaos

Engineering is the best *proactive* method for improving availability and security in the software industry."

Whether you are considering adopting Chaos Engineering in your organization, or seeking to improve an existing practice, this part of the book will offer guidance and provide context about how to marry the science of Chaos Engineering with the pragmatism of business in order to create value.

CHAPTER 13

ROI of Chaos Engineering

> *"No one tells the story of the incident that didn't happen."*
> —John Allspaw

Chaos Engineering is a pragmatic discipline designed to provide value to a business. One of the most difficult aspects of running a successful Chaos Engineering practice is *proving* that the results have business value. This chapter enumerates the difficulties of establishing a connection to business values, describes a model for methodically pursuing return on investment (ROI) called the Kirkpatrick Model, and provides an objective example of establishing ROI taken from Netflix's experience with ChAP, the Chaos Automation Platform.

Ephemeral Nature of Incident Reduction

Imagine that you measure the uptime of your service in some consistent way, and find that you have two nines[1] of uptime. You implement a Chaos Engineering practice, and subsequently the system demonstrates three nines of uptime. How do you prove that the Chaos Engineering practice should be credited and not some contemporaneous change? That attribution issue is a hard problem.

There is another confounding obstacle: the nature of the improvement that Chaos Engineering provides is self-limiting, because the most obvious benefits are ephemeral. Instead of establishing long-lasting benefits to system safety, improvements

---

1 "Nines" are a common way of measuring uptime. Two nines corresponds to the service being up for 99% of the time, three nines corresponds to 99.9% of the time, and so on. The more nines, the better. Five nines corresponds to less than 5.5 minutes of downtime per year. Note that this small amount is extremely difficult to measure, and any number of nines above this is meaningless for most systems, even if it is measured in some consistent manner over time.

triggered by Chaos Engineering tend to open the gates to other business pressures. If Chaos Engineering improves availability, chances are good that the business will respond by releasing features faster. That in turn will raise the bar for how difficult it is for those teams to navigate complexity, which in turn can make maintaining that level of availability even more difficult.

So if Chaos Engineering works, the benefit might be invisible. And if it works noticeably well, the benefits will be erased by competing pressures. On the surface this may seem like a no-win situation, but all hope is not lost. Extra effort has to be expended to explicitly capture the value. Sometimes the value can be directly tied to a business outcome; sometimes it cannot. This often depends on how much effort can be put toward measuring this value, as well as the method for going about capturing the value.

Kirkpatrick Model

The Kirkpatrick Model offers one way to evaluate ROI. The model has been around since the 1950s and the most common iteration can be deconstructed into the following four levels:

- Level 1: Reaction
- Level 2: Learning
- Level 3: Transfer
- Level 4: Results

The levels are a progression, where Level 1 is relatively simple and low value, while Level 4 is often difficult to implement but high value.

The model is used in educational settings like academia and corporate training programs to evaluate the effectiveness of a teaching or training program. Since Chaos Engineering teaches people about their own systems, we can think of it as an educational endeavor. Much of the Kirkpatrick Model therefore applies to the results of Chaos Engineering.

Level 1: Reaction

We enter the model with a very basic assessment: How did the trainees respond to the training? We can assess the trainees' response through questionnaires, interviews, or even informal conversation. In the context of Chaos Engineering, the owners and operators of the system are the people we want to educate about systemic vulnerabilities. They are the trainees as well as stakeholders in the safety of the system. We want these stakeholders to tell us whether the experiments were helpful or not. Did they feel like they learned something from the experiments? Did they enjoy Game Day exercises? How do they feel about the Chaos Engineering program as implemented? Would they recommend continuing or expanding the program? If the answers are positive, we consider that a positive Level 1 evaluation in the Kirkpatrick Model and this is a minimal demonstration of the ROI of Chaos Engineering. If the answers are not positive, then the Kirkpatrick Model tells us that the program is likely ineffective and the Chaos Engineering program as implemented should be discontinued or significantly changed. Education rarely occurs when the stakeholders do not value the training program.

Level 2: Learning

It is all well and good if the operators as stakeholders feel good about the program. This next level in the model takes it a step further to establish proof that they learned something. During a Game Day, this might be one of the explicit functions of a facilitator. They may write down discoveries, like: "Team learned that Production has an unanticipated dependency on the Kafka cluster in Staging." Or, "Team learned that the failure of two Tier-2 services will bring down a Tier-1 service, which would result in catastrophic failure." (Hopefully items like those are learned with proper minimization of blast radius.) In non-Game Day experiments, the lessons learned might be more difficult to identify. If there is a mechanism to record hypotheses that are disproved, this would at least provide a starting point for enumerating things learned by the program. Enumeration of the lessons learned establishes this level of ROI for Chaos Engineering according to the Kirkpatrick Model.

Level 3: Transfer

Enumerating the lessons learned in Level 2 is a solid start to establishing ROI of a training program and it is even better when that is followed up by translating it to practice. Level 3 in the Kirkpatrick Model seeks to establish that translation of information into behavior. If Chaos Engineering teaches the operators and stakeholders where the system is vulnerable, we expect to see an impact on their behavior somewhere. We can look for behavior changes in operators, engineers, other stakeholders, and even managers such as:

- Do they fix the vulnerabilities?
- Do they change the operational strategy regarding their systems?
- Do they build services in a more robust manner?
- Do they enhance the adaptive capacities that contribute to system resilience?
- Do they allocate more resources toward safety like code reviews and safer continuous delivery tooling and additional Chaos Engineering?

If we can establish changes in behavior as a result of the Chaos Engineering, then according to the Kirkpatrick Model we have strong evidence that the Chaos Engineering program is working.

Level 4: Results

This final level of assessing effectiveness of a training program in the Kirkpatrick Model is the most difficult to establish. Correlating one specific effect with a business outcome is not a clean comparison to make, since so many factors contribute to business outcomes. Whether the goal is less downtime, fewer security incidents, or less time spent in a noticeably degraded mode, the business has a reason for instituting the program in the first place. Does the organization get the result that it paid for? The Chaos Engineering program costs money. Can a reduction in downtime, fewer security incidents, or less degradation be correlated with the implementation of a Chaos Engineering program? If so, then the business case is made, and it is simply a matter of comparing the cost of the program to the value of the outcome. This is the final and most important level pursued according to the model.

The levels in the Kirkpatrick Model establish progressively stronger evidence for ROI from Level 1 to Level 4. They also get progressively more difficult to carry out. The Kirkpatrick Model assumes that the extent to which you need to demonstrate ROI will correspond to the effort you expend, and will therefore determine the level to which you aspire. For example, if you have a very light-weight program and it does not cost an organization too much, then Level 1 might suffice in assessing the ROI. It might be enough to send a questionnaire to participants of a Game Day, to see if they feel they benefited from the experience. On the opposite end of the scale, if you have a team of many engineers dedicated completely to the program, then you may need to pursue Level 4. You might need a way to classify incidents, and show that certain classes of incidents are decreasing over time in frequency, duration, or depth.

Alternative ROI Example

The Chaos Engineering program at Netflix has been described elsewhere in this book. The application ChAP (discussed in Chapter 16) in particular was a large investment, and needed a corresponding demonstration of ROI. Several efforts to improve availability were continuously ongoing at Netflix, so it was not enough to record an improvement in availability. The contribution of ChAP had to be isolated from these other efforts.

ChAP generated hypotheses along the lines of, "Under conditions X, customers will still have a good time." Then it tried to disprove these hypotheses. Most were unable to be disproved, which gave more confidence in the system. Every once in a while, a hypothesis was disproved. Each disproved hypothesis was a lesson. Stakeholders thought that the system behaved one way; ChAP showed them that it did not. That was the primary value of the application.

Each disproved hypothesis corresponded to some amount of the business's key performance indicators (KPIs) that differed between the variable group and control group. In ChAP's case, the primary KPI was how many videos start streaming per second, referred to as SPS. For every disproved hypothesis, an impact on SPS was recorded. That might be a 5% impact, or 100%, etc.

Actual incidents also had a recorded SPS impact. For example, an incident that showed a 20% drop in SPS might last fifteen minutes on average. Using this probability distribution, we could roughly bucket the disproved hypotheses into durations of actual incidents. Summing the lost SPS over time gave us a best guess of the impact of that vulnerability, had it actually manifested in Production.

Using the method for each disproved hypothesis just described, we could project the "saved" hypothetical SPS impact due to discovering these vulnerabilities in ChAP safely, before they manifested in Production and had the chance to affect all of the customers. Summing these "SPS saved" over time gave a chart that showed this metric going up and to the right every month, provided that at least one hypothesis was disproved. This showed that ChAP was continually adding value. There is an implied congruence between this metric and the point of the practice in the first place. This established the ROI of ChAP as part of the Chaos Engineering program at Netflix.

Judging by the Kirkpatrick Model, this evaluation of ChAP's ROI only attained Level 2, because it captured demonstrable learning. No effort was made to show that engineers behaved differently over time because of the vulnerabilities discovered, and no correlation was established with better availability. Had it been necessary to establish a stronger case for ROI, changes in engineer behavior would have to be found and recorded for Level 3, and somehow the lessons learned by disproved hypothesis would have to be correlated with better availability or other business goals for Level 4. As it stood, the "SPS saved" method of establishing ROI was convincing.

Collateral ROI

This example with ChAP shows a tangible result measured by a fundamental metric from a business-goal perspective. Many lessons learned from Chaos Engineering are independent of the primary goals of the exercises. These connections occur in proximity to the Chaos Engineering, and often not during the actual hypothesis evaluation. We call this "Collateral ROI": benefits accrued that are different from the primary goal of the exercise but nonetheless contribute to the "return" on the investment.

A great place to see this is in the conversations leading up to a Game Day exercise. During the design phase of a Game Day, people are selected to participate. The stakeholders in the relevant systems are identified and brought together. One of the first questions asked of this group should be: under conditions *X*, what do you think should happen?

Two "collateral ROI" benefits fall out of this process. The more obvious is the ideation of potential scenarios. Isolated pockets of knowledge are surfaced: what seems like an obvious outcome to one person is often a revelation to another. Many Game Days are modified at this stage because what seems to some facilitators like a worthy hypothesis for analysis turns out to have a high probability of failure. In these cases, it does not make sense to go through with that particular experiment. The underlying vulnerability should be addressed, and then verified with a future Game Day, and another hypothesis can be considered for the current one.

Another benefit of this process is more difficult to characterize. It is often the case that people brought together for this exercise have not previously collaborated. Sometimes they have not even met before. This offers the opportunity to surface islands of knowledge; it also lays the groundwork for humans to interact, working toward a common goal of improving the safety properties of the system. This is practice. Practice working together makes teams function together better during actual incidents.

Continuing with our example, imagine that the first time these people are brought together is during an ongoing incident in Production. Imagine the time saved even in just making introductions and adjusting to individual idiosyncrasies of communication. This is an additional source of "collateral ROI."

Incident response can be intimidating and is often confusing for participants. Since humans are mostly creatures of habit, practice is the best method for preparing engineers to be on call for a system. Just like the response to a fire drill, or CPR, or any more thorough practice like athletic training, putting a human through a simulated situation gives them a foundation to address the real thing when it happens. This cannot all be captured in documentation. Relying on runbooks is insufficient. Exposure to the tools and process of an incident and the ensuing response builds an unspoken context. That unspoken context does a better job of communicating expectations than anything that can be written out.

As with all Chaos Engineering, the purpose here is not to cause chaos. The point is not to cause discomfort either. Incident response can be chaotic on its own. The purpose of Chaos Engineering here is to provide a controlled situation in which humans can learn to navigate the chaos toward the result that they want, which in this example is quick and lasting incident remediation.

Conclusion

Demonstrating the ROI of Chaos Engineering is not easy. In most cases, you will feel the value of experiments almost immediately, before you can articulate that value. If that feeling is sufficient to justify the program, then there is no point in engineering a more objective measure. If an objective measure is required, dig into the Kirkpatrick Model as described in this chapter. The four levels provide a framework to establish progressively more compelling evidence of ROI with commensurate effort to reveal that value. It can be hard work, but the tools are here to establish a solid case for the ROI of Chaos Engineering.

CHAPTER 14

Open Minds, Open Science, and Open Chaos

Russ Miles

Chaos Engineering is science. You seek evidence of system weaknesses that are hidden in the essential complexities of modern, rapidly evolving systems. This is done through empirical experiments that inject controlled but turbulent conditions into a combination of your infrastructure, platforms, applications, and even your people, processes, and practices.

Like all science, Chaos Engineering is at its most valuable when it is highly collaborative: where everyone can see what experiments are being pursued, when they are happening, and what findings have surfaced. But, like science, this can all collapse like a house of cards if the collaborative nature is in any way stymied.

Collaborative Mindsets

Imagine two mindsets. In the first, engineers think along the following lines: "I just like to find weaknesses. I can't wait to take everyone's systems and inject all sorts of interesting harm on them to show everyone why they should be improving their systems."

A team with this mindset is focused on doing chaos *to* other people's systems. The goal is still to learn, but this is easily lost in the conflict-style relationship that is likely to be established when the Chaos Team starts to run experiments against other people's systems. That's the key problem—it is done to *other people's systems*. This team's remit tends to end with "Here's the problem!" and even if it goes as far as "Here are some potential solutions," it's still going to meet intense resistance from the teams who actually own those systems.[1] Can you hear, "But the Chaos Team is slowing us down…"? With this style of relationship things can swiftly deteriorate to the point where Chaos Engineering is seen as yet another thing to circumvent, and eventually may even be rejected, as seen in Figure 14-1.

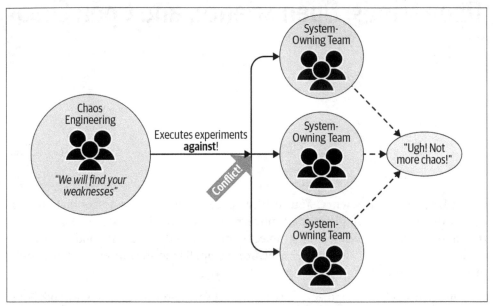

Figure 14-1. A poisonous "Chaos Engineers versus Us" relationship

Contrast that with the following mindset: "I can't wait to help the teams improve their systems. Running their systems is hard, and so I'm looking forward to helping them find weaknesses in their systems so they can learn from that evidence and get an opportunity to build more resilient systems which just might make their lives a little easier."

In this second example, the Chaos Engineer is working *with* the engineering teams. They are exploring their own system's weaknesses, and Chaos Engineering is providing support through help and tooling. The chance of a poisonous "them versus us" relationship is much reduced when everyone is part of surfacing the dark debt, and participating in the solution as well, as seen in Figure 14-2.

---

1 Exactly this sort of conflict-style relationship is common when there is a difficult Quality Assurance versus Development Team setup. By separating quality out into being "someone else's job," you have developers focused on features and testers focused on quality, which means something will suffer (usually the people involved, as well as the quality of the code and the feature velocity!). This is why quality should be the Development Team's responsibility, as it is one of the core practices of development and not an adjunct to developing features.

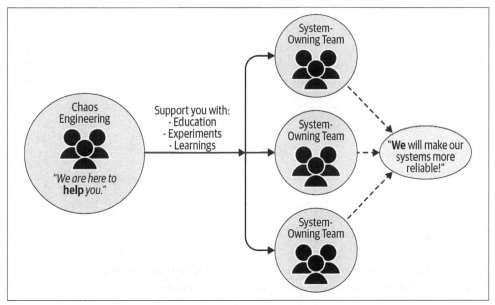

Figure 14-2. A supportive relationship between a Chaos Engineering capability and the teams that take ownership of finding and meeting the challenges of weaknesses in their systems

Two very different approaches, and it might at first glance feel very subjective to project the difference between the two. Which would you want to kick off the Chaos Engineering initiative in your company? As it happens, one of those teams can easily lead to Chaos Engineering not being successful in your organization, and the other sets you up for success. Collaboration and co-ownership are requirements for a healthy Chaos Engineering program.

Open Science; Open Source

Collaboration goes beyond co-ownership as well. Even if you manage to amass evidence of system weaknesses, if this information is locked away in proprietary systems, proprietary protocols, or stored in proprietary formats, then its true value can be undermined. In order for Chaos Engineering to flourish in an organization, and indeed for science itself to flourish in society, it's not enough to ensure anyone is enabled to do it.

Chaos Engineering needs to be *open* to even have the possibility of meeting its true potential. The full value of Chaos Engineering relies on open learning about the experiments people design and choose to execute; making it possible to share the findings of those experiments across a team, a department, an organization, and even potentially publicly.

Science has the same need. Although it has a long history of struggling with commercial and societal constraints when it comes to openness, various fields have met and dealt with those challenges. The Open Science movement "make[s] scientific research (including publications, data, physical samples, and software) and its dissemination accessible to all levels of an inquiring society, amateur or professional,"[2] and it does this through six principles:

- Open Educational Resources
- Open Access
- Open Peer Review
- Open Methodology
- Open Source
- Open Data

You and your organization can get the same benefits from openness through your Chaos Engineering efforts by following similar principles.

Open Chaos Experiments

In order to share experiments between all interested parties, a definition of what needs to be in an experiment is specified. One group that I helped launch called the Open Chaos Initiative (*https://openchaos.io*) defines an experiment as comprising:

Experiment Description
An Experiment is the first-class, top-level concept for Chaos Engineering. It contains a list of Contributions, a Steady-State Hypothesis, a Method, and (optionally) some Rollbacks. The description may also contain a title, tags for identification, and any sourced configuration useful to the execution of the experiment.

Contributions
This defines what important system concerns this experiment attempts to help build trust and confidence in.

Steady-State Hypothesis
A Steady-State Hypothesis describes "what normal looks like" for your system in order for the experiment to surface information about weaknesses when compared against the declared "normal" tolerances of what is measured. Normally

---

2 Ruben Vicente-Saez and Clara Martinez-Fuentes, "Open Science Now: A Systematic Literature Review for an Integrated Definition," *Journal of Business Research*, Vol. 88 (2018), pp. 428–436.

this contains Probes that, along with a tolerance measure, declare that the system is measurably within tolerance.

Method

A Method introduces the turbulent conditions that are being explored by the Chaos Engineering experiment. Through a collection of activities, the right turbulent conditions can be introduced in a controlled or random way. Activities can be either Actions or Probes.

Probes

A Probe is a way of observing a particular set of conditions in the system that is undergoing experimentation.

Actions

An Action is a particular activity that needs to be enacted on the system under experimentation.

Rollbacks

Rollbacks contain a sequence of actions that revert what was undone during the experiment.

How these concepts are implemented is dependent on the context and can vary greatly, however there are reference implementations of this approach in the wild.[3]

The execution of the experiment is declared as seen in Figure 14-3.

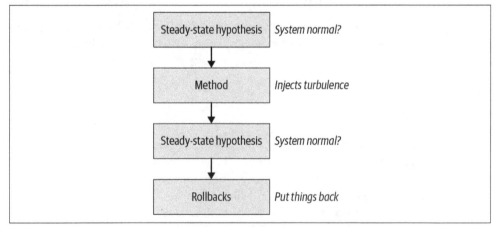

Figure 14-3. Open chaos experiment execution flow

---

3 A concrete example of these concepts in action can be found in the Open Chaos Public Experiment Catalog: *https://oreil.ly/dexkU.*

One interesting part of this experiment execution flow is that the *Steady-State Hypothesis* is used twice. It is used once at the beginning of the experiment to ensure that the system is recognizably "normal" before the experiment is allowed to continue. Then it is used again when the turbulent conditions being explored using the experiment have been applied. This second assessment of the *Steady-State Hypothesis* is crucial as it either shows that the system has "survived" the turbulent conditions, and therefore is robust to them, or that it has "deviated" from normality, in which case there is evidence of a potential weakness being present.

Experiment Findings, Shareable Results

Defining experiments so that they can be executed and shared is half the battle. If you can't share your experimental findings, your potential evidence of weaknesses, then collaboration is once again blocked.

For this reason, the Open Chaos Initiative also defines the concepts of what should appear in a journal of an experiment's execution. The key concepts are:

- Information about the experiment itself
- The status and duration of the experiment execution.

An example of a real-world journal is not provided here, but even a simple record of the execution of an experiment will contribute to open collaboration, even if each case is context- and implementation-specific.

The opportunity to share and collaboratively learn from what is being explored *and* what weaknesses are being surfaced across various systems is possible. This is an example of what can be achieved in a community like the one forming around Chaos Engineering.

Conclusion

Chaos Engineering requires freedom so that everyone can explore and surface evidence of weaknesses in their own systems. This requires open tooling and open standards, and this is where the concept of Open Science can help. Through Open Chaos standards we can all collaborate and share our Chaos Engineering experiments and findings, perhaps even through open APIs. Learning from each other's experiments, we can overcome system weaknesses before they hurt our users. The reliability provided by Chaos Engineering should not be a differentiator. Working together we will all be stronger.

About the Author

Russ Miles is CEO of ChaosIQ.io, where he and his team build products and services that help their customers verify the reliability of their system. Russ is an international consultant, trainer, speaker, and author. His most recent book, *Learning Chaos Engineering* (O'Reilly), explores how to build trust and confidence in modern, complex systems by applying Chaos Engineering to surface evidence of system weaknesses before they affect your users.

CHAPTER 15

Chaos Maturity Model

When the team at Netflix wrote the first book on Chaos Engineering,[1] they introduced the "Chaos Maturity Model." This was initially a joke, playing on the CMM from the late '80s/early '90s—the "Capability Maturity Model" developed at Carnegie Mellon University to analyze the software development process. That framework was a very heavy-handed process, which stood in stark contrast to the culture at Netflix where "process" was a bad word.

As the team at Netflix played with the model, it actually made sense. Turns out that the joke was not a joke. The Chaos Maturity Model actually provides value, particularly to organizations looking for ways to assess and increase their investment in Chaos Engineering practices.

In very broad terms, the software industry as a whole is not homogenous enough to support industry standards around Chaos Engineering. Infrastructures, cultures, expectations, and maturity are too different for a drop-in solution that would provide some base level of functionality comparable across different companies. In lieu of industry standards, the Chaos Maturity Model presents sliding scales on which different Chaos Engineering practices can be evaluated for comparison and refinement.

This chapter illustrates the Chaos Maturity Model (CMM) as a framework. This can be used to plot a map of a team or organization's position. The map visually suggests where the team can go to improve if the path of others in Chaos Engineering is any indication of the potential for progress. There are two axes in the CMM map: Adoption and Sophistication. Both aspects can be explored independently.

---

1 Ali Basiri et al., *Chaos Engineering* (Sebastopol, CA: O'Reilly, 2017).

Adoption

One of the most frequently asked questions about Chaos Engineering is how to convince management to buy into the concept. Winston Churchill famously quipped, "Never let a good crisis go to waste." This applies very well to the adoption of Chaos Engineering. As described in Introduction: Birth of Chaos, the discipline itself was born from crisis at Netflix. Chaos Monkey was invented during the outages that plagued the migration from the datacenter to the cloud in 2008. Chaos Kong was invented after the Christmas Eve outage in 2012.

It may feel a bit like ambulance chasing, but sometimes the best opportunity to help someone is just after they feel the repercussions of not having the help they need. We have seen several instances where management was reluctant to pursue Chaos Engineering until just after an availability or security incident. Immediately following, there was strong alignment and budget to prevent a similar occurrence. As one of the few proactive methods to improve reliability, this is often the best chance to introduce Chaos Engineering.

As the discipline as a whole matures, eventually we will reach a point where companies mandate a certain level of Chaos Engineering as a matter of policy. The verification of robustness alone has great implications for compliance processes. But before we get there, adoption will usually proceed from a ground-up model.

Adoption can be split into four considerations:

- Who bought into the idea
- How much of the organization participates
- The prerequisites
- The obstacles

Who Bought into Chaos Engineering

Early in the adoption cycle, it is likely that the individual contributors (ICs) who are closest to the repercussions of an outage or security incident are most likely to adopt Chaos Engineering or seek out the discipline for obvious reasons. This is often followed by internal championing, with advocacy often found in DevOps, SRE, and Incident Management teams. In more traditional organizations, this often falls to Operations or IT. These are the teams that understand the pressure of being paged for an availability incident.

Of course, the urgency around getting the system back online sets up obstacles for learning. Much effort is put into optimizing the incident review or learning review process, and very few organizations have yet found a comfortable path to Resilience

Engineering: learning from work-as-done to enable the adaptive capacity of the people in a sociotechnical system.

Instead, we typically see a continued focus on reducing time-to-detect and time-to-remediate. Working on reducing both of these is great and a necessary effort, but it is also *reactive*. Eventually by rational argument, example, or consequence, the pressure for choosing a *proactive* strategy to reduce incidents reaches higher in the management chain.

At some forward-looking institutions Chaos Engineering has become an edict. This top-down alignment comes from the SVP, CIO, or CISO level and generates strong adoption incentives usually within specific parts of the organization tasked with technical operational health.

This illustrates the most common progression of adoption: from those most impacted by incidents (the ones carrying the pagers) up to management, and then back down as a policy directive.

How Much of the Organization Participates in Chaos Engineering

Regardless of how Chaos Engineering is introduced into an organization, the spread of the practice is another metric by which adoption can be measured. Organizational alignment is reflected by commitment, and commitment is reflected in the resource allocation.

Chaos Engineering can start with an individual on an application team, or in a centralized operation team. Perhaps it is not even a full-time job at first, but a practice invoked to improve the operational properties of a specific system. As adoption increases, we expect Chaos Engineering to be taken up across several applications or systems. This requires more people to be involved.

Eventually it makes sense to centralize the role either in full-time positions for Chaos Engineering or an actual team with that title. This function then implicitly has a cross-functional domain, otherwise it would be wholly embedded within one team. The allocation of resources to this team signals to the broader organization that proactive recovery of incidents is a priority, and that is a fairly high level of adoption.

Since Chaos Engineering can be applied to infrastructure, inter-application, security, and other levels of the sociotechnical system, there are many opportunities for the practice to spread to different parts of the organization. Ultimate adoption occurs when practicing Chaos Engineering is accepted as a responsibility for all individual contributors throughout the organization, at every level of the hierarchy, even if a centralized team provides tooling to make it easier. This is similar to how in a DevOps-activated organization, every team is responsible for the operational properties of their software, even though centralized teams may specifically contribute to improving some of those properties.

Prerequisites

There are fewer prerequisites for Chaos Engineering than most people think. The first question to ask an organization considering adopting the practice is whether or not they know when they are in a degraded state. Most organizations can easily distinguish when they are offline. Not all organizations can tell when they are in a degraded state, or about to go offline.

If they cannot distinguish between levels of degradation, then any results from Chaos Engineering will be fleeting. A control group and an experimental group cannot be contrasted without being able to discern a difference in degradation between the two, so the value of the experiment is questionable from the start. Equally important, any prioritization of results will be impossible. Without levels of degradation to distinguish between effect sizes, it won't be clear whether a Chaos Experiment indicated something should be pursued further or not.

Monitoring and Observability are the antidote. Fortunately, this pursuit can have the unintended and significant consequence of improving insight tooling in and around the system.

While any instrumentation is being improved, this would be a good time to spread awareness of Chaos Engineering as a practice. Not every experiment should have a warning. Ideally, the experiments become so routine that no one thinks about them until they violate a hypothesis. This should happen with little to no impact on the system KPI, and it should teach the operators something new about the system properties.

Chaos Engineering should be actively discussed when first introduced into any system or subsystem. It is important to be very explicit with all parties involved what is being done, to what end, and the expectation for the outcome. Chaos Engineering often teaches us new things that we did not expect, but surprise itself is not the virtue. Surprising an involved party via an experiment would only create animosity and friction.

Another way to cause friction would be to introduce a variable when the outcome is known to be undesirable. Chaos Engineering cannot be productive unless the hypothesis can be tested with an honest expectation that it will be upheld. If statements cannot be made along the lines of, "This service will meet all SLOs even under conditions of high latency with the data layer," then the experiments should not be run in the first place. New knowledge is not generated if the process only confirms that a suspected broken component is indeed broken. Fix what is known to be broken before Chaos Engineering comes into play.

Finally, the discipline requires that the organization has the alignment to respond to the new information generated by Chaos Engineering. If vulnerabilities are found and no one does anything with that information, then it is not really information, just noise.

Summary of prerequisites:

- Instrumentation to be able to detect degraded state
- Social awareness
- Expectations that hypothesis should be upheld
- Alignment to respond

Obstacles to Adoption

There is a recurring question of whether or not having the word "Chaos" in the name of the discipline discourages adoption, or scares off executives. In the experience of the authors, this is rare if it ever occurs. People seem to understand intuitively that the word "Chaos" refers to uncovering the complexity already inherent in the system, not creating additional frenetics.

There are some legitimate obstacles to adoption, however. The primary objection is that the business model cannot afford the side effects of experimentation in production traffic. This is a valid argument from a psychological perspective because change and introducing risk are uncomfortable. If the system does not suffer from availability or security incidents, then perhaps it is also a rational argument. No need to mess with a system that never breaks.

If the system does have outages or security incidents, then avoiding Chaos Engineering on these grounds is no longer rational. The options then are (a) continue with reactive methods, incur the inevitable incident, and repeat; or (b) adopt the proactive method, control the potential damage by limiting the blast radius, and avoid incidents. The latter solution is strictly better. Chaos Engineering swaps uncontrolled risk for controlled risk.

Chaos Engineering does not always have to occur in production anyway. More sophisticated programs usually end up operating in production, but that is an advanced principle. Many teams have learned critical insights from running experiments first in a staging or test environment. When things can be done in a safer manner, they should be.

Compliance is another potential obstacle. Outdated requirements do not always take into account the benefit of preventing uncontrolled, large incidents when dictating rules about introducing controlled, small risks. This can be particularly thorny when security controls are being tested in a live environment.

The current state of operational stability in a system is a not-uncommon obstacle. People often joke that they do not need Chaos Engineering because the system provides enough of its own chaos. If a system is indeed unstable, then learning new ways in which it is unstable does not seem like a useful application of resources. This creates confusion about priorities and can have a negative effect on team morale. If the queue is always growing faster than workers can process items from the queue, then there is no reason to make that problem worse.

One of the trickiest obstacles to adoption is determining ROI for a Chaos Engineering program (this is addressed in more depth in Chapter 13). No one is in a rush to hear the story about the incident that never happened. Likewise, it can be difficult to garner alignment and resources for a practice that may be improving things significantly, but silently.

Summary of obstacles:

- Experimenting in Production carries some risk
- Compliance prevents experimentation in some cases
- Insurmountable instability in the existing system
- Difficulty in measuring ROI

Sophistication

The axis of measuring the sophistication of a Chaos Engineering practice within an organization is analogous to determining where it is on the scale of being a consultative service versus being a set of tools. When it was created at Netflix, the Chaos Engineering team existed within a consultative organization. Casey, the manager of the team, made the explicit decision to drive the team toward productization of tools. This is reflected in the advanced principles, like automating the experiments.

Both consulting and tooling can be initiated by a small, centralized team. Software infrastructure is so heterogeneous across the industry that there cannot be a prepackaged tool that satisfies sophisticated Chaos Engineering use cases in all of these disparate environments. It is natural that the practice starts off with heavy human involvement, with bespoke solutions being developed over time.

The progression often looks like the following:

1. Game Days
2. Fault injection consultation
3. Fault injection self-service tools
4. Experimentation platforms
5. Automation of the platforms

Game Days

Game Days are a great way for an organization to dip its toes into the waters of Chaos Engineering. From a technical point of view, they are easy to set up and don't have to be sophisticated in terms of implementation. A facilitator or project manager can run a Game Day by doing the following:

1. Get a bunch of people in a room who are responsible for a system or set of systems.
2. Shut off a component that the system should be robust enough to tolerate without it.
3. Record the learning outcomes and bring the component back online.

The benefits of this type of exercise can be enormous, especially the first few times they are done. The burden is almost entirely on the people, though. The stakeholders are the engineers who own the system. If something goes sideways during the experiment, they are the ones who presumably can rectify the system. The coordination is entirely up to the facilitator: to schedule the event, preview the process, record the learnings, disseminate that information, and so on. This is all highly valuable, but it consumes one of the most valuable resources of any organization—people's time—and does not scale to a large number of services.

Fault injection consultation

With the initial success of Game Day learning outcomes, the next step is to build some tools that can be reused throughout the organization to run manual experiments. This often takes the form of a fault injection framework. A fault injection framework ideally can interfere with the inter-process communication (IPC) layer of the system. Concentrating requests, delaying them, flapping connections, and cutting off downstream message passing are all great examples of experiments that can be built around IPC manipulation.

> ## Examples of Experiment Types
>
> Other methods of sophistication in experiment type include returning errors, changing status codes in response headers, changing the order of requests, and changing request data payloads. Having access to all of these methods is not always useful and depends on the function of the system. The general set of availability-related variables are increased latency, error, and failure to respond. Arguably the last one is just a case of infinite latency.
>
> There is also a class of experiments that do not fit within the realm of fault injection, which is one of the reasons such a hard distinction is made between fault injection and Chaos Engineering. Sending more traffic than usual to one instance in a cluster is a great experiment. In the real world this can be caused by underprovisioning, an unexpected hashing pattern, unusual load balancing, an inconsistent sharding strategy, misunderstood business logic, or even by a sudden burst in customer traffic. In each of these cases, calling increased traffic a "fault" is a mischaracterization of the behavior.

Similar to a Game Day experience, the consulting facilitator will sit down with a team, use the fault injection framework to kick off an experiment, and record learnings. If vulnerabilities are found in the robustness of the system, the process will often be repeated in cycles, iterating on new solutions until the vulnerability is verifiably removed. This is also effective, like the Game Day, with the added benefit that one tool can be used to perform experiments with multiple teams. Here we see more cross-functional learning, as experiments that proved fruitful with one team can be easily replicated using the fault injection framework on other teams.

Fault injection self-service tools

After a period of success with this type of tooling the automation process begins. The fault injection framework is wrapped in a self-service interface so that several teams can use it simultaneously, without always needing the help of the facilitator. The consultation usually continues at this stage in setting up the experiments and interpreting results, but they can now scale out a little better since they are not required to sit down with every team during an experiment's run.

Experimentation platforms

The progression of sophistication can take one of two paths here: more automation or better experimentation. In most cases the tooling progresses into better experimentation first. Experiments are set up with a control group and a variable group. A subsample of traffic is directed to these two groups. The blast radius is minimized to just the variable group. Request-stickiness is often implemented so that the agent initiating a request is consistently forced to either the control or the variable. This allows for not only safer experiments, but deeper insights. An effect that might be lost during an experiment on an entire system can often be brought into focus when it's performed on a small subsample that has a direct comparison in the control group.

At this point, the team might still be consulting to set up and start experiments and to interpret results. The power of an experimentation platform allows multiple experiments to be run simultaneously, even in Production. The number of experiments being run can now increase geometrically with the number of consultants. Each experiment has to be created and monitored.

Automation of the platforms

Automation of the experimentation platform poses several novel technical challenges. Features like KPI monitoring can enable a "dead robot's switch," so that experiments that find something interesting can be stopped immediately. This removes the need for humans to monitor each experiment, but does still require them to view the results afterwards and interpret any anomalies. System introspection allows the platform to build experiments without intervention by a facilitator; for example, when a new service comes online it automatically detects it and queues it for experimentation. Of course, it also needs context to only run experiments where there is a quantifiable expectation for hypothesis such as a known fallback statement in code. This removes the need for humans to create each experiment.

Finally, heuristics are codified to prioritize experiments so that time and resources are spent on the experiments that are most likely to teach something previously unknown about the system. At this point the automation is complete enough that it can run fully automated: creating, prioritizing, executing, and terminating experiments. We consider this a very high level of sophistication in the state-of-the-art for Chaos Engineering tools.

Experiment Prioritization Example

An important item to keep in mind while you are building an algorithm to prioritize and run experiments is to give teams insight into what is running and how priority is being decided. Providing this level of observability can help teams understand where their mental models deviate from what is actually happening in their system.

Let's go through an example. Imagine that you work at a company that provides the ability to stream TV shows and movies. Let's make the following assumptions:

- The company's key performance indicator is the ability for someone to stream video.
- This KPI is measured by stream starts per second.

- Traffic is fairly predictable, meaning that if the stream starts per second deviates (either an order of magnitude higher or lower than expected), teams will get paged and triage whether or not there is a problem.

Imagine that you work on a team that operates the "Bookmarks" service. "Bookmarks" is responsible for knowing where in the video stream a person is currently watching, in case they leave the video and want to come back to where they left off. If someone asked you whether or not "Bookmarks" impacted stream starts per second (i.e., whether or not "Bookmarks" was considered "critical") you would say "no." In fact, you are so sure of this that you have implemented a fallback for when your service fails to get the correct place in time in the stream where the user left off. If it fails, it restarts the stream at the beginning of the video.

Now let's go back to the algorithm that prioritizes experiments. This algorithm should first keep in mind whether something is "safe to fail" in order to properly design the experiment. To simplify for the sake of example, let's assume that this algorithm looks through all of the services that exist in the system, and empirically determines whether or not they have a fallback associated with them. If no fallback exists, it can assume they are *not* safe to fail.

We have "Bookmarks" and we have our prioritization algorithm. The algorithm has determined that the "Bookmarks" service *is* safe to fail and successfully designs and subsequently runs an experiment. During the experiment, it's important that its success is measured against the company's KPI, stream starts per second.

The experiment automatically gets designed, and runs, and then fails. What happened?

Remember how "Bookmarks" has a fallback that redirected users to the beginning of the video? It turns out that many users still want to find where they are in the stream. This means the KPI, stream starts per second, still dipped as they were looking for their place.

This is a great example of a mental model being recalibrated and it's important that the team designing the chaos automation takes mental model recalibration and observability into account. This may be in the form of collecting session data that shows a user's behavior as the experiment was going on, as well as a place for a service owner to make note of how their assumptions changed.

That is not to say that the road ends there. The platform can be extended and polished in many ways:

- Automatically identify the correct person to notify when a vulnerability is found.
- Implement a "chaos budget" so that only a certain number of KPI can be missed in a given time period, ensuring that experimentation never inadvertently causes more disruption than the business is willing to tolerate. This can increase

confidence that the platform is controlled, focused on identifying chaos, and not creating it.

- Construct experiments with combinatorial variables. While this is extremely rare given the small windows of failure that most components see, it can discover patterns caused by exhaustion of common resources, for example.

- Automatically remediate the vulnerability. In theory this is possible. In practice, this might require an entirely different book to explore the topic.

At some point during this journey, it makes sense to include security experiments as well as the traditional availability experiments. Security Chaos Engineering is covered in depth in Chapter 20.

 There are antipatterns in sophistication as well. The most common antipattern is developing new ways to fail an instance. Whether an instance dies, runs out of memory, has a pegged CPU, or fills up its disk, that is likely to manifest as increased latency, error, or failure to respond. Typically, nothing new is learned from failing the instance in multiple ways. This is a common feature of complex software systems, and so those types of experiments can generally be avoided.

Another way to understand the development of Chaos Engineering sophistication is to consider the layer in which the variable is introduced. Typically, experiments start at the infrastructure layer. Chaos Monkey famously started by turning off virtual machines. Chaos Kong took a similar approach at the macroscopic level, turning off entire regions. As the tooling grows more sophisticated, it moves up into application logic, affecting requests between services. Above that, we see even more sophisticated experiments when the variable affects business logic, for example, delivering a plausible but unexpected response to a service. The natural progression of experimentation is Infrastructure -> Application -> Business Logic.

Putting It All Together

Drawing the two properties, Adoption and Sophistication, as axes orthogonal to each other provides us with a map (see Figure 15-1). Starting in the lower-left quadrant of this map we have Game Days run by individual SREs or other interested folks. Depending on which axis develops first, the discipline either moves toward higher sophistication with perhaps a fault injection framework, or higher adoption with dedicated resources to Chaos Engineering. Generally, Adoption and Sophistication are going to develop together. A tension exists that discourages the tooling from becoming too sophisticated without widespread adoption, and likewise from reaching widespread adoption without better tooling.

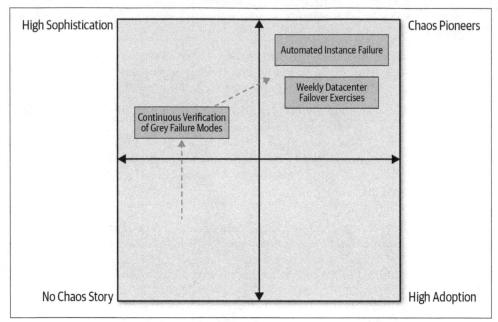

Figure 15-1. Example CMM map

Mapping your organization's position could help you understand your context within the discipline, and could suggest areas of investment to make the next leap. The ultimate goal of any of this is to return value to the organization. As seen in the map (Figure 15-1), moving up and to the right is where Chaos Engineering provides the most value. Highly sophisticated, pervasive Chaos Engineering is the best *proactive* method for improving availability and security in the software industry.

PART V

Evolution

By definition, a human cannot understand a complex system well enough to make accurate predictions about its output. Chaos Engineering certainly lives within a complex system of interacting practices, needs, and business environments. That said, clear trends have emerged that outline the future directions of this practice and its place within broader industry. This part of the book speaks to those trends.

The first chapter in this part of the book, Chapter 16, "Continuous Verification," situates Chaos Engineering within a larger category of software practices. "Like CI/CD (continuous integration/continuous delivery), the practice is born out of a need to navigate increasingly complex systems. Organizations do not have the time or other resources to validate that the internal machinations of the system work as intended, so instead they verify that the output of the system is inline with expectations." Many companies have already embraced the term "continuous verification" (CV) and interest is growing in the full complement of practices "CI/CD/CV," particularly at companies that operate software systems at scale.

The following chapter, Chapter 17, "Let's Get Cyber-Physical," takes a half-step away from software into the realm of hardware with cyber-physical systems (CPSs). "It turns out that when you get a lot of highly experienced, cross-disciplinary people together over a long enough period of time to undertake an activity like [Failure Mode and Effects Analysis], they actually do a pretty good job of having enough context from their experience, and the number of iterations they take, to squeeze out an awful lot of uncertainty." Nathan Aschbacher explores the considerations CPSs need to grapple with in situations where the outcome has a direct impact on the physical world around us and could literally be a matter of life and death.

In Chapter 18, "HOP Meets the Chaos Monkey," Bob Edwards takes us even further outside the world of software and into manufacturing. The Human and Organizational Performance (HOP) approach to improving systems in manufacturing shares many foundational roots with Chaos Engineering, and this overlap can help inform us about the practice in our domain. "The Chaos Engineering approach teaches us to modify the simulation control room parameters and software so that the actual degraded state of the site is better represented in the simulations."

Closer to home for software engineers, most Chaos Engineering practices are focused on the application layer. For a perspective on another layer in the stack, we have Chapter 19, "Chaos Engineering on a Database," by Liu Tang and Hao Weng from the database company PingCap. This chapter contains the deepest technical dive in the book, taking us through the application of Chaos Engineering to the database TiDB in order to improve its fault tolerant properties. "In TiDB we apply Chaos Engineering to observe the steady state of our system, make a hypothesis, conduct experiments, and verify those hypotheses with real results."

The final chapter in this part of the book takes us into the realm of cybersecurity. In Aaron Rinehart's Chapter 20, "The Case for Security Chaos Engineering," we see the application of Chaos Engineering to security, which from a system safety perspective is the other side of the coin to availability. When people discuss Chaos Engineering today, they mostly talk in terms of reliability and uptime. With Aaron's foray into the field, that may soon change. In the near future, Chaos Engineering may find most of its activity in security.

Across industries and disciplines, Chaos Engineering is finding a foothold and influencing how people understand the safety properties of their complex systems. The chapters in this part of the book illuminate a few of those corners.

CHAPTER 16

Continuous Verification

Continuous verification is a discipline of proactive experimentation in software, imple-mented as tooling that verifies system behaviors.
—Casey Rosenthal

The challenges posed by complex systems encouraged a natural evolution from con-tinuous integration to continuous delivery to continuous verification. The latter is the subject of this chapter, describing the nascent field and the room for opportunity, and following up with a real-world example of one of the systems in production at Netflix called ChAP. Where the industry decides to take continuous verification is wide open, but the general areas of focus for future development are reviewed at the end of this chapter.

Where CV Comes From

When a gap of expectations exists between two or more engineers separately writing code, then the interaction of that code may produce unexpected and undesirable results. The quicker that can be caught, the more likely it is that the next code written will have fewer gaps. Conversely, if that gap is not caught early on, then the next code written will likely diverge even further, multiplying the opportunities for undesirable outcomes.

One of the most efficient methods for uncovering that expectations gap is to put the code together and run it. Continuous integration (CI) was promoted heavily as part of the XP methodology (*https://oreil.ly/I5XIS*) as a way to achieve this. CI is now a common industry norm. CI pipelines encourage the development of integration tests, which specifically test the functionality of the combined features of the code written by separate developers or teams.

With each edit to code published to a common repository, a CI pipeline will compile the new amalgamation and run the integration test suite to confirm that no breaking changes were introduced. This feedback loop promotes reversibility in software: the ability to promote code quickly, change your mind, and revert that change. Reversibility[1] is an advantageous optimization for navigating complex software systems.

The practice of continuous delivery (CD) builds on the success of CI by automating the steps of preparing code and deploying it to an environment. CD tools allow engineers to choose a build that passed the CI stage and promote that through the pipeline to run in production. This gives developers an additional feedback loop (new code running in production) and encourages frequent deployments. Frequent deployments are less likely to break, because they are more likely to catch additional expectation gaps.

A new practice is emerging that builds on the advantages established by CI/CD. Continuous verification (CV) is a discipline of proactive experimentation, implemented as tooling that verifies system behaviors. This stands in contrast to prior common practices in software quality assurance, which favor reactive testing,[2] implemented as methodologies that validate[3] known properties of software. This isn't to say that prior common practices are invalid or should be deprecated. Alerting, testing, code reviews, monitoring, SRE practices, and the like—these are all great practices and should be encouraged. CV specifically builds on these common practices in order to address issues that are unique to complex systems:

- There are very few *proactive* practices that address optimization of systemic properties.

- Complex systems require practices that favor method of exploration of the unknown (experimentation) over the known (testing).

- Tools are required in order to scale, whereas methodologies (Agile, DevOps, SRE, etc.) necessitate digital transformations and cultural changes along with expensive investments in staff to implement them.

- Verification addresses business outcomes, which are a more pragmatic focus when operating a complex system than validation, which focuses on the correctness of software.

---

1 See the section "Economic Pillars of Complexity" on page 20 in Chapter 2 for more about the advantages of Reversibility in software engineering.

2 See the section "Experimentation Versus Testing" on page 26 in Chapter 3.

3 See the section "Verification Versus Validation" on page 27 in Chapter 3.

- Complex system properties are open ended and in a constant state of flux, which necessitates different approaches than those required to understand known properties of software like output constraints.

CV does not aim to develop a new paradigm in software engineering. Rather, it is a recognition of a confluence of development efforts and practices toward solutions that have a lot of things in common. It is an observation that this new category has emerged that differs substantially from the way that we commonly thought about software development and operation up to this point (Figure 16-1).

Much like Chaos Engineering, CV platforms can include availability or security (see Chapter 20) components and often express these as hypotheses. Like CI/CD, the practice is born out of a need to navigate increasingly complex systems. Organizations do not have the time or other resources to validate that the internal machinations of the system work as intended, so instead they verify that the output of the system is inline with expectations. This is the preference for verification over validation that hallmarks successful management of complex systems.

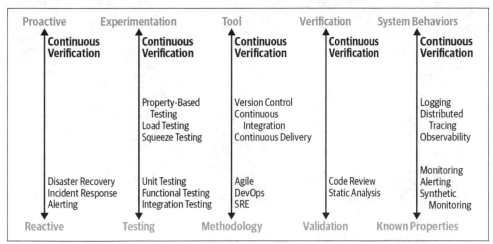

Figure 16-1. Continuous verification (top) versus prior common practices in software quality (bottom)

Types of CV Systems

Tooling in this category is still nascent. On one end of the spectrum, we have sophisticated Chaos Engineering automation platforms. These run explicit experiments usually during business hours. The specific example of ChAP is discussed in the next section.

Automated canaries also fall into this category, and can be considered a subcategory of automated Chaos Engineering platforms. Automated canaries run an experiment in which the variable introduced is a new code branch and the control is the currently deployed branch. The hypothesis follows: customers will have a good experience, even under the conditions of the new code. If the hypothesis is not disproven, then the CD automatically promotes the new code to replace the current code running in production.

On the other end of the spectrum in CV, we have tools that provide holistic views of the system. Some of these fall into the discipline of Intuition Engineering. Netflix's tool Vizceral (Figure 16-2) is a great example of a tool that provides an immediate, visual, high-level signal to a human about the overall state of a system.

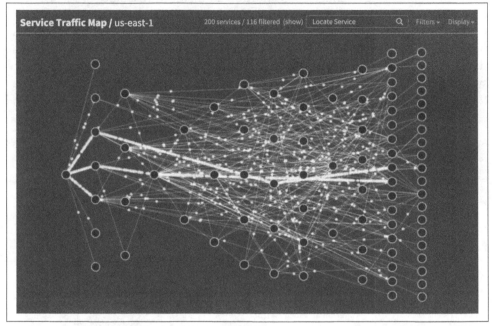

Figure 16-2. Screenshot of Vizceral[4]

In the case of Vizceral, the visual interface itself provides a continuously updating representation of the system that holistically gives an impression of its health or output. This allows a human to verify assumptions about the state of the system with a glance, potentially developing additional context about ongoing operational properties. Vizceral on its own does not run experiments, but it can interface with simulations and it certainly provides a proactive tool to verify system behaviors.

---

4 Vlad Shamgin, "Adobe Contributes to Netflix's Vizceral Open Source Code," Adobe Tech Blog, Dec. 6, 2017, *https://oreil.ly/pfNlZ*.

On one end of the CV spectrum we have empirical tools that provide verification through experimentation. On the other end we have qualitative tools that provide verification through assisted human interpretation. The space between these two poles is currently being explored and poses a rich field for research and for practical tool development in industry.

CV in the Wild: ChAP

The most prominent example of CV to date is also the most sophisticated example of Chaos Engineering in the industry. The Chaos Automation Platform (ChAP)[5] was developed at Netflix while Nora was an engineer and Casey was manager of the Chaos Engineering Team. It exemplifies the advanced principles highlighted throughout this book as well as the feedback loop we expect in CV.

ChAP is fully automated. It introspects the microservice architecture, selects microservices for inspection, constructs experiments for that microservice, and runs the experiment during business hours. The experiment hypotheses take the following form: under conditions X for microservice Y, customers still watch a normal amount of video streams. X is usually an amount of downstream latency, and normal is defined by a control group.

ChAP: Selecting Experiments

As part of ChAP's rollout, a product called *Monocle* was created. Monocle provides the ability to prioritize experiments and also allows users to get insight into that process of prioritization.

Monocle calls out to Netflix services to collect information about its dependencies. In this case, a *dependency* refers to either a configured RPC client or a Hystrix command. Monocle integrates data from multiple sources: the telemetry system, the tracing system (an internally built system based conceptually on Google's Dapper), and by querying running servers directly for configuration information such as timeout values.

Monocle presents these insights through a UI that summarizes information about dependencies. For each Hystrix command, Monocle displays information like its timeout and retry behavior along with whether or not ChAP thinks it is safe to fail. Specifically this means whether or not the system owner has things to fix before they can safely run a chaos experiment. If it is safe to fail, then that microservice may be added to the list and prioritized for experimentation.

---

5 Ali Basiri et al., "ChAP: Chaos Automation Platform," The Netflix Technology Blog, *https://oreil.ly/Yl_Q-*.

ChAP: Running Experiments

Through integration with Netflix's CD tool Spinnaker, ChAP is able to introspect the code deployed for the chosen microservice in the prioritization process provided by Monocle. For this microservice, there are a number of instances running in a cluster. ChAP will spin up two additional instances. One acts as the control, the other as the variable. A small amount of requests from production traffic is siphoned off and evenly split between these two instances.

The variable group gets the treatment. This is often an injection of latency to down-stream dependencies.

As responses are emitted from the system back to clients, the responses are checked to see if they participated in either the control or variable group. If they did partici-pate, then a KPI is called for that request. The default KPI for Netflix is video starts per second (SPS).

As long as the KPI for the control and variable group track together, ChAP has a strong, high-level signal that supports the hypothesis. Experiments typically run for 45 minutes (with a minimum being 20 minutes).

If, on the other hand, the KPIs deviate, then the experiment is immediately shut down. No more requests are routed to the experiment. The control and variable instances are torn down. Most importantly, the team responsible for that microser-vice is notified that under conditions X for their microservice, customers have a bad time. This discovery informs the team about their own safety margin and it is up to them to figure out why customers have a bad time under those conditions and what to do about it.

The Advanced Principles in ChAP

Notice how ChAP applies the advanced principles from Chapter 3:

Build a hypothesis around steady-state behavior
   At Netflix the steady state behavior is modeled using the KPI of how many video streams start per second. This is a metric that all engineers can easily access, and it correlates strongly with the health of the service and the business value. Cus-tomers who watch a lot of Netflix tend to recommend it to others. The hypothe-sis, "Under conditions X for microservice Y, customers still watch a normal amount of video streams," captures this notion of the desired steady-state behavior.

Vary real-world events
   Most incidents in a complex, distributed system can be modeled using latency, because in the real world this is how most node failures manifest. Contrast that with modeling a CPU pegged at 100% utilization or OOM error. These aren't

really helpful, because at a system level they will manifest as a service getting slow or a lack of response.

Run experiments in production
ChAP runs in the production environment. The Netflix distributed system is too large, complex, and fast changing to have an accurate alternative in a staging environment. Running in production provides certainty that we are building confidence in the system we care about.

Automate experiments to run continuously
ChAP runs continuously during business hours, without requiring human intervention. Experiments can be added manually, but this is not necessary since Monocle (described earlier) can generate a list of prioritized experiments daily.

Minimize blast radius
The mechanisms that spin up a new control and variable instance, and redirect a small amount of Production traffic to them, safely reduce the blast radius. If the hypothesis is disproved and something goes horribly wrong with the requests in the variable group, not only will the experiment stop immediately, but only a small amount of traffic was exposed to those conditions to begin with. This has the added benefit that many different experiments can be run simultaneously, since each is safely quarantined from the rest.

ChAP as Continuous Verification

There are some important features to note about ChAP as a CV tool as well:

- It runs continuously, during business hours, generating new knowledge whenever a hypothesis is disproved.

- It runs autonomously, prioritizing experiments using heuristics and static code analysis in Monocle to run experiments in an order designed to maximize the rate at which insights are generated.

- With minor modifications, ChAP could be configured as a stage in the CI/CD tooling pipeline that would represent a deep integration of CI/CD/CV.

CV Coming Soon to a System Near You

There are at least three categories for future use cases for CV: performance testing, data artifacts, and correctness.

Performance Testing

Countless tools exist for load testing along multiple dimensions of performance (speed, deviance of latency, concurrency, etc.). Not many of these are tied into platforms that continuously run them against a frequently changing state of the world. Most of them establish how much traffic the entire system can withstand for one particular utilization pattern. Not many of them vary the utilization pattern in real time based on observations of real production traffic. Not many of them test the performance of subsystems, or squeeze test individual microservices to establish provisioning and capacity data. Smarter tools are on the horizon, and will give operators more information about their systems.

Data Artifacts

Databases and storage applications make many claims about the properties of writes and retrieval, and offer many guarantees for their products. Jepsen (*https://jepsen.io*) is a great example of an experimentation platform that verifies these claims. Jepsen sets up an experimentation platform, generates load on the database, and then looks for various things like violations of commutativity in eventually consistent databases, violations of linearizability, incorrect isolation level guarantees, and so on. For systems like critical payment processing services where transactional properties need to be preserved, having a continual pulse on the presence of data side effects is important.

Correctness

Not all forms of "right" manifest as state or desirable properties. Sometimes different parts of a system have to agree, either by contract or by logic or even in some cases by rationale. In "Example 1: Mismatch Between Business Logic and Application Logic" on page 3 in Chapter 1, we saw an example of a breakdown in correctness when Service P received a 404 response for an object that it knew existed. This breakdown in correctness occurred because the logic encoded in different levels was internally consistent, but not consistent between layers. Three common layers of correctness in software are:

Infrastructure
> This is sometimes referred to as "undifferentiated heavy lifting." Common infrastructure correctness scenarios include resource allocation, autoscaling, and provisioning within SLA.

Application
> In most scenarios, infrastructure has no knowledge of what applications run on top of it. Application correctness can be captured in API contracts between services, types in programming languages, or the interface description language of

Protocol Buffers. These specifications of correctness can be rigorously applied to application logic to show that a piece of code is provably correct using a solver. Unfortunately, even if all of the components of a complex system are provable correct, the system as a whole can still emit undesirable behavior.

Business

This is often implicit in assumptions made apparent in a user interface. In order for a business to be competitive, it will often have to innovate. If the business logic is innovative, then it is not practical to rigorously specify it since it will likely change in response to conditions in an uncertain environment. Business logic therefore is the most difficult to verify, and mismatches between business, application, and infrastructure logic are an inevitable possibility in any situation with resource constraints.

If the guarantees of the three layers above are out-of-sync, then issues of correctness will manifest over time. This can quickly lead to incidents, both in security and availability.

As these categories and additional use cases develop, continuous verification will mature with them. New opportunities to apply CV will be found throughout the industry. Chaos Engineering is a cornerstone of this work, and in many ways CV will be founded on the tooling built in the Chaos Engineering space.

CHAPTER 17

Let's Get Cyber-Physical

Nathan Aschbacher

Much of the attention around Chaos Engineering currently focuses on the creation, deployment, and management of infrastructure and applications that underpin various internet-centric products and services, such as Netflix, AWS, and Facebook. These are domains where innovative, large-scale, complex, and interconnected software-driven systems dominate the landscape.

The goal of Chaos Engineering in these IT and cloud-dominated ecosystems is the discovery and removal of questions about system behavior in the pursuit of achieving more reliable and robust systems. By applying Chaos Engineering practices to complex systems you're attempting to learn where you have blind spots. Sometimes this takes the form of discovering you can't actually detect when something has gone wrong. Other times you are discovering that your assumptions about your system's behavior don't hold up at all. You may find you are reverse-engineering your implementation's real model and finding out just how far away it is from the design you imagined.

In this chapter we will explore four topics:

- Facets of traditional Functional Safety practice
- Where there is overlap between Functional Safety and Chaos Engineering (e.g., performing Failure Mode and Effects Analysis)
- Where Functional Safety practices leave a lot of room for improvement with respect to the new generations of software-intensive systems currently being developed

- Where Chaos Engineering principles can be applied to fill those gaps to enable engineers to safely push the boundaries of technology while chasing the next great breakthrough innovations

We consider these topics within the context of cyber-physical systems.

The Rise of Cyber-Physical Systems

There are many ecosystems unfamiliar to most software engineers where software is still the centerpiece driving innovation. Cyber-physical systems (CPSs) comprise one such ecosystem. A CPS is an interconnected hardware-software system that is deployed into, and interacts with, the physical world around it. Examples of such systems range from avionics systems or autonomous vehicles to traditional operational technology deployments like industrial control systems in a chemical refinery. Typically they're composed of a menagerie of sensors, embedded devices, communication transports and protocols, and half-a-dozen different obscure operating systems, and often they have critical dependencies on numerous proprietary black box components.

Modern IT and cloud-based systems are often already strained by necessary complexity. This is the case even when the deployment considerations are limited to x86 servers, communicating unanimously via common TCP/IP interfaces, with only one or two operating system targets. CPS adds multiple additional layers of complexity through both diversity and opacity. As if that wasn't enough already, there is an increasing demand to integrate CPS more cohesively into enterprise IT and cloud operations. So, take all the complexity you know now, add a few wild permutations, and then deploy it out into the physical world where the risk of failure could literally be a matter of life or death.

Against that backdrop, if you consider that the goal of Chaos Engineering is to remove questions and challenge assumptions in pursuit of understanding both system complexity and its impact in order to produce more reliable and resilient systems, then CPSs present fertile ground for Chaos Engineering on all fronts.

Some of the tenets of Chaos Engineering align so well with the need to remove unknown unknowns from systems interacting with their environment, that facets of it are already represented in the age-old engineering practice called Functional Safety. The discipline of Functional Safety attempts to remove unacceptable risk of causing physical harm to people and property from machines, processes, and systems. Designers and developers of CPSs, especially those deployed in critical environments, often leverage Functional Safety practices to assess and manage risk associated with what they're creating.

Functional Safety Meets Chaos Engineering

Functional Safety standards and practices come in many forms. There are multiple industry-specific standards. For instance, I am an SGS-TÜV certified Automotive Functional Safety Professional, which means that I am certified as having a working knowledge of the ISO 26262 standard. As you might have guessed from the lengthy credential name, this is the standard for the automotive industry. This particular standard is specifically for automotive electric and electronic systems in passenger vehicles. The "electronic systems" part happens to be why software gets lumped under this standard since many of those electronic systems are little embedded computers performing tasks like coordinating Automatic Emergency Braking (AEB) or keeping your kids pacified on long trips through the magic of in-vehicle "infotainment" systems.

Other industries have their own standards too, like aviation (DO-178C and DO-254) and nuclear power (IEC 61513). All these myriad standards tend to descend from a common root known as "IEC 61508: Functional Safety of Electrical/Electronic/ Programmable Electronic Safety-related Systems." The most important thing to recognize here is that there is not any particular special magic or science in these standards. By and large they are codifications of engineering best practices that have accumulated over many decades and sometimes in the aftermath of tragedy, controversy, or both. Because these are collections of best practices, there are some things in these standards that you might do in the normal course of engineering irrespective of whether or not what you are creating is subject to regulation.

One such activity is called Failure Mode and Effects Analysis (FMEA). Based purely on the name you might already be imagining that this sounds at least superficially related to Chaos Engineering. After all, one of the things you do when practicing Chaos Engineering is induce degradations in your system and then attempt to analyze the effects of doing so. Let's review what an FMEA is and what it isn't.

The following steps are typical of conducting an FMEA:

1. Define the scope of what you're analyzing (e.g., whole-system, subcomponent, design, development process, etc.).

2. Identify all the pieces of functionality that are within that scope.

3. Brainstorm an exhaustive list of all the things that could fail with each piece of functionality.

4. Enumerate all the effects of each potential failure mode for each piece of functionality.

5. Assign number rankings for severity, likelihood, and detectability (before failure) of each potential failure mode.

6. Multiply the rankings for each failure mode together to calculate something called risk priority numbers.

7. Write it all down in a spreadsheet, and revisit as you iterate on your system.

The theory goes that the higher the risk priority number, the more attention you should give to those failure modes until you've accounted for all of them in your design and/or implementation. However, a few things might jump out to you when looking over the preceding steps that can seriously impact the validity and usefulness of an FMEA:

- It's highly probable that whatever scope you selected to analyze may actually be missing some critical consideration.

- It's very challenging to actually identify every piece of functionality within a given scope.

- Outside of trivial cases it is very unlikely you've completely exhausted the list of things that can go wrong.

- It is even less likely that you've completely explored the space of what the effects of failure will be, and certainly so for the failure modes you didn't think of.

- The rankings are inherently somewhat arbitrary, even with guidelines, and thus not necessarily representative of reality.

- The somewhat arbitrary nature of the rankings means the calculated priority is also likely to be askew.

- A spreadsheet full of your best ideas and intentions isn't actually exercising your real system. It doesn't make sure that any of what you've written down is actually true.

This process itself is highly susceptible to a variety of failures due to simple miscalculation of what to analyze, failure of imagination for what can go wrong, the limits of being able to accurately assess the scale and depth of what the effects of failure will be, the fairly arbitrary nature of the rankings, and a slightly more subtle issue related to multipoint failures (we will discuss this later in the chapter). For the most part, when you're doing an FMEA you're making a whole bunch of educated guesses.

For a process with so many potential pitfalls, why is it often such an essential part of our historical attempts at building reliable and resilient systems? First, for really critical systems performing something like an FMEA is just one among many, many different processes. Many reviews and double- and triple-checking are required to meet standards compliance. Second, it's hard to undersell one of the most significant values of going through with a process like this: namely, it puts you in a failure-first mindset.

It turns out that when you get a lot of highly experienced, cross-disciplinary people together over a long enough period of time to undertake an activity like FMEA, they actually do a pretty good job of having enough context from their experience, and the number of iterations they take, to squeeze out an awful lot of uncertainty.

FMEA and Chaos Engineering

If Functional Safety practices like FMEA have done a good job so far, then what value is there to be gained from adopting Chaos Engineering in these systems? The most obvious possibility is that Chaos Engineering experiments can be used to validate or invalidate every assumption made in your FMEA:

- You can assemble multiple, diverse groups of experts to independently perform the FMEA and look for discrepancies in their results.
- You can inject failures in out-of-scope areas and observe whether or not they should have been considered in-scope.
- You can induce the failures you enumerated and attempt to measure their real, rather than imagined, effects.
- You can use the findings from your Chaos Engineering experiments to directly inform revisions to your FMEA.

In more formalized development processes, you would typically be required to establish a test plan and show evidence of testing to verify your FMEA before releasing your product out into the wild. There are some extremely sophisticated means of testing the components of a system currently commercially available. There are numerous equipment vendors that sell various kinds of failure injection units capable of doing things like simulating shorts in electrical interfaces, faulty mechanical connectors, and so on.

Chaos Engineering adds something significant to creating reliable and resilient CPSs by helping both Functional Safety and Systems Engineers better understand the effects of the interactions between complex software and complex hardware merged together in increasingly complex systems. This is especially true for systems that are being highly automated, where human operators are either removed entirely from the loop or are interacting at much further distance, often through multiple system abstractions, from the critical interfaces and operations within.

Software in Cyber-Physical Systems

Software has some unique properties that make it especially problematic when there are residual faults in its implementation (known issues), latent faults in its implementation (bugs you don't know about), or systematic faults in its design (issues that require you to fundamentally reconsider something about your system specifications).

Software is reused pervasively in ways that cannot be done with mechanical or electrical components. You might call a software function 1,000 different times from 1,000 different places, and it's the exact same function every time. By contrast, a single physical instance of a resistor isn't being used in 1,000 different ways across a 1,000 different circuit boards. You get a bad resistor and you have one failure. You get a bad software function and now everything that depends on it everywhere has problems.

This fairly unique aspect of software is fantastic when the function is implemented and behaving how you expect it to. It's quite the opposite situation when something goes wrong. Now you have exactly the same unexpected behavior throughout your system all at once. To add insult to injury, the effects that this unexpected behavior can have on the rest of your system can vary dramatically depending on not only where it's occurring, but also along an almost infinite timeline of possibilities based on the state of the rest of the system when it occurred.

We interact with software at a very high-level abstraction. An enormous number of underlying models must hold up for us to be capable of reasoning about what software will actually do when operating in a live system. Every abstraction obfuscates complexity for convenience, but that obfuscation also introduces new dimensions of uncertainty. It is also easy in software to accidentally create tightly coupled dependencies and relationships between different pieces of functionality without even realizing it.

Finally, not only is it possible for software to exhibit symptoms that are uniquely software problems, it can also have an impact on system behavior that resembles failing hardware. Consider the common case of an interconnected system with a spastic TCP/IP stack or misconfigured network interface. Depending on the nature of the issue this can look like a byzantine or malicious actor to other parts of your system, or it can look like a severed network cable, or both. All of these things combined make it entirely too easy to introduce latent failure modes, and trivial to create multiple simultaneous failure modes otherwise known as multipoint failures.

It is worth highlighting a subtle point of concern about the traditional FMEA process: normally when you conduct an FMEA you don't consider simultaneous multipoint failures in your analysis. For each enumerated facet of functionality, you perform the analysis assuming that the rest of the system isn't failing at all, and only one thing is failing at a time in the area you're analyzing. When you consider that conducting an FMEA is a framework designed for humans to arrive at better—not perfect—understanding, then this seems like a reasonable approach. Grappling with the combinatorial complexity of failure modes and effects in any nontrivial system with multipoint failures might be intractable.

This is not a complete indictment of typical approaches like FMEA for assessing the risks in your system. After all, consider that even for the domain of Functional Safety the expectation is "to remove unacceptable risk," and from the perspective of electro-mechanical systems it's considered *extremely unlikely* to have a system experience independent multipoint failures at the same time. The self-imposed constraints on an FMEA make complete sense from this point of view. Experiencing multiple simultaneous independent failures in a system is seen as unlikely because you probably don't have two completely independent mechanical or electrical components that are going to randomly fail at the same time. On top of that, the results of such overlapping failures are considered to be so unrecoverable and catastrophic as to not warrant spending energy analyzing. It's a bit like if you were attempting to assess the impact of your authentication system going offline due to your servers being struck by lightning, your data center flooding, and the Earth being struck by an asteroid. The fact that your authentication system is offline becomes immaterial and there's probably not much you can do about it.

However, intensive use of software changes the game. Unlike a single failed electrical component, the ease with which software issues spread like a contagion has the nasty side effect of making accuracy difficult to impossible when assessing failure modes, their effects, their severity, their likelihood, and their detectability. This is where the empirical verification provided by Chaos Engineering can offer new insights through experimentation and exploration.

Chaos Engineering as a Step Beyond FMEA

Some of the FMEA procedures have corollaries to the Chaos Engineering principles (*https://principlesofchaos.org*):

Define your scope and functionality == Hypothesize about steady state
Brainstorm about what could go wrong == Vary real world events
Assign scores to severity, likelihood == Minimize blast radius

The FMEA process provides some guidance and prioritization about where to look more deeply and perhaps create experiments to verify assumptions. Looking at the highest risk priority numbers, one might get the most value out of introducing chaos experimentation to explore the real risks latent in both your assumptions and your systems.

However, there's an enormous amount of overhead and ceremony associated with going through all that. There are other valuable approaches that can be used to identify points for experimentation to maximize information and insights. We can do this by reflecting on how we design and engineer things and what assumptions and assurances we critically depend on in doing so.

For example, it's unbelievably difficult to create something on the back of undefined or nondeterministic behavior. Say I gave you the task of developing a system in a programming language where the only operators that worked correctly and deterministically were "addition" and "assignment," but everything else was unpredictable. If you didn't just outright decline the job on the basis of its insane requirements, you would go *way* out of your way to lean as hard as possible into using *only* addition and assignment for absolutely everything if you could get away with it. Eventually to get anything useful done you'd have an enormous tower of clever tricks and abstractions built on top of nothing but addition and assignment because they're the only bits you would have any faith in.

When people start designing chaos experiments there's a tendency to want to go after the biggest "black box" first. It seems reasonable at first: on the one hand, you've got a bunch of stuff that you implicitly trust; and on the other, you have an amorphous heap of opaque uncertainty. But consider this decision in the context of the contrived example just discussed. Given what you've been told to expect about the programming language you used, the design of your system would likely end up using addition and assignment everywhere it was critical for the system to behave as you expect, and you'd use other operators as a convenience where it's more acceptable if the results or side effects are fuzzy. In effect, you would implicitly bias some parts of your system to be resilient to nondeterminism, and bias others not to be.

Given this, it doesn't make sense to start out by experimenting on what you have fair reason to believe is wobbly. Instead, start out by exploring whether there is latent uncertainty in the things you believe to be absolutely true. Known knowns that are unverified are really just unknown unknowns of the worst kind. You are not only unaware of their existence, but you critically depend on them everywhere. In this example, a great initial chaos experiment might look like purposely breaking the guarantees you've been told will hold up. If you've constructed this massive edifice on the back of addition and assignment always working as you expect, then introduce error into your system in multiple locations and multiple layers so that assumption doesn't hold up anymore. Fiddle with the source code. Break the compiler's code generation. Simulate a CPU that does something seemingly impossible. Then you can see how much risk you're exposed to just by way of potential unknowns in your basic assumptions and critical dependencies.

In order to build something robust, engineers tend to build as much as possible on top of what we think we can count on as being reliable in our systems. In this contrived example, by leveraging so heavily the only two facets of our programming language that we're told we can depend on we've introduced a tremendous amount of brittleness. In order for anything to work we *really* need addition and assignment to *never* do something weird or unexpected. For the other parts of our system, we anticipated failure and implicitly work reliability into our design, use case, or both. We end up with this strange paradox: the parts of the system we trust to be reliable become enormous vectors for risk if they do fail, and the parts least trusted end up being the most robust.

The world of CPSs exacerbates this problem by having *a lot* of things that must work just right inside of really tight and consistent tolerances in order for anything above it to have any prayer of working as intended. One area where huge towers of expectations can build up is around timing, specifically around "hard real-time" constraints. Unlike most IT systems where the tolerances of timing can have relatively wide margins for error, in CPSs there are often strict operational boundaries and tolerance requirements because it's unacceptable for certain things to *eventually* happen when the tolerance is exceeded. In the physical world, you might not be able to simply try again in a little while; by then you might be literally on fire or underwater.

The good news is that electrical engineers have gotten really good at building very reliable local clocks and timing circuits. The bad news is that they've gotten so good at it that they rely utterly on these behaviors as the bedrock upon which systems are designed and built. As I'm designing my system, I start to think of timing in the same way that I thought about adding two numbers in my programming language example. I bias my design to depend on timing because I have more confidence in the reliability of that one component.

The ways in which this assumption can produce catastrophic cascading problems with even subtle deviations in the real behavior are enormous. Timing requirements get baked into considerations around control loops. Small errors in timing can now bubble throughout my system and affect the functions that are responsible for actuating the physical parts of a CPS. They're baked into scheduling concerns that can be as banal as running a nonessential process at the wrong time, but it can also mean not running an absolutely essential function exactly when you need to. Timing errors can cause watchdog timers to trigger when they shouldn't or trigger an emergency failsafe reaction like power-cycling a component or a whole system. Persistent timing issues can cause a subsystem to bounce itself, come back, bounce itself again, and just drop in and out of existence like this in perpetuity.

Distributed systems engineers have an inherent distrust of wall clocks. They understand that in a distributed software system it is unlikely that clocks will agree on the same time and frequency. This deep distrust and skepticism isn't shared widely with other kinds of systems engineers, so they build very large and complex systems on top of an assumption that these timing guarantees will hold up. Historically they did: the systems were smaller, the functions were simpler, and the local clocks were pretty reliable. Global clocks weren't often shared across large distances or diverse requirements. Embedded engineers and safety-critical system engineers are slowly coming to the realization that they are no longer component engineers building a self-contained piece of local functionality in a box. We are all distributed systems engineers now. Chaos Engineering's origins in distributed software systems can help CPSs because distributed systems engineers are predisposed to worrying about things that are just now entering the radar of embedded engineers.

Working with engineers in the autonomous vehicle development space, I often suggest going after timing constraints as a first target for Chaos Engineering and experiments. Not once has it left anybody wanting for interesting and in some cases existential insights about how their system behaves when their clocks play tricks on them. For anybody reading this who works on critical software-intensive systems of systems looking for a place to start applying Chaos Engineering practices: start with timing. Many of the components you're likely to work with are pretty good already at handling or at least noticing things like data corruption, bit flips, message drops, and so on. Timing issues can be subtle, are often cascading, and can be the difference between life and death in a CPS.

Probe Effect

The extreme tolerances and expectations of reliability in embedded and life-critical systems pose practical challenges for applying Chaos Engineering to the devices and systems themselves. Putting something in place to create a fault in a system and something else in place to take measurements to try to assess the impact usually isn't free. Consider a situation where you are working on an extremely sensitive electrical device. The signal level is very low compared to the noise floor. You want to take a measurement of this system to verify something, so you wire up your oscilloscope to the signal path. Unfortunately, there is no such thing as a perfect probe. There will be probe tip resistance, capacitance, and the ground clip will have some amount of inductance. The very presence of your probe will affect your measurements.

This is commonly referred to as "probe effect": The condition of unintended side effects due to trying to take a measurement. In the realm of Chaos Engineering, this bites us twice. There is a probe effect in taking the measurements, and another in the layer of the system in order to inject a fault or other variable. Consider a software system where you want to perform some chaos experiments deep in the Linux kernel on some kind of low-latency IO interface. You wire up a piece of software somewhere in the "signal path" of the IO interface to give yourself a man-in-the-middle. On the output you want to flip some bits so that any upstream application depending on this interface is affected by your chaos probe, but you don't want it to be active all the time, so you need to be able to turn it on and off. In the naive case you've stuck yourself in the middle. Now for every bit that goes out this interface you've inserted a conditional, "Am I running a chaos experiment right now or not?" question into the critical path. What cost does this have, what are the side effects in the system, and what are the side effects of those side effects? Did this conditional interact with optimization hardware in the CPU like the branch-predictor? If it did, then did that impact the performance of something else as a pipeline needed to be flushed?

The more layers and abstractions there are in the system, the more these probe effects can come into play. Recall that we are not even injecting faults yet. We're just laying the groundwork. Now imagine we start injecting faults to flip every third bit. Not only do I have the chaos I'm intending by flipping every third bit, but I'm also constantly calculating when I'm at every third one, and I've introduced a longer code path down this branch, so I'm definitely having an impact on timing and CPU caches. I made a thing to inject one kind of fault to see how it would affect the behavior of the system, but I actually injected all kinds of unintended faults to other resources in the system beyond just this IO interface.

Addressing the Probe Effect

The closer my system is to operating at its limits, and the more my design and implementation depends on those really tight tolerances, the more this probe effect is itself likely to be a significant problem. Fortunately, there are a handful of methods to deal with it; unfortunately, none of them is satisfying if you seek absolute precision in understanding the nuances of your system's behavior.

The solution to this problem will sound simultaneously trite and impossible. You need to take care to understand what the impact of your probe is going to be. With an oscilloscope we have the benefit of physics and understanding the electrical properties of the thing we're using as a probe to help us out. In a multilayered pile of leaky abstractions from the CPU microarchitecture all the way up to your application stack, potentially distributed across N-number of devices, this can be extremely challenging.

There are lots of ways to understand the initial impact of what your probe can do. For example, you could make a piece of formally verified software that ensured that your probe will always consume an amount of memory that is always above and below some bounds, or that your probe would never suddenly crash, or that your probe path took exactly and always four CPU instructions to complete its function. That's a useful number of known knowns. You know the extent of your probe's local footprint. You could also do this through empirical measurements of your probe to get similar confidence in its behavior without the associated verification proof to go along with it. What you don't know is what sticking that footprint into the system will be even when it's not doing anything to create chaos on purpose. To address that, you can make dummy probes that put similar loads on the system even when you're not injecting chaos. Once you do that you can characterize your system with the dummy probe load to understand, to some degree of confidence, what the probe effect itself is on your system's behavior. Then you can put in the real probes to run real experiments and take real measurements. This will materially adjust for the interaction of the test "equipment" on the analysis.

Another approach trades precision in return for convenience. Consider the property of your system that you are most interested in assessing. For example, if you are really concerned about your system's reliability in terms of communications issues, then perhaps it doesn't matter that probes may be causing side effects on CPU utilization.

This could provide an interesting avenue of experimentation as long as your belief that your system is insensitive to variations in CPU usage is true. As another example, perhaps you are interested in understanding what happens when your processes can't allocate more memory. In that case it might not matter if your measurement collection function saturates network capacity. By focusing on the dimensions or operational constraints your system is most sensitive to, it's possible to triangulate whether or not the probe effect is likely to matter in the results of your measurement. There might be a significant effect in one corner, but it's not a corner you're interested in evaluating. You have reason to believe through experimentation that the effects of the probe itself are sufficiently independent from the effects you are otherwise trying to measure by using the probe to introduce variables into the system.

All that said, there's always the easy route: Build your system with all the probes built in, deployed all the time, always putting passive load on the system even when they're not doing anything to change the system behavior on purpose. Get all the probes in there, set static RAM allocations for them, have all code paths do real work or pointless dummy work that's a suitable approximation of the real work, and just have the whole system running in steady-state equivalent to the worst case in terms of resource utilization. This is like running your entire system in debug mode all the time, and obviously not an option for systems where efficiency is paramount.

As they say, there's no free lunch. That includes when you're feeding probes to your system and asking for its culinary opinions of your cooking.

Conclusion

My bias as a former mechanical and manufacturing engineer may be showing, but one of the things I've always remained nostalgic for from my former life is the idea of "material properties." These are things like tensile strength, magnetoresistance, surface tension, flash point, and so on. There are no corollaries to things like this in the world of software engineering. This significantly holds back the sophistication and complexity of the things we can reliably build, understand, and integrate as software-intensive systems. This first struck me as I listened to two different Chaos Engineering talks: one by Nora Jones when she was at Netflix, and another by Heather Nakama when she was at Microsoft.

Listening to those two speakers, I realized that they had both built up very valuable knowledge about their respective systems. Outside of some know-how about pursuing that knowledge by means of Chaos Engineering, there wasn't really much in the way of directly transferable knowledge from the systems Nora dealt with day to day and the systems that Heather dealt with day to day. Certainly there are some similar components in those systems, but if Nora wanted to take a Netflix subsystem and plop it into Heather's infrastructure at Microsoft to provide the same functionality there, it would be very hard for either of them to know ahead of time whether or not that would work. What would the impact be? What stresses would it place on other aspects of Heather's infrastructure? Understanding software systems as we deal with them today depends so much on context.

"Material properties," on the other hand, are stable across use cases and across contexts. We measure how titanium behaves in materials testing laboratories. We bend it. We break it. We shake it. We rapidly heat it and cool it. We take consistent measurements about its behavior and learn a set of things about titanium that we can use to not only guide us as to its viability for a given application. But with enough of these measurements we can also project failure modes, stresses, and effects on models without the time and expense of actually making them.

This is like what Finite Element Analysis tools enable Mechanical Engineers to do. They can design something as a virtual model. They can parameterize the model with which parts are made of what materials. They can define load sources and stresses that they expect to be applied to the design when put to real life use, and because we've characterized and measured so many material properties in repeatable and consistent ways, it's possible to predict how the thing will behave long before physically producing one. Because of these kinds of consistent measurements and properties we can virtually create whole aircraft frames, simulate crumple zone deformation in vehicle collisions, and design underwater turbines that will minimally disrupt the environment they're deployed into. This has fundamentally raised the bar on the sophistication and complexity of things that mechanical engineers can reliably make.

I see Chaos Engineering practices as a path to this kind of world for software-intensive systems. To some extent, basic properties and characteristics have surfaced in different corners of the software systems world. We consider properties like "availability." We note metrics like CPU utilization and network throughput. We are not bereft of places to start defining measurements and meaning. Formalizing Chaos Engineering will create the equivalent of "material properties" for software-intensive systems. It will create the empirical methods that let us discover the values for context-independent measurements for all kinds of systems. Chaos Engineering tools are like the materials testing laboratories where we learn how things behave when we push them to their limits. If we do this right, then Chaos Engineering will move incidents from late-stage operations impacts to early-stage design considerations. Software-intensive systems have reached levels of complexity where the complexity itself is holding back innovation in software systems. Chaos Engineering provides a path that can lead us to answers beyond that problem.

About the Author

Nathan Aschbacher began his career writing programs for CNC machines where overlooked edge cases resulted in mangled heaps of metal, broken tools, and lasting impressions of catastrophic failure. Since those early days he has gone on to design fault-tolerant distributed data platforms and global transaction processing networks. Nathan first applied Chaos Engineering principles to problems in the FinTech space, later transferred the practice to autonomous vehicle platform development, and now focuses on developing products and technology, through his company Auxon, which leverages formal methods and sophisticated fault injection to enable engineers to verify and validate complex, highly automated systems.

CHAPTER 18

HOP Meets Chaos Engineering

Bob Edwards

What Is Human and Organizational Performance (HOP)?

HOP is an approach to improving organizational structures and functional processes to optimize for business-critical properties such as safety. Perhaps because of its roots in manufacturing, it is often mistaken for a process, but it's not prescriptive in that sense. There is a flexibility and art to it, based on the five principles outlined in this chapter.

As an approach commonly applied in the manufacturing world, we have an opportunity to learn from Chaos Engineering and incorporate techniques that have shown value in software systems. Both Chaos Engineering and HOP have philosophical roots in what is known as the "new view"[1] philosophy in safety science. This is a fundamental shift in our understanding of accidents, human factors. HOP is an application of new view models to accident investigations and organizational change for the purpose of building safer systems.

---

1 The "new view" is a rough philosophy (not rigorously defined) that draws a contrast with the "old view" of safety science, promoted in many of Sidney Dekker's books and via his coauthors. Roughly this philosophy corresponds to the latest research and trends in Safety Science and Resilience Engineering since the early 2000s, including concepts like "Safety-II" and "Safety Differently" popularized in the academic and popular literature on the subject. See Sidney Dekker, "Reconstructing Human Contributions to Accidents" (*Journal of Safety Research* 33 (2002), pp. 371–385), for an early exposition of "new view" safety.

Key Principles of HOP

We have taken five key principles that we adapted from research in the Human Performance Technology[2] field of study and fitted them for practical use in the world of general industry. These principles are our guide to improving operational reliability and resilience in industries such as manufacturing, utilities, chemical, oil and gas, and even the medical world. These five principles are applicable to just about any organization:

- Error is normal.
- Blame fixes nothing.
- Context drives behavior.
- Learning and improving is vital.
- Intentional response matters.

Principle 1: Error Is Normal

All humans make mistakes. Many times, the people who make the most mistakes are those who do the most work. I once saw a sign in a machine shop that said, "He who makes no mistakes, doesn't make anything." If we expect humans in the work environment to perfectly perform their tasks for success, we are setting ourselves up for failure. We need to prevent the errors that we can; however, we also need to build in the capacity to fail safely. Automotive manufacturers adopt this way of thinking in the way they build defenses to help prevent drivers from having accidents and simultaneously build the cars to be remarkably safe to wreck. Car designers want drivers to be as safe as they can, but they also know that all accidents are not preventable. They build in warning systems and even automated steering correction and brake assist to help prevent accidents. In addition to these types of prevention strategies, the auto manufacturers also design and build in crumple zones, airbags, and survivable space for the times when the prevention doesn't work. They are counting on accidents to occur and they are planning for wrecks to occur so they make the car both hard to wreck and safe to wreck.

---

2 Think of process management and process improvement methods such as Lean, Six Sigma, knowledge management, training, and so on. In the software world, this would include XP, Agile, and DevOps, but the term *HPT* (*https://oreil.ly/U_7Tm*) usually applies to manufacturing and is not commonly applied to software.

Principle 2: Blame Fixes Nothing

Blame not only fixes nothing; it also drives important conversations and necessary information underground. If it feels like a person could be blamed for something, they will be very reluctant to talk about it especially if they think they might be the one who messed up. This doesn't mean we aren't accountable for our actions; we are. It is time to shift to a different way of thinking about accountability. All too often when people say, "I need to hold employees accountable," what they are really saying is that they need someone to pin the blame on. When we stop focusing on blame and instead start focusing on learning and improving and restoring, we begin to build a work environment where the workers are not afraid to talk about issues, even if they played a role in how the issue unfolded. It is hard not to blame, because we are humans and humans are exceptionally good at inferring connections between things, even if that inference isn't backed by objective evidence. HOP cannot prevent blame from happening; but blame cannot make you or your organization better. If your goal is to improve then you will need to make a deliberate effort to direct your organization towards learning and improving, and away from blame and punishment.

Principle 3: Context Drives Behavior

Many different conditions and components create the context surrounding work. Some of these components are the systems we work with daily; systems such as safety, quality, production, environmental, metrics, and so on. Pick any of them and look at what behavior they drive. If safety tells you that you must reach zero injuries, this creates a pressure to under-report. The more the system drives to lower that number, the less people will report their injuries. If the context around your production pressure says to make one thousand parts by the end of the shift, then it will be less important how you achieved that goal and more important that you did. The context set around work often drives behavior that is disjointed from the goal of the business. We need these systems and we need metrics; however, it is very important to be open and honest about what sort of behavior those systems are driving. If we find that they are driving the right sort of behavior, that's great, if not, we should do something different. We should also be aware that the context of work that drove a certain behavior yesterday or last year may have drifted into a less desirable behavior now. For example, if we implement an observation program in order to get leaders out on the floor to see what was going on, that seems like a good thing. We may add a metric to make sure they do at least a certain number of observations per week. It is easy for that weekly metric to become more of the focus than what we are learning when we go to observe the work.

Principle 4: Learning and Improving Is Vital

Many of us have some sort of continuous improvement process in our organization. It may be working well; it may need a tune-up. The methods we use to learn and improve need to be usable by participants and effective in practice not just theory. One of the methods we have created for this learning process is what we call a "Learning Team." Part of the learning and improving process requires making sure they help by checking results against pre-planned goals. In some cases, it may not even be a complete fix, but rather an improvement for now based on what the work looks like now. In order to know if what we have put in place is working, we need to have effective testing or analysis of the improvements. This is where the Chaos Engineering approach can really help: by verifying that the system is producing the desired output.

Principle 5: Intentional Response Matters

The last of the five principles is about how we think about our response. When an incident happens or nearly happens, when we are not clear about some process, or when we are not sure if we were lucky or good, we need to respond. We need to set into motion operational learning that will lead us toward a deeper understanding of our workplace and encourage us to improve. This needs to be done thoughtfully and intentionally. Simultaneously, how we respond needs to direct our organization away from blaming the worker or blaming the supervisor or blaming the manager. Remember, "Blame Fixes Nothing." When we model a healthy response to some event or issue, it will set the tone for those around us. How we respond throughout our organization, at all levels, matters—a lot!

HOP Meets Chaos Engineering

In my world of manufacturing, when some event happens, it could be safety, quality, or some sort of operational upset, we want to fix things and make it better. We want to make sure that our action items are in fact acted upon in a timely manner and that they will work. We usually track these action items to closure with an owner and closure target date and hold meetings about why some items haven't been closed yet. Sound familiar? I am not saying this is bad, it's just that I often see more focus on getting the items closed than I see focused on effectiveness and sustainability, especially if it is considered a compliance item.

This process plays out at most organizations and it does have some value. That said, I want to shift the focus more toward effectiveness and resilience of the solutions, fixes, improvements, and action items coming from our learning and improving efforts. I want my team and my leadership to have confidence that the improvements being made will really add more reliability and resilience into the workplace. Did what we do really make a difference in the work environment? This thinking is largely summed up with what I am learning from the work of the Chaos Engineering folks.

Here is what I've learned so far from Nora Jones, Casey Rosenthal, and their colleagues. There are some key principles they apply in the Chaos Engineering approach, used to better understand their products' reliability. These are the principles I want to apply to better understand defenses and capacity with my improvement efforts. If you take these principles and apply them more broadly to our processes and our organization, see if we can apply this way of thinking to better characterize what defenses and capacity we have built at our place of business.

Let's start with my understanding of the Chaos Engineering overall experimentation philosophy. The intent is not to do away with standard testing that is used to ensure the product or process complies with regulatory requirements and meets basic operational criteria. Chaos Engineering is used to push the product or process beyond its normal expected conditions and to see if we can learn something new about the reliability of the product or process or perhaps to uncover the lack thereof, by seeing the system operating within the "chaos" of life. We are experimenting to learn something new.

Experimenting to learn something new, not just test for the known, is brilliant.

I'm reminded of a simple example of putting this in action. Let's say, as a part of a learning and improving effort, we decide we need to install a safety rail in place. I paint it safety yellow. I bolt it down with concrete anchors through anchor plates at the bottom of each leg (making sure there are four bolts per plate). It has to be 42 inches tall and have a mid-rail and a toe-guard if elevated. It must withstand a certain side loading force, etc. This railing needs to meet these requirements and should be tested for them. These are the "known" requirements. What Chaos Engineering has taught me is that I also need to know how well this rail is working when actually in use. Does it get in the way? Is it blocking access to valves or gauges? Does it cause workers to have to walk out into other hazard areas to get around it? Does it slow down the workflow? What do we know about how well the railing works in the area when there are frequent equipment breakdowns, or a take-cover alarm goes off or a fire drill takes place? These are the things that are becoming more interesting to me than just whether it passes the regulatory requirements or whether it was closed out in the action tracker within 30 days.

Now, armed with the Chaos Engineering approach to system experimentation and defense and capacity building, the equation changes. As I began to think about this new approach to understanding products and processes, I realized that this could be a real game changer with the work that we are doing with HOP. When Learning Teams come up with improvements and solutions, we can verify them with Chaos Engineering. After our Learning Team sessions, we know a lot more about the chaos of work. Now armed with this information, as we put improvement ideas in place, we can verify them. This will give us a much better idea if the improvements we made brings the process, product, or operations to a more reliable state. Admittedly, at the time of this writing, we are at the early stages of this new thinking; however, I wanted to share what we are already doing and ideas of what we are planning on doing.

Chaos Engineering and HOP in Practice

Here's an example of Chaos Engineering in the HOP world. Many of the companies that we work with have simulation training rooms. They are usually set up as close to the real control room as possible. Operators, as a part of their training, spend countless hours in the simulation room just as they would in real life work. The trainers can throw problems at a new operator and see how they solve them. They can fail, learn, and try again. This is a great way to build confidence and competence for the work they are about to begin performing. A problem shows up on the simulation control board and the operator closes valve 3 and diverts the flow through the bypass and into the overflow tank. Problem solved and good job. There is definite value to this training. The problem is, we have a simulator that does what it's supposed to do. Valve 3 closes, and the flow diverts to the overflow tank.

The problem in real life is that valve 3 has been hanging up and only closing 80% of the way, which won't fully divert the flow and will continue to allow a significant flow down the section of pipe where the issue is. This is reality but it's not in the simulator. The Chaos Engineering approach teaches us to modify the simulation control room parameters and software so that the actual degraded state of the site is better represented in the simulations. Now when the new operator attempts to close valve 3 it shows that it closed; however, they are still seeing flow downstream of the valve. Now they have to think, in real time, about other options and solutions. This is real-time problem solving with the stress of the system not doing what it's supposed to do. It is the chaos inherent in the work. We are learning this information in our Learning Team sessions and can apply them to the software of the simulator.

I think we will be able to even create code that will randomize the issues for different simulations. Maybe some sort of "decay" algorithm that makes different components wear out and not function as originally designed to. This will add a real sense of the chaos of actual operations in a control room at a power company or at a chemical processing plant or any place where the process is controlled by computer-based systems.

Now consider how this example relates to the principles of HOP:

Error is normal
> We expect trainees to make suboptimal decisions in the simulation. Real-time problem solving is hard, especially when you are still building foundational experience. They will fail, and that is okay.

Blame fixes nothing

In a simulation, it is easier to suppress the cultural impulse to blame people for decisions that don't lead to the desired outcome. The stakes are lower because business outcomes aren't really impacted in this environment.

Context drives behavior

The realism of the simulation establishes context, and that interplay between the interface of the simulation and human behavior makes a great learning platform for trainers as well as trainees. This is also an opportunity for user experience (UX) designers to better understand the interplay between human operators and technical parts of the system. The disparity between the action taken (close valve 3) and the result seen (flow is still happening in the problematic pipe) informs the human operator, but it also signals an opportunity to improve the tool.

Learning and improving is vital

The entire point of the simulation is to provide a safe learning environment. This is core to the HOP approach.

Intentional response matters

In a realistic simulation, trainers can look for intentionality, encourage it, and facilitate better conversations about the decision-making process.

The goals of Chaos Engineering and HOP dovetail beautifully. Focusing on empirical data, actually trying to operate the system in turbulent conditions, speaks directly to the principles of HOP.

Conclusion

HOP is designed to help pull together the best of all we know about how humans and organizations perform together and then build a better workplace. It also encourages organizations to challenge what they are currently doing to see if what they are doing is making them better, or perhaps is giving them a false sense of security instead. Chaos Engineering complements this approach philosophically and practically, by verifying that we get what we want out of a system and that the output tracks with the intention of the response.

About the Author

Bob Edwards is a Human and Organizational Performance (HOP) practitioner. Bob works with all levels of an organization, teaching HOP fundamentals and training and coaching Learning Teams. Bob has a bachelor's degree in mechanical engineering from Tennessee Technological University and a master's in advanced safety engineering management from the University of Alabama Birmingham. His work experience includes time as a maintenance man, soldier in the US Army, design engineer, maintenance and technical support leader, safety leader, and assistant plant manager.

CHAPTER 19

Chaos Engineering on a Database

Liu Tang and Hao Weng

Why Do We Need Chaos Engineering?

Ever since Netflix open sourced Chaos Monkey (*https://oreil.ly/H2ouw*) in 2011, this program has become more and more popular. If you want to build a distributed system, letting Chaos Monkey go a little crazy on your cluster can help build a more fault-tolerant, robust, and reliable system.[1]

TiDB (*https://oreil.ly/n5xBc*) is an open source, distributed, Hybrid Transactional/ Analytical Processing (HTAP)[2] database developed primarily by PingCAP. It stores what we believe is the most important asset for any database users: the data itself. One of the fundamental and foremost requirements of our system is to be fault-tolerant. Traditionally we run unit tests and integration tests to guarantee a system is production ready, but these cover just the tip of the iceberg as clusters scale, complexities amount, and data volumes increase by PB levels. Chaos Engineering is a natural fit for us. In this chapter, we will detail our practices and the specific reasons why a distributed system like TiDB needs Chaos Engineering.

Robustness and Stability

To build users' trust in a newly released distributed database like TiDB, where data is saved in multiple nodes that communicate with each other, data loss or damage must be prevented at any time. But in the real world, failures can happen any time, anywhere, in a way we can never expect. So how can we survive them? One common way

---

1 Some contents of this chapter were previously published on the PingCAP blog (*https://oreil.ly/-P8tK*).

2 HTAP means the capability of a single database to perform both online transaction processing (OLTP) and online analytical processing (OLAP) for real-time operational intelligence processing.

is to make our system fault-tolerant. If one service crashes, another fallover service can take charge immediately without affecting online services. In practice we need to be wary that fault tolerance increases the complexity for a distributed system.

How can we ensure that our fault tolerance is robust? Typical ways of testing our tolerance to failures include writing unit tests and integration tests. With the assistance of internal test generation tools, we have developed over 20 million unit test cases. We also utilized a great number of open source test cases such as MySQL test cases and ORM framework test cases. However, even 100% unit coverage does not equal a fault-tolerant system. Likewise, a system surviving well-designed integration tests does not guarantee that it will work well enough in an actual production environment. In the real world, anything can happen, such as disk failures, or Network Time Protocol (NTP) out of sync. To make a distributed database system like TiDB more robust, we need a method to simulate unpredictable failures and test our responses to these failures.

A Real-World Example

In TiDB we use the Raft consensus algorithm to replicate data from the leader to followers to guarantee data consistency among replicas. When a follower is newly added in a replica group, the chances are good that it will lag behind the leader by multiple versions. To keep data consistent, the leader sends a snapshot file for the follower to apply. This is one place where things might go wrong. Figure 19-1 shows a typical case we encountered in a production environment.

```
[root@10-180-0-22 data]# ls -lt snap/* | grep 16986
-rw-r--r-- 1 ops ops       58 Jul 18 23:42 snap/rev_1129386_18_16986.meta
-rw-r--r-- 1 ops ops        0 Jul 18 23:42 snap/rev_1129386_18_16986_write.sst
-rw-r--r-- 1 ops ops        0 Jul 18 23:42 snap/rev_1129386_18_16986_lock.sst
-rw-r--r-- 1 ops ops  8499200 Jul 18 23:42 snap/rev_1129386_18_16986_default.sst
```

Figure 19-1. A real-world bug found in TiDB snapshot. The _write.sst and _lock.sst files should not be 0 bytes according to the information in the .meta file.

As seen in Figure 19-1, the snapshot consists of four parts: one meta file (with the suffix of .meta), and three data files (with the suffix .sst). The meta file contains the size information for all data files and corresponding checksums, which we can use to check whether the received data files are valid for applying.

For a newly created replica, Figure 19-2 displays how snapshot consistency is verified among the Raft Leader and the followers. As you can see in the log, some sizes are zero, but in fact they are not zero in the meta file. This means the snapshot is corrupted.

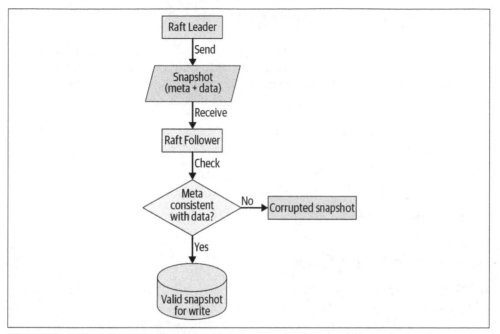

Figure 19-2. Snapshot consistency verification in a Raft group. The leader sends a snapshot to the follower, where the meta file is compared against the data files to decide whether they are consistent with each other.

So how did this bug happen? In the Linux debug message, we found an error in the Linux kernel:

```
[17988717.953809] SLUB: Unable to allocate memory on node -1 (gfp=0x20)]
```

The error happened when Linux operated the page cache,[3] which functions as the main disk cache that the kernel refers to when reading from or writing to disk. When we write data to a file in Linux without using the direct IO mode, the data will be written to the page cache at first, then flushed to the disk through a background thread. If the flushing process fails due to system crashes or power outage, we might lose the written data.

This failure was tricky because it was not isolated to TiDB itself. It could only be encountered in the full context of a production environment, which has a greater amount of complexity and unpredictability. Solving this one problem is easy, but no matter how many unit tests or integration tests we write, we still can't cover all the cases. We need a better way: we need Chaos Engineering.

---

3 Marco Cesati and Daniel P. Bovet, *Understanding the Linux Kernel*, Third Edition (Sebastopol, CA: O'Reilly, 2005), Chapter 15.

Applying Chaos Engineering

Not only did Netflix invent Chaos Monkey, it also introduced the concept of Chaos Engineering, a methodical way to help us identify failure modes. To apply Chaos Engineering, we combine the following experimentation guidelines (from the "Principles of Chaos" site (*http://principlesofchaos.org*)) with our specific approach:

- Define the "steady state" as some measurable output of a system that indicates normal behavior.
- Develop a hypothesis based on steady state.
- Introduce variables that reflect real-world incidents.
- Disprove the hypothesis by detecting deviations from steady state as failures.

Our Way of Embracing Chaos

In TiDB we apply Chaos Engineering to observe the steady state of our system, make a hypothesis, conduct experiments, and verify our hypothesis with real results.[4] Here is our five-step Chaos Engineering methodology based on the core principles:

1. Define the steady state based on metrics. We use Prometheus as the monitor, and define the system's steady state by observing and collecting critical metrics of a stable cluster. Typically, we use QPS and latency (P99/P95), CPU, and memory. These are key indicators of quality of service for a distributed database like TiDB.

2. Make a list of hypotheses of certain failure scenarios and what we expect to happen; for example, if we isolate a TiKV (the distributed key-value storage layer of TiDB) node from a three-replica cluster, the QPS should drop first, but will soon recover to another stable state. Another example is we increase the number of regions (the storage segmentation unit in TiKV) to 40,000 on a single node. The CPU and memory utilization should remain normal.

3. Pick a hypothesis to verify.

4. Inject faults into the system, monitor the metrics, and verify whether the metric change is expected. If there are major deviations from the steady state, there must be something wrong. To continue with the QPS hypothesis (Figure 19-3), in a TiKV node failure if the QPS never returns to the normal level, it means that either the failed leaders caused by the partition are never re-elected or the client is constantly requesting response from the missing leader. Both cases indicate bugs, or even design defects in the system.

---

4 See Chapter 3 for more about the template for experimentation.

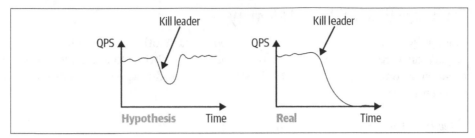

Figure 19-3. Hypothesis and reality

5. Rinse and repeat on another hypothesis from our list, and automate the process via a test framework called Schrodinger.

Fault Injection

Fault injection (https://oreil.ly/84uqP) is a technique for improving the coverage of a test by introducing faults to test code paths, in particular error-handling code paths. Working on TiDB we have accumulated lots of ways to perform fault injection to disturb the system and better understand its complexity. While performing fault injection, it's important to isolate parts of the system and understand their components to minimize the blast radius. Based on the impact scope, we divide our fault injection methods into four major categories:

- Fault injection in applications
- Fault injection in CPU and memory
- Fault injection in a network
- Fault injection in a filesystem

Fault Injection in Applications

In the application level, killing or suspending the process is a good method to test the fault tolerance and concurrency processing abilities (see Table 19-1).

Table 19-1. Fault injection in applications

Purpose	Method/step
Fault tolerance/recovery	Randomly kill a process forcefully (with SIGKILL) or gracefully (with SIGTERM) and restart it
	Stop a process with the SIGSTOP signal and then resume it with SIGCONT
Concurrency bugs	Use `renice` to change the priority of a process.
	Use `pthread_setaffinity_np` to change the affinity of a thread.

Fault Injection in CPU and Memory

Since CPU and memory are closely related to each other, and both have a direct impact on thread operations and performance, it's fitting that we place CPU and memory as one category. Table 19-2 lists the steps and purposes of fault injection in CPU and memory.

Table 19-2. Fault injection in CPU and memory

Purpose	Method/step
Saturation and performance issues	Run utilities like the `while (true){}` loop to max out the CPU (100% utilization)
Performance under restricted conditions	Use `cgroup` to control the CPU and memory usage of a certain process

CPU and memory are generic parts for fault injection. Since we are building a distributed database where data is saved in multiple machines that communicate with each other, we focus more on fault injection into the network and filesystem.

Fault Injection in the Network

After analyzing 25 famous open source systems, Ahmed Alquraan et al.[5] identified 136 faults attributed to network partition. In these faults, 80% are catastrophic, with data loss being the most common (27%) category. This is especially relevant for a distributed database. Network partitions are not to be taken lightly. With fault injection in network, we can detect as many networking problems as possible to build our understanding and confidence in our database before its deployment in production.

There are three types of network partition, as shown in Figure 19-4:

a. Complete partition: Group 1 and Group 2 can't communicate completely.

b. Partial partition: Group 1 and Group 2 can't communicate directly, but they can communicate through Group 3.

c. Simplex partition: Group 1 can connect to Group 2, but Group 2 can't connect to Group 1.

---

5 Ahmed Alquraan et al., "An Analysis of Network-Partitioning Failures in Cloud Systems," *13th USENIX Symposium on Operating Systems Design and Implementation* (OSDI 18), USENIX Association.

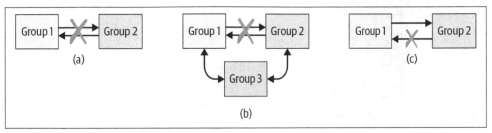

Figure 19-4. Network partitioning types

For TiDB we not only use the basic network partition types to simulate network failures, but also add several other variations:

- Use tc[6] to increase network latency.
- Use tc to reorder network packets.
- Start an application to run out of the bandwidth.
- Use a proxy to control specific TCP connection.
- Use iptable to restrict specific connections

With these methods to inject faults into network, we are able to detect major network issues mostly related to a distributed database, such as latency, packet loss, network partition, and so on. Of course, these are not all of the conditions we explore; for example, sometimes we unplug the network cable to cause immediate full network partition for a specified period of time.

Fault Injection in the Filesystem

Pillai et al.[7] found that the filesystem may cause data inconsistency as a result of crashes, like the snapshot problem we mentioned earlier. To better understand the filesystem and protect the data against filesystem faults, we need to run chaos experiments with those as well.

Because it is hard to inject faults to the filesystem directly, we use Fuse (Figure 19-5) to mount a directory and let our application operate data in this directory. Any I/O operation will trigger a hook so we can do fault injection to return an error or just pass the operation to the real directory.

---

6 tc (traffic control) is the user-space utility program used to configure the Linux kernel packet scheduler (*https://oreil.ly/d8uOy*).

7 Thanumalayan Sankaranarayana Pillai et al., "All File Systems Are Not Created Equal: On the Complexity of Crafting Crash-Consistent Applications," *Proceedings of the 11th USENIX Symposium on Operating Systems Design and Implementation*, October 2014.

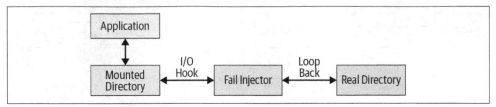

Figure 19-5. Fuse architecture

In the Fail Injector, we define rules such as for path /a/b/c, impose a delay of 20 ms on each read/write operation; or for path /a/b/d, impose a `return NoSpace error` action on each write operation. Faults are injected per these rules via the mounted directory. Operations that don't match bypass these rules and interact with the actual directory.

Detecting Failures

Developing experiment hypotheses and injecting faults to systems based on that are enlightening, but they are just the start of the process to understand the complexity and unpredictability of the system. For the experimentation to actually work, we need methods to detect failures efficiently and accurately in production. In the meantime, we need a way to help us detect failures in production automatically.

An easy way to detect failures is to use the alert mechanism of Prometheus. We can define some alert rules, and receive an alert when something goes wrong and triggers the rule. For example, when a given number of errors per second exceeds a predefined threshold, the alert would trigger and we can respond accordingly.

Another way is to learn from history. We have a long time span of metrics data on user workload. Based on this historical data, we can infer whether current indicators, like a surge in the saving duration, are normal or not because user workload is fixed most of the time (see Figure 19-6).

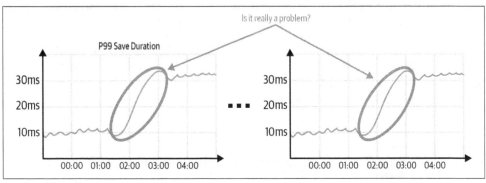

Figure 19-6. Indicator over history

For critical errors, we use Fluent Bit (*https://fluentbit.io/*), an open source log processor and forwarder to collect logs across TiDB components, and parse the logs before later processing and debugging in Elasticsearch. To streamline log collection, parsing and query in a structural manner, we have defined a unified log format called TiDB Log Format, structured as follows:

```
Log header: [date_time] [LEVEL] [source_file:line_number]
Log message: [message]
Log field: [field_key=field_value]
```

Here is a sample log:

```
[2018/12/15 14:20:11.015 +08:00] [WARN] [session.go:1234]
["Slow query"]
[sql="SELECT * FROM TABLE WHERE ID=\"abc\""] [duration=1.345s]\n
[client=192.168.0.123:12345] [txn_id=123000102231]
```

In this example, we have a keyword "Slow query". From the log message part, we can know the SQL statement in question and its txn_id (a unique ID for a SQL query), based on which we can get all the associated logs and know why the SQL is slow.

Automating Chaos

In 2015, when we first began to develop TiDB, every time we committed a feature we would do the following:

1. Build the TiDB binary.
2. Ask the administrator to allot some machines for testing.
3. Deploy the TiDB binaries and run them.
4. Run test cases.
5. Inject faults.
6. Clean up everything and release the machines after all tests are finished.

Although this worked back then, all these tasks involved manual and tedious operations. As the TiDB codebase and userbase grew, more and more experiments needed to run concurrently. The manual way simply couldn't scale. We needed an automatic pipeline that solves this pain.

Automated Experimentation Platform: Schrodinger

The famous thought experiment Schrodinger's cat (*https://oreil.ly/eV42N*) presented a hypothetical cat that may be simultaneously alive and dead, by being linked to a subatomic event that may or may not occur. Various interpretations aside, we found the unpredictability in the experiment and the device that caused it perfectly apply to our practices of Chaos Engineering. With this inspiration, we built Schrodinger, an experimentation platform that performs Chaos Engineering automatically. All we need to do is write experiments and configure Schrodinger to perform the specific testing tasks, and it would take everything else from there.

The overhead of creating an environment with a clean slate on physical machines was one of the larger pain points involved in running these experiments. We needed a solution for running our Chaos Engineering experiments that could do away with this toil so we could focus on what matters: understanding our systems. Schrodinger is based on Kubernetes (K8s), so we don't depend on physical machines. K8s hides the machine-level details and helps us schedule the right job for the right machines.

As shown in Figure 19-7, Schrodinger consists of the following components:

Cat
A TiDB cluster of specified configurations

Box
A template to generate configurations for the cluster and related experiments; it's an encapsulation of an *Experiment*, or a test to run

Nemesis
The fault injectors that inject errors to disturb the system, with the target to "Kill the cat," or fail the test

Test Case
Specifies the testing procedure, inputs, and expected outputs

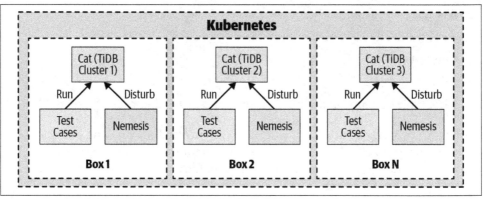

Figure 19-7. Schrodinger architecture on K8s

With the Schrodinger platform, we streamline our methodology of Chaos Engineering workflow so that we could scale the experiments as we need, automatically.

Schrodinger Workflow

Now, if we want to use Schrodinger to experiment on our newly developed features, we only need to:

1. Prepare the test case:

   a. Download the testing code via *git clone*, compile, and specify the running parameters.

   b. Specify the running sequence for multiple experiments, for example, serial or parallel, and determine whether to inject errors using Nemesis either randomly or based on experiment scenarios.

2. Create the Cat. Cat is the TiDB cluster we want to test. Set the number of different TiDB components in the cluster, the code branch, and configurations of the component in the configuration file.

3. Add the Box, and put the configured TiDB cluster and test cases in the Box.

After we finish these steps, Schrodinger begins to prepare the resource, build the corresponding release, deploy, and run the cluster. Then it will run the Experiment (with Nemesis injecting errors or not) and give us a report in the end.

Prior to Schrodinger, for even a simple experiment like account transfer we needed to manually deploy the TiDB cluster, configure the test, inject faults, and finally detect the failures. With Schrodinger, whether it's a simple experiment like this or much more complicated ones, these manual steps can run automatically at a few clicks. Schrodinger can now run experiments in seven different clusters simultaneously, 24/7 without stopping.

Conclusion

Our implementation of a Chaos Engineering platform, Schrodinger, has helped us locate issues more efficiently and comprehensively in all components of TiDB, including third-party ones such as RocksDB. We firmly believe that Chaos Engineering is a great way to detect systematic uncertainty in a distributed system and build confidence in the system's robustness.

For our next steps, we will continuously expand upon our current implementation by making our platform more versatile, smart, and automatic. For example, we want to be able to do kernel-level fault injections, and use machine learning to make Schrodinger "study" the history log of the cluster and figure out how to inject fault intelligently. In addition, we are also considering providing Schrodinger as an experimentation service via Chaos operator,[8] or Chaos as Customer Resource Definition (CRD) (*https://oreil.ly/eV42N*) via K8s, so that more users outside of PingCAP could detect their issues with our methodologies, simply by providing their own Helm charts (*https://oreil.ly/iH4Ca*).

About the Authors

Liu Tang is the chief engineer at PingCAP. He has been the team leader and a senior maintainer of the TiKV project since it started in 2015. He is also a long-time advocate and practitioner of Chaos Engineering. Outside PingCAP, he is an open source enthusiast who authored go-ycsb and ledisdb.

Hao Weng is the content strategist and internationalization project coordinator for the TiKV project at PingCAP. He has many years of technical writing experience in tech companies like Spirent and Citrix. Besides conveying complicated technologies through understandable language, he is also passionate about marathons and musicals.

---

8 By the time of publication, Chaos Mesh (*https://oreil.ly/pPDLn*), a cloud native Chaos Engineering platform for orchestrating chaos experiments on K8s, has already been open sourced by PingCAP.

CHAPTER 20

The Case for Security Chaos Engineering

Aaron Rinehart

> Definition of Security Chaos Engineering: The identification of security control failures through proactive experimentation to build confidence in the system's ability to defend against malicious conditions in production.[1]

According to the Privacy Rights Clearinghouse (*https://www.privacyrights.org*), an organization that tracks data breaches, the frequency of security incidents as well as the number of impacted consumer records is exponentially rising. Failure to correctly implement basic configurations and appropriate technical controls lead the pack of contributing factors to security incidents.[2] Organizations are being asked to do so much with so few resources, just to maintain the security status quo. All the while there is a conflict in the way we approach security engineering and the way systems are being built in tandem.

The need to think differently about information security is paramount as the movement toward complex, distributed systems threatens the ability of security to keep pace. Engineering practices have reached a state where the systems we are designing are impossible for the human mind to mentally model. Our systems are now vastly distributed and operationally ephemeral. Transformational technology shifts such as cloud computing, microservices, and continuous delivery (CD) have each brought forth new advances in customer value but have in turn resulted in a new series of future challenges. Primary among those challenges is our inability to understand our own systems.

---

1 Aaron Rinehart, "Security Chaos Engineering: A New Paradigm for Cybersecurity," Opensource.com, Jan. 24, 2018, *https://oreil.ly/Vqnjo*.

2 IBM/Ponemon Institute, "2018 Cost of a Data Breach Report," 2018, *https://oreil.ly/sEt6A*.

If we have a poor understanding of how our systems are behaving in general, how is it possible to affect good security upon the same system? Through planned, empirical experimentation. This chapter applies Chaos Engineering to the field of cybersecurity. We call this Security Chaos Engineering (SCE).

SCE serves as a foundation for developing a learning culture around how organizations build, operate, instrument, and secure their systems. The goal of these experiments is to move security in practice from subjective assessment into objective measurement. As they do in the DevOps world, chaos experiments allow security teams to reduce the "unknown unknowns" and replace "known unknowns" with information that can drive improvements to security posture.

By intentionally introducing a failure mode or other event, security teams can discover how well instrumented, observable, and measurable security systems truly are. Teams can see if security functions are working as well as everyone assumes they are, objectively assessing abilities and weaknesses, moving to stabilize the former and eliminate the latter.

SCE proposes that the only way to understand this uncertainty is to confront it objectively by introducing controlled signals. If you introduce an objective controlled signal by injecting incidents into the system, it becomes possible to measure things like how good the team is at different types of incidents, how effective the technology is, how aligned runbooks or security incident processes are, and so on. Now you are able to truly understand when an incident began, measure, track, and compare outcomes across different periods of time, and even assess and encourage different teams to better understand attack preparedness.

A Modern Approach to Security

Chaos Engineering is the only established, proactive mechanism for detecting availability incidents before they happen. In that tradition, SCE allows teams to proactively, safely discover system weakness *before* they disrupt business outcomes. This requires a fundamentally new approach to cybersecurity, one that keeps pace with the rapidly evolving world of software engineering.

Human Factors and Failure

In cybersecurity the attribution of "root cause" is still a widely held cultural norm.

> What you call "root cause" is simply the place where you stop looking any further.
>
> —Sydney Dekker[3]

---

3 Sydney Dekker, *The Field Guide to Understanding "Human Error"*, 3rd ed. (Abingdon and New York, NY: Routledge, 2014).

There is no single root cause for failure, much like there is no single root cause for success. The root cause analysis (RCA) approach results in unnecessary and unhelpful assignment of blame, isolation of the engineers involved, and ultimately a culture of fear throughout the organization.

Mistakes will always happen. Rather than failing fast and encouraging experimentation, the traditional RCA approach to postmortem analysis diminishes the ability to derive a deeper understanding of what events and actions might have contributed to the outcome of the adverse event. At the end of the day, RCA is not reducing the number or severity of security defects in our products. Our current mindset and processes are making the problem worse, not better.

The reactionary state of the industry means that we quickly use the "root cause" as an object to attribute and shift blame. Hindsight bias often confuses our personal narrative with truth, and truth is an objective fact that we as investigators can never fully know. The poor state of self-reflection, human factors knowledge, and the nature of resource constraints further incentivize this vicious pattern.

Most reported "root causes" of data breaches[4] are not due to malicious efforts or criminal activity. The Ponemon Institute refers to "malicious attacks" as being "caused by hackers or criminal insiders (employees, contractors or other third parties)." In other words, the definition for "malicious or criminal attacks" can be fairly broad to include attacks spawned from allies and/or enemy nation-states, hacktivism, organized crime, cyberterrorism, corporate espionage, and other acts of criminal destruction. Yet if "human factors" and "system glitches" are the more frequently cited "root causes" of data breaches then why are these issues neglected in deference to the aforementioned criminal destruction?

According to a story that reflects on the sophistication of cybercriminals, the BBC reported:[5]

> Attacks like that do happen. But more often than not, the hackers and cybercriminals hitting the headlines aren't doing anything magical. In fact, they're often just wily opportunists–like all criminals.

The reality is that the vast majority of malicious code such as viruses, malware, ransomware, and the like habitually take advantage of low-hanging fruit. This can take the form of weak passwords, default passwords, outdated software, unencrypted data, weak security measures in systems, and most of all they take advantage of unsuspecting humans' lack of understanding of how the complex system in front of them actually functions. Our industry needs a new approach.

---

4 IBM/Ponemon Institute, "2018 Cost of a Data Breach Report."

5 Chris Baraniuk, "It's a Myth that Most Cybercriminals Are 'Sophisticated,'" BBC.com, July 26, 2017, *https://oreil.ly/qA1Dw*.

Remove the Low-Hanging Fruit

If the majority of malicious code is designed to prey on the unsuspecting, ill-prepared, or unknowing humans, aka "the low-hanging fruit," then it makes sense to ask: How many of the data breaches attributed to criminal and malicious attacks would still be successful if there wasn't such a large surface area to begin with?

What if the "low-hanging fruit" is actually the sweetest? Consider the situation just described where criminals prey on the weak through their accidents, mistakes, and errors. Could it be possible that this "low-hanging fruit" is the key to proactively understanding how our systems and the humans that build and operate them behave?

If we always operated in a culture where we expect humans and systems to behave in unintended ways, then perhaps we would act differently and have more useful views regarding system behavior. We might also discover that the inherent failures within the sociotechnical ecosystems we operate might be just what we need to move the security trends in the opposite direction. Assume failure, and design the system expecting said failures.

We should be focusing on our ability to learn from the failures in our systems because we now expect this as our new operational state. Through this shift in thinking we can begin to understand what it takes to build more resilient systems. By building resilient systems in this context, rather than trying to catch all mistakes, we make unsophisticated criminals and attackers work harder for their money.

Ponemon cites "system glitches" as a contributing factor: "System glitches include application failures, inadvertent data dumps, logic errors in data transfer, identity or authentication failures (wrongful access), data recovery failures, and more."

The stone-cold reality of these "system glitches" is that failure is the normal behavior of our systems and their security. No doubt failures come as unpleasant surprises, but the real surprise is that our systems work at all to begin with. If "system glitches," failure, and surprises are frequent enough to be normal, then the success of our systems teeters on the edge of chaos every day.

Instead of simply reacting to failures, the security industry has been overlooking valuable chances to further understand and nurture incidents as opportunities to proactively strengthen system resilience. What if it were possible to proactively identify an incident before it happens? What if we didn't have to only rely on hope and instead approached security proactively and purposefully?

Feedback Loops

Even as modern software becomes increasingly distributed, rapidly iterative, and predominantly stateless, the approach to security remains predominantly preventative and dependent on point-in-time. Today's security practices lack the rapid iterative feedback loops that have made modern product delivery successful. The same feedback loops should exist between the changes in product environments and the mechanisms employed to keep them secure.

Security measures should be iterative and agile enough to change their behavior as often as the software ecosystem in which they operate. Security controls are typically designed with a particular state in mind (i.e., production release on Day 0). Meanwhile, the system ecosystem that surrounds these controls is changing rapidly every day. Microservices, machines, and other components are spinning up and spinning down. Component changes are occurring multiple times a day through continuous delivery. External APIs are constantly changing on their own delivery schedules, and so on.

> In order for security to improve, it's important to evaluate what you do well and learn to *Do Less, Better*.
>
> —Charles Nwatu, Netflix security engineer (former CISO, Stitch Fix)

Charles Nwatu describes SCE as a mechanism for organizations to proactively assess the effectiveness of their security precautions. Whether it be due to increasing compliance requirements or the evolving attack landscape, security organizations are increasingly being asked to build, operate, and maintain an ever-increasing number of security controls. As the former CISO of Stitch Fix, Charles was tasked with building out a high-performing cybersecurity organization. In the process of building the company's security apparatus he expressed the need to "Do Less, Better" instead of blindly deploying security measures in a paint-by-number fashion. His "Do Less, Better" motto came as a response to his desire to proactively and continuously verify that the security measures being built ("do less") were indeed effective at performing their intended functions ("better").

Charles was well aware that security tools and methods must be flexible enough to match the constant change and iteration in the environment in order to be effective. Without a feedback loop for security, the system's security risks the eventual drift into a state of unknown failure, just as a system without a development feedback loop would drift into unreliable operational readiness.

The most common way we discover security failures is when a security incident is triggered. Security incidents are not effective signals of detection, because at that point it's already too late. The damage has already been done. We must find better ways of instrumentation and observability if we aspire to be proactive in detecting security failures.

SCE introduces observability plus rigorous experimentation to illustrate the security of the system. Observability is crucial to generating a feedback loop. Testing is the validation or binary assessment of a previously known outcome. We know what we are looking for before we go looking for it. Experimentation seeks to derive new insights and information that were previously unknown. These new insights complete the feedback loop and continue the learning. This is a higher level of security maturity.

Injecting security events into our systems helps teams understand how their systems function as well as increase the opportunity to improve resilience. SREs,[6] product teams, and security teams are all expected to implement security. They should all be coding their services to withstand potential failures and gracefully degrade when necessary without impacting the business. By running security experiments continuously, we can evaluate and improve our understanding of unknown vulnerabilities before they become crisis situations. SCE, when properly implemented, becomes a feedback loop informing the security posture of the system.

Security Chaos Engineering and Current Methods

SCE addresses a number of gaps in contemporary security methodologies such as Red and Purple Team exercises. It is not the intention to overlook the value of Red and Purple team exercises or other security testing methods. These techniques remain valuable but differ in terms of goals and techniques. Combined with SCE, they provide a more objective and proactive feedback mechanism to prepare a system for an adverse event than when implemented alone.

Red Teaming[7] originated with the US Armed Forces.[8] It has been defined in different ways over the years, but it can be described today as an "adversarial approach that imitates the behaviors and techniques of attackers in the most realistic way possible." Two common forms of Red Teaming seen in the enterprise are ethical hacking and penetration testing, which often involve a mix of internal and external engagement. Blue teams are the defensive counterparts to the Red teams in these exercises.

Purple Team exercises[9] were intended as an evolution of Red Team exercises by delivering a more cohesive experience between the offensive and defensive teams. The "Purple" in Purple Teaming reflects the mixing or cohesion of Red and Blue teaming.

---

6 Betsy Beyer, Chris Jones, Jennifer Petoff and Niall Richard Murphy, eds., *Site Reliability Engineering* (Sebastopol: O'Reilly, 2016).

7 Margaret Rouse, "What Is Red Teaming," WhatIs.com, July 2017, *https://oreil.ly/Lmx4M*.

8 Wikipedia, "Red Team," *https://oreil.ly/YcTHc*.

9 Robert Wood and William Bengtson, "The Rise of the Purple Team," RSA Conference (2016), *https://oreil.ly/VyVO0*.

The goal of these exercises is the collaboration of offensive and defensive tactics to improve the effectiveness of both groups in the event of an attempted compromise. The intention is to increase transparency as well as provide a conduit for the security apparatus to learn about how effective their preparation is when subjected to a live fire exercise.

Problems with Red Teaming

Problems with Red Teaming include the following:

- Results frequently consist of reports. These reports, if shared at all, rarely suggest actionable followup. Nor do they provide alignment or incentive to the engineering teams to change their priorities.
- Primarily focused on malicious attackers and exploits instead of the more common systemic vulnerabilities.
- Teams are incentivized by their ability to outfox the opposing Blue Team rather than participate in a shared understanding:
  - Success for a Red Team frequently looks like a big, scary report indicating a large, vulnerable surface area.
  - Success for a Blue Team often looks like the right alerts fired, indicating that the preventative controls all worked.
- For Blue Teams, many alerts can be misunderstood to mean that detection capabilities are operating effectively, when in fact the situation may be much more complex than that.

Problems with Purple Teaming

Problems with Purple Teaming include the following:

- Running Purple Team exercises is highly resource intensive, which means:
  - Only on a small percentage of applications in the business portfolio are addressed.
  - The exercises are run infrequently, usually on an annual or monthly basis.
- The resulting artifacts lack a mechanism to reapply past findings for the purpose of regression analysis.

Benefits of Security Chaos Engineering

SCE addresses these problems and offers a number of benefits, including the following:

- SCE has a more holistic focus on the system. The principal goal is not to trick another human or test alerts; rather, it is to proactively identify system security failures caused by the nature of complex adaptive systems and build confidence in operational security integrity.

- SCE utilizes simple isolated and controlled experiments instead of complex attack chains involving hundreds or even thousands of changes. It can be difficult to control the blast radius and separate the signal from the noise when you make a large number of simultaneous changes. SCE significantly reduces the noise.

- SCE yields a collaborative learning experience that focuses on building more resilient systems instead of reacting to incidents. It is considered a best practice in Chaos Engineering to not perform experiments during an active ongoing incident or outage. It's not difficult to grasp that doing so will likely be disruptive to response team efforts but additionally it's important to recognize that people operate differently during active incidents due to time pressure, cognitive load, stress, and other factors. An active incident situation is not an ideal learning environment, as the focus is typically on restoring business continuity instead of learning about what might have contributed to the adverse event. We execute SCE experiments in the absence of adverse events and outages when the system is thought to be running optimally. This results in facilitating a better and more collaborative learning environment as teams are focused on building more resilient systems as an alternative to reacting to incidents.

SCE does not necessarily compete with the findings or intent of Red or Purple Teaming. It does, however, add a layer of efficacy, transparency, and reproducibility that can significantly enhance the value of those practices. Red and Purple Team exercises are simply unable to keep pace with CI/CD and complex distributed computing environments. Software engineering teams now deliver multiple product updates within a 24-hour period. The relevance of results obtained in Red or Purple Team exercises quickly diminishes because the system may have fundamentally changed in the meantime. With SCE, we can have a signal of security posture that keeps pace with the changes that software engineers continually make to the underlying system.

Security Game Days

The backup almost always works; it's the restore you have to worry about. Disaster recovery and backup/restore testing provide classic examples of the devastating potential of a process that isn't exercised. The same goes for the rest of our security controls. Rather than wait to discover that something is not working, proactively introduce conditions into the system to ensure that our security is as effective as we think it is.

A common way to get started is to use a Game Day exercise to plan, build, collaborate, execute, and conduct postmortems for experiments. Game Day exercises typically run between two and four hours and involve a cross-functional team who develop, operate, monitor, and/or secure an application. Ideally, they involve members working collaboratively from a combination of areas.

The intent of a Game Day exercise is to introduce failure in a controlled security experiment to determine:

- How effectively your tools, techniques, and processes detected the failure
- Which tools provided the insights and data that led to detect it
- How useful the data was in identifying the problem
- Whether the system operates as intended

You cannot predict the manifestation of future events, but you can control your ability to understand how well you respond to situations that you cannot predict. SCE provides the tooling and process to practice incident response.

Example Security Chaos Engineering Tool: ChaoSlingr

There is a growing community of security professionals who are both advocating SCE and developing experiments through open source and other community initiatives. As general-purpose Chaos Engineering tools mature, those experiment libraries will include more security-specific experiments. Today, however, security professionals should be prepared to design and build their own experiments through scripting or leverage existing open source software tool sets such as ChaoSlingr as a framework.

The Story of ChaoSlingr

ChaoSlingr, as seen in Figure 20-1, is a security experiment and reporting framework created by a team at UnitedHealth Group led by Aaron Rinehart (this chapter's author). It was the first open source software tool to demonstrate the value of applying Chaos Engineering to cybersecurity. It was designed, introduced, and released as open source with the intention of demonstrating a simplified framework for writing security chaos experiments.

One experiment at UnitedHealth Group involved misconfiguring a port. The hypothesis for this experiment was that a misconfigured port should be detected and blocked by the firewall, and the incident should be appropriately logged for the security team. Half of the time, that's exactly what happened. The other half of the time, the firewall failed to detect and block it. But a commodity cloud configuration tool did always catch it and block it. Unfortunately, that tool did not log it in such a way that the security team could easily identify where the incident had occurred.

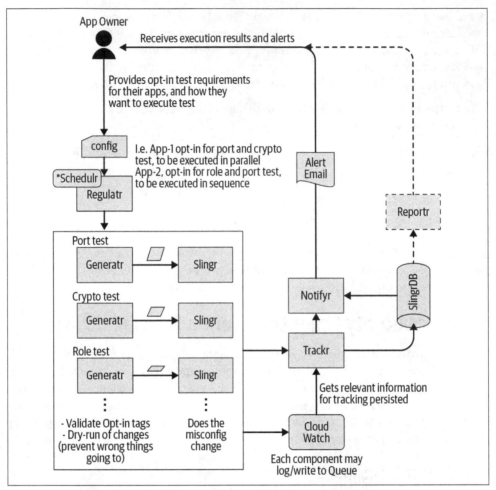

Figure 20-1. ChaoSlingr's high-level context and design

Imagine that you are on that team. Your fundamental understanding of your own security posture would be shaken by this discovery. The power of ChaoSlingr is that the experiments prove whether your assumptions are true or not. You aren't left guessing or assuming about your security instrumentation.

The framework consists of four primary functions:

Generatr

   Identifies the object to inject the failure on and calls Slingr.

Slingr

   Injects the failure.

Trackr
    Logs details about the experiment as it occurs.

Experiment description
    Provides documentation on the experiment along with applicable input and output parameters for Lambda functions.

ChaoSlingr was originally designed to operate in Amazon Web Services (AWS). It proactively introduces known security failure conditions through a series of experiments to determine how effectively security is implemented. The high-level business driver behind the effort was to improve the company's ability to rapidly deliver high-quality products and services while maintaining the highest level of safety and security possible.

The safety critical systems that are being built today are becoming so complex and distributed in nature that no single entity can account for the entirety of its operational nature. Even when all of the individual services in a distributed system are functioning properly, the interactions between those services can cause unpredictable outcomes. Unpredictable outcomes, compounded by rare but disruptive real-world events[10] that affect production environments, made these distributed systems inherently chaotic. ChaoSlingr was developed to uncover, communicate, and address significant weaknesses proactively, before they impacted customers in production.

Features of ChaoSlingr (*https://github.com/Optum/ChaoSlingr*) include:

- Open source
- Big red button: automatically shuts down ChaoSlingr if it's not behaving or during an active incident
- Configurable timeframes and frequency of experiment runs
- Written in Python
- Runs as Lambda functions
- Auto-configuration for setup written in Terraform script form

ChaoSlingr demonstrates how Chaos Engineering experiments can be constructed and executed to provide security value in distributed systems. The majority of organizations utilizing ChaoSlingr have since forked the project and constructed their own series of security chaos experiments using the framework provided by the project as a guide.

---

10 David Woods and Emily S. Patterson, "How Unexpected Events Produce an Escalation of Cognitive and Coordinative Demands," in *Stress Workload and Fatigue*, Hancock and Desmond, eds. (Hillsdale, NJ: Lawrence Erlbaum, 2000).

Conclusion

As enterprises adopt cloud native stacks and the DevOps model, their security programs must evolve to meet new demands such as the frequency of system-wide changes enabled by continuous deployment. Traditional security testing, while valuable, is insufficient to meet these new challenges.

The mindset of the approach to security must also change. "System glitches" are the normal operating conditions of complex systems. Focusing on "human error," "root cause," or sophisticated attackers won't get you nearly as far in security as a better understanding of your basic security posture, in an ongoing way, with instrumented feedback loops. SCE creates these feedback loops, and can expose previously unknown unknowns, limiting the surface area for attackers.

The tool ChaoSlingr proves that Chaos Engineering can be applied to cybersecurity. The experience of utilizing ChaoSlingr at UnitedHealth Group proves that there is value in this approach. When applied in a security context, Chaos Engineering has the potential to reveal valuable, objective information about how security controls operate, allowing organizations to invest in security budgets more efficiently. Given that benefit, all organizations should consider when and how to implement this discipline, especially those operating complex systems at scale.

Contributors/Reviewers

Charles Nwatu, Netflix
Prima Virani, Pinterest
James Wickett, Verica
Michael Zhou, Verica
Grayson Brewer
Chenxi Wang, Ph.D., Rain Capital
Jamie Lewis, Rain Capital
Daniel Walsh, Rally Health
Rob Fry, VP Engineering JASK (former Netflix security lead)
Gerhard Eschelbeck, CISO, Google (retired)
Tim Prendergast, Chief Cloud Officer Palo Alto (founder, Evident.io)
Lenny Maly, VP Security Engineering, TransUnion
DJ Schleen, Aetna
Enrique Salem, Bain Capital Ventures
Rob Duhart, Cardinal Health
Mike Frost, HERE Technologies

About the Author

Aaron Rinehart is the CTO and cofounder of @Verica.io. He works to expand the possibilities of Chaos Engineering in its application to other safety-critical portions of the IT domain, notably cybersecurity. He began pioneering the application of security in Chaos Engineering during his tenure as the chief security architect at the largest private healthcare company in the world, UnitedHealth Group (UHG). While at UHG Aaron released ChaoSlingr, one of the first open source software releases focused on using Chaos Engineering in cybersecurity to build more resilient systems. Aaron resides in Washington, DC, and is a frequent author, consultant, and speaker in the space.

CHAPTER 21

Conclusion

Resilience is created by people. The engineers who write the functionality, those who operate and maintain the system, and even the management that allocates resources toward it are all part of a complex system. We each play a role in creating resilience, bringing to bear our experience and focused attention to this property of the system.

Tools can help. Chaos Engineering is a tool that we can use to improve the resilience of systems. As practitioners in this industry, our success depends not on removing the complexity from our systems, but on learning to live with it, navigate it, and optimize for other business-critical properties despite the underlying complexity.

When we illustrate the distinction between the tools and the people around the tools, we refer to the tools as being "below the line." The people and the organization that put the tools in place are "above the line." As software professionals, too often we focus on what's happening below the line. It's easier to see problems there, and easier to point a finger at those problems. There is a psychological satisfaction in being able to reduce an incident to a single line of code, and then just fix that one line of code. There is a temptation to stop there, but we must resist that temptation.

Throughout this book, we delved into work both below and above the line. We laid out how that work contributes to building better systems. People, organization, human interaction, tools, automation, architecture, innovation, and digital transformation have all been explored. We think of the people and technology coming together in a "sociotechnical" system that can't be fully understood without exploring both sides of the coin and putting into context how they interact.

This can have some unexpected side effects. For example, it isn't always possible to make our systems more reliable by writing more code. Often the best strategy to improve the robustness of a system is to create better alignment around how to react to hazards. Alignment can't be engineered, or at least, it can't be engineered in the same way that software is.

After decades of research spanning the gamut of sociology, to decision theory, to organizational sociology and psychology, to human factors and engineering, Jens Rasmussen wrote:

> The most promising general approach to improved risk management appears to be an explicit identification of the boundaries of safe operation together with efforts to make these boundaries visible to the actors and to give them an opportunity to learn to cope with the boundaries. In addition to improved safety, making boundaries visible may also increase system effectiveness in that operation close to known boundaries may be safer than requiring excessive margins which are likely to deteriorate in unpredictable ways under pressure.[1]

The consequence of this conclusion is that the contextualization of incident reviews and resilient properties is more pragmatic and actionable than hunting for a "root cause" or enforcing rules.

In fact, enforcing rules for increasing reliability can lead you astray. For example:

- Intuitively, it makes sense that adding redundancy to a system makes it safer. *Unfortunately, experience shows us that this intuition is incorrect.* Redundancy alone does not make a system safer, and in many cases it makes a system more likely to fail. Consider the redundant O-rings on the solid rocket booster of the Space Shuttle *Challenger*. Because of the secondary O-ring, engineers working on the solid rocket booster normalized over time the failure of the primary O-ring, allowing the *Challenger* to operate outside of specification, which ultimately contributed to the catastrophic failure in 1986.[2]

- Intuitively, it makes sense that removing complexity from a system makes it safer. *Unfortunately, experience shows us that this intuition is incorrect.* As we build a system, we can optimize for all sorts of things. One property we can optimize for is safety. In order to do that, we have to build things. If you remove complexity from a stable system, you risk removing the functionality that makes the system safe.

- Intuitively, it makes sense that operating a system efficiently makes it safer. *Unfortunately, experience shows us that this intuition is incorrect.* Efficient systems are brittle. Allowance for inefficiency is a good thing. Inefficiencies allow a

---

1 Jens Rasmussen, "Risk Management in a Dynamic Society: A Modelling Problem," *Safety Science*, Vol. 27, No. 2/3 (1997), *https://lewebpedagogique.com/audevillemain/files/2014/12/maint-Rasmus-1997.pdf*.

2 Diane Vaughan, *The Challenger Launch Decision* (Chicago: University of Chicago Press, 1997).

---

system to absorb shock and allow people to make decisions that could remediate failures that no one planned for.

The list of intuitive but incorrect rules for building safe systems could go on. It's a long list. Unfortunately, we don't have many generalized rules that can be universally applied.

That's why humans are so important in the equation. Only humans can contextualize each situation. Only humans can improvise during an incident, and find creative solutions within unpredictable circumstances. These are the human factors we need to consider in our complex systems.

As software engineers, we often like to think of ourselves as behaving in a logical manner. Humans are not logical. At best, we are rational. But most of the time, we are simply habitual, repeating the patterns that worked for us in the past. This book has explored and illustrated the rich habits, patterns, interactions, and inner workings of the sociotechnical system that allow Chaos Engineering to work.

We hope we have convinced you that in order to successfully improve your resilience, you need to understand the interplay between the human elements who authorize, fund, observe, build, operate, maintain, and make demands of the system and the technical "below the line" components that constitute the technical system. With Chaos Engineering you can better understand the sociotechnical boundary between the humans and the machines; you can discover the safety margin between your current position and catastrophic failure; you can improve the reversibility of your architecture. With Chaos Engineering, you can fundamentally improve the qualities of your sociotechnical system that support the value of your organization or business.

Tools don't create resilience. People do. But tools can help. Chaos Engineering is an essential tool in our pursuit of resilient systems.

Index

About the Authors

Casey Rosenthal is CEO and cofounder of Verica; formerly the Engineering Manager of the Chaos Engineering Team at Netflix. He has experience with distributed systems, artificial intelligence, translating novel algorithms and academia into working models, and selling a vision of the possible to clients and colleagues alike. His superpower is transforming misaligned teams into high performance teams, and his personal mission is to help people see that something different, something better, is possible. For fun, he models human behavior using personality profiles in Ruby, Erlang, Elixir, and Prolog.

Nora Jones is the cofounder and CEO of Jeli. She is a dedicated and driven technology leader and software engineer with a passion for the intersection between how people and software work in practice in distributed systems. In November 2017 she keynoted at AWS re:Invent to share her experiences helping organizations large and small reach crucial availability with an audience of ~40,000 people, helping kick off the Chaos Engineering movement we see today. Since then she has keynoted at several other conferences around the world, highlighting her work on topics such as Resilience Engineering, Chaos Engineering, Human Factors, Site Reliability, and more from her work at Netflix, Slack, and Jet.com. Additionally, she created and founded the www.learningfromincidents.io movement to develop and open source cross-organization learnings and analysis from reliability incidents across various organizations.

Colophon

The animal on the cover of *Chaos Engineering* is the common marmoset (*Callithrix jacchus*). This small species of New World monkeys lives in the treetops of the forests of northeastern Brazil.

Common marmosets average just over seven inches tall, and weigh eight to nine ounces. They are mostly brown, grey, and white, with long banded tails and distinctive white ear tufts. In the wild, they live an average of twelve years. They are omnivores, eating primarily insects and tree sap, but also eat many other things, such as fruit, seeds, bird eggs, and small reptiles.

As with other primates, common marmosets are social animals. They live in groups of nine or more that feature complex social dynamics such as dominance hierarchies, which are communicated through vocalizations as well as visual signals. Because of this, these marmosets are sometimes used in laboratory studies of social behavior.

The IUCN rates the conservation status of the common marmoset as being of least concern. Many of the animals on O'Reilly covers are endangered; all of them are important to the world.

The cover color illustration is by Karen Montgomery, based on a black and white engraving from *Meyers Kleines Lexicon*. The cover fonts are Gilroy Semibold and Guardian Sans. The text font is Adobe Minion Pro; the heading font is Adobe Myriad Condensed; and the code font is Dalton Maag's Ubuntu Mono.

O'REILLY®

There's much more
where this came from.

Experience books, videos, live online
training courses, and more from O'Reilly
and our 200+ partners—all in one place.

Learn more at oreilly.com/online-learning

Printed in the USA
CPSIA information can be obtained
at www.ICGtesting.com
JSHW050242151123
R13091100003B/R130911PG51980JSX00003B/1